P9-DDR-259

FORTY-TWO FACES

OTHER BOOKS BY JOHN HETHERINGTON

FICTION

The Winds are Still

GENERAL

Airborne Invasion

Australian Soldier

Blamey

Australians: Nine Profiles

Booklets

Norman Lindsay (*Australian Writers and Their Work* Series)

Sir John Monash

JOHN HETHERINGTON - 1907-

Forty-Two Faces

Biography Index Reprint Series

BOOKS FOR LIBRARIES PRESS
Freeport, New York

Reprinted in this edition 1969

First published in Australia 1962 by
F. W. Cheshire Publishing Pty Ltd
Melbourne, Canberra, Sydney

Library of Congress Catalog Card Number 73-75719

CONTENTS

* *Efforts having failed to establish when D'Arcy Niland and Ruth Park were born (D'Arcy Niland writes: ". . . a writer's age, we consider, is a private and not a public affair"), they are placed in this index by guess.*

PORTRAITS

TO

Brin Newton-John

INTRODUCTION

MANY Australians still deny the existence of an Australian literature. With all respect to their sincerity, I am baffled by their reasoning. It seems to me that anybody living in Australia who can remain insensible of the emergence and growth of a national literature should take his place with the man who exclaimed, on first seeing a giraffe, 'There ain't no such beast!' It is true that Australian writing has not yet found the world recognition that Australian painting has done. Some of the most trustworthy European critics rank Patrick White among the best living novelists, but White is the only Australian of today to have won such notice—indeed, the only Australian to have done so since Henry Handel Richardson was belatedly acclaimed, when *Ultima Thule*, the third volume of her trilogy, *The Fortunes of Richard Mahony*, came out in 1929.

World recognition aside, I sometimes wonder if the extravagant claims which intellectual chauvinists have made, and continue to make, for Australian writing have not discouraged many Australians from reading Australian books. I do not imagine I am alone in detesting the cultural missionary who seizes me by the coat lapels and tells me I must read Australian books (or any kind of books, for that matter), not necessarily for pleasure or for profit, but as a patriotic duty. I read, and have read every year for many years, a good number of Australian books, both fiction and non-fiction, but never as an act of duty. If a day should ever come when I find myself reading Australian books as a duty, I shall change my reading habits.

To me however the existence of an Australian literature is indisputable. The foundation of it, as something peculiarly Australian, not something deriving from Europe, was laid little more than a century ago, and its subsequent growth has been reasonably steady. This is not to say that the process has been uninterrupted; there have been checks, digressions and hesitations, and now and then an appearance of retrogression. For much of the period separating the two world wars Australian literature looked to be, if not dead, then sleeping, but a handful of writers went on writing, even when, as often happened, they knew their work was more likely than not to go unpublished; they continued, in the teeth of an apathy so profound that it stifled the creative enthusiasm of all but those few men and women to whom the act of writing was hardly less necessary than the act of breathing. Some of that few are in this book, but not many of them will be found here, because most of those who refused to throw away their typewriters in that doleful period have since died; and all those whose profiles appear in this book are living, or were living when the book was made ready for the printer, and are still building the literature of Australia in the middle of the twentieth century. Some, like Frank Dalby Davison and Leonard Mann, have been building it for a long time, while others, like Randolph Stow and David Forrest, did not publish their first work until the 1950s, when World War II was already a diminishing speck on the horizon of history. To that extent then, this book is a walk behind the scenes of Australian literature today. It is also an acknowledgment of the truth of Ralph Waldo Emerson's words: 'Talent alone cannot make a writer. There must be a man behind the book.'

Since the subjects of these profiles are all still actively writing, and, for good or ill, adding to the body of their published work, all these profiles are tentative. I claim no more for them than that. It is statistically inevitable that many of these writers will be forgotten, except by anthologists and literary historians, in twenty-five years, that the names of others will be fading, and that not more than three or four will still be spoken of with respect. In short, only a few of them will outlive their own time; more could not be expected of any group of forty-odd writers drawn from a population of fewer than eleven million people. Some of them will probably be forgotten well within their own time, but they appear here because the least of them has made some contribution to Australian literature; a contribution which, although possibly trivial in itself, appears to be symptomatic of a development in one aspect or another of Australian twentieth century writing. Only time will tell whether the period spanned by this series of profiles has produced a writer, or writers, to rank with, above, or near Lawson, Furphy or Richardson. I make no forecast on this point. Many a literary critic, esteemed for the supposed infallibility of his judgment, must look back upon opinions, lauding this writer or damning that one, which he expressed a mere five or ten years earlier and cringe with embarrassment to see what time has done to make his findings appear ridiculous. I prefer to leave to others such feats of prognosis.

Most of these profiles were originally published in a weekly series, Australian Writers in Profile, which appeared in the Saturday Literary Supplement of the Melbourne daily newspaper, *The Age*, from July,

1960, to May, 1961; the full series was published also in the Perth *West Australian*, and about half of it in the Sydney *Daily Telegraph*. The idea of Australian Writers in Profile was conceived by Keith Sinclair, Editor of *The Age*, and when the series started neither he nor I guessed it would continue for as long as ten months, and would even then omit perhaps a dozen or more Australian writers who, on any measure of merit, should have been included. The series owed a great deal to Keith Sinclair, not only in conception, but also for the unfailing cooperation he offered as it grew and developed.

Thirty-eight of the forty-one profiles in this book (forty-one profiles but forty-two faces, because D'Arcy Niland and his wife, Ruth Park, are portrayed in a single profile), are adapted from the series published in *The Age*; all these thirty-eight have been more or less modified, some heavily so, but in modifying them I have tried to keep the spirit of the original, and to sharpen, but not to alter in any basic way, the portrait of any subject. A few of the original profiles have been omitted, for reasons which seem valid either to the publishers or to me, and three new ones—those of Randolph Stow, Cyril Pearl and David Martin—specially written for the book. No poets, as such, are included. Some of the subjects of these profiles have published verse, but they are in this book as writers of prose. To me, verse and prose seem to be different media of expression, having little in common merely because each consists of an arrangement of words, and I felt it would be artificial and unreal to make bed-fellows of poets and prose writers here. The book's validity would, I believe, have suffered, for me at any rate, if I had forced into it profiles of, say, ten or twelve poets in an effort to 'broaden its appeal'. One further word on omissions. A number of prose writers, whom anyone even casually acquainted with Australian writing of today would expect to meet in this book, are missing. Marjorie Barnard, Norman Lindsay, Ernestine Hill, Russell Braddon, Donald Stuart, Godfrey Blunden, Tom Ronan, T. A. G. Hungerford, and two or three others are omitted, not because I wished to omit them, but for reasons outside my control. I regret this, but if I had put off finishing this book until I could include in it everybody who should have been included, it would probably never have appeared at all. In this case I felt three-quarters of a loaf was better than none.

Several criticisms, often directed at me when these profiles were appearing as a newspaper series, will doubtless be directed at me also as the author of this book. One was that I shirked the obligation of making any estimates of the worth of these writers' work. My reply is that I do not consider the profilist has a right to make such estimates; if he attempts to do so, he forsakes his own field for that of the critic.

I have occasionally quoted the finding of one critic or another on the work of some subject, but only when this appeared to help in depicting the personality of the writer under consideration. To me, the paramount task of a profilist is to project his subject's personality; he must obviously mention the subject's work, but must never let the work overshadow the human aspects of the portrait. A second criticism was that I often 'permitted' my profile subjects to make statements of opinion and philosophy which would have been better omitted—whatever the words 'better omitted' might mean in that context. As for that, let me say I often disagreed with views on life, letters, politics and other matters expressed by one or another of my subjects in the course of conversation with me, but I reported what I rejected, along with what I accepted, wherever it seemed to me that this was pertinent to an understanding of the subject's character. I can imagine no reading more wearisome than a collection of profiles written by an author who would not set down any opinions expressed by his subjects which conflicted with his own. Such acts of censorship are not for the profilist, but for those who believe themselves qualified to play God. Then, some people challenged the inclusion in the original newspaper series of the profiles of Alan Moorehead, James Aldridge and Paul Brickhill, on the ground that each of these writers is almost entirely concerned in his books with overseas settings and themes. Let us look first at the merits of the case: Moorehead's only Australian book is *Rum Jungle*. Aldridge has published only a few short stories about Australians in Australia, and only one novel—*The Sea Eagle*, a war story with a Mediterranean locale—in which Australians appear as anything but supernumerary figures. Brickhill's documentary books, concerned with his own wartime experiences and the war experiences of other men, mention Australians only incidentally, and the one novel he has written—*The Deadline*, published this year—has an Australian as a central figure in a French setting. Having admitted so much, I make no apology for including any of these writers. All three were born in Australia and spent their formative years here, and each writes as he does, irrespective of what he writes about, largely because of his Australian background. To exclude any of them from this book would be as logical as to exclude Walter Murdoch from it, because he was born in Aberdeenshire, Scotland.

While these profiles were appearing in *The Age* I received a few indignant letters asking, by implication at any rate, what importance some of my subjects could possibly have to Australian literature. I surmised that most of those letters came from people who can never find any merit in what is, but only in what has been. Some of them seemed to feel that, by even appearing to look for a potential Australian literary giant of the present, I was somehow disparaging Australian literary giants of the past. This I do not admit. A Patrick White or a Katharine Susannah Prichard is not necessarily the same kind of giant as a Henry Lawson or a Joseph Furphy, but giants come in many guises, and Australian literature, that large, awkward, sprawling, sparsely populated land (in those respects, not unlike Australia itself) has room for all of them. It is unlikely to be overcrowded with giants for quite some time to come.

JOHN HETHERINGTON

Walter Murdoch

PREACHER EXTRAORDINARY

A TYPEWRITER stands on the desk of Walter Murdoch's book-lined study. It is a tangible symbol of the mental youthfulness that makes him willing to use any modern tool he has found to be efficient. 'I type all my own stuff straight on to the machine,' he says. 'I don't find that my work is any better, or any different, if I draft it by hand.' To those dedicated writers who believe every word must be hand-written with pen or pencil, if it is not to suffer some subtle loss of quality, Professor Murdoch's approval of the typewriter is probably a kind of treason; to him, it is merely a piece of common sense. Although he was born in 1874, he differs from many men old in years in refusing to despise new-fangled things merely because they are new-fangled. This does not mean he is one of those people who endeavour to cling to youth long after youth has gone. He tries to delude neither himself nor anyone else by pretending he is not an old man, and writes frankly on every aspect of old age. For example, in one short essay, published when he was eighty-six, he said: '. . . I think the chief trouble of old age is the passing of so many contemporaries, men who were boys when I was a boy, women whom I knew as young girls. That is what makes one feel that one has lived too long.' In March, 1962, after ten years of widowerhood, he married his secretary-companion. Asked by a journalist what he felt about octogenarian marriages, he replied: 'Eighty-seven is the best age for a man to marry. At eighty a man is an octogenarian, but too young.'

Walter Murdoch, essayist, biographer, anthologist, and occasional poet, has always been one for standing off and examining himself, then describing what he has seen in terms of gentle ridicule. In the preface to one of his books he named 'the vice of preaching' as his besetting sin; he claimed to have inherited it from 'some ancestral theologian who used to compose sermons while he was being chased across the heather by Claverhouse's dragoons', and went on: 'You may be a secret tippler or a secret murderer, but you cannot be a secret preacher. You cannot shut yourself up in a sanctum (whatever a sanctum may be) and preach to the table and the chairs. When you have fallen into the grip of this vice, there is no concealment possible.'

Australian literature would have been poorer if Professor Murdoch had done his preaching—as he chooses to call it—in secret. The first essay he ever published appeared in the Melbourne *Argus* over sixty years ago. That essay discussed Australian poets, and, although some readers (including one or two of the poets concerned) disliked his conclusions and wrote angry letters damning them, it caused a stir. He has been writing essays ever since. These have been collected into a dozen volumes. One of the earliest volumes, *Speaking Personally*, which was first published in 1930, has sold the large total, for any book of essays, of nearly twenty-two thousand copies.

Since about the time World War II ended, however, he has written few orthodox essays. For many years a weekly essay by him was published in newspapers throughout Australia, but in 1945 he replaced this by a weekly column of answers to questions which readers asked him. Over the years he has given his opinions on such questions as 'Can one be a snob and a Christian?'; 'What is a perfect day?'; 'Does it ever rain cats and dogs?'; and 'Are you afraid of death?'. He calls these replies 'essays in miniature', and it would be hard to find a better name for them; they reflect, no less than his longer essays do, his philosophy of life and his personality. 'I began by undertaking to answer questions for three months,' he says, 'but I have never wished to stop. The idea came as a godsend. I had grown tired of finding subjects; now my readers find subjects for me.'

When I wrote from Melbourne, asking if I might call and see him on a visit I intended making to Perth, he replied: 'I shall be glad to be as useful as I can. I must warn you, however, that I am old and intellectually somewhat decrepit; so that a visit to me may turn out quite unprofitable to the visitor.' In fact, as every word that he writes attests, his mind is as active as quicksilver and as fresh as a southerly breeze. He is a short man, and his shoulders sag a little under the weight of his years. The hair on his disproportionately large head is snow-white and unruly, his nose is prominent, and his blue-grey eyes under strongly arched brows are birdlike; the heavy white moustache does not hide the lines of humour engraved about his mouth. It is the face of a man who finds the world and the antics of men perpetually interesting and often amusing, and who has learned most of the lessons life can teach, except how to be a cynic. Search Walter Murdoch's writings line by line, and you will find no cynicism in them; they are often ironic, sometimes acidulated, occasionally indignant, but never cynical.

Portraits of forty-two faces

WALTER MURDOCH

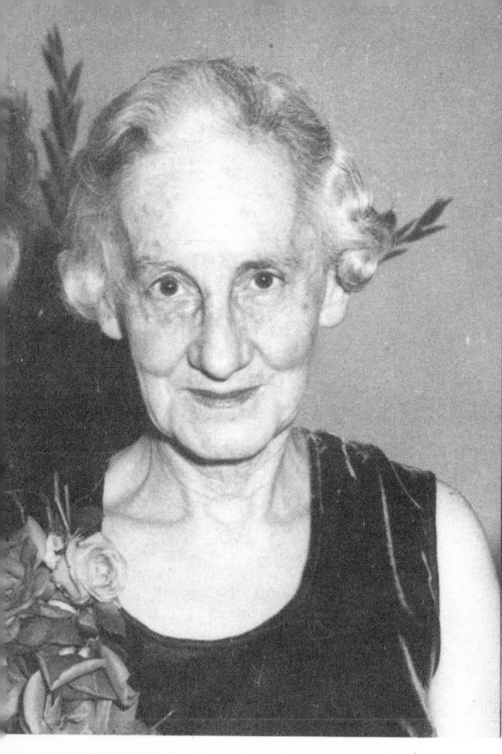

KATHARINE SUSANNAH PRICHARD

ION L. IDRIESS

ARTHUR UPFIELD

JOHN TIERNEY

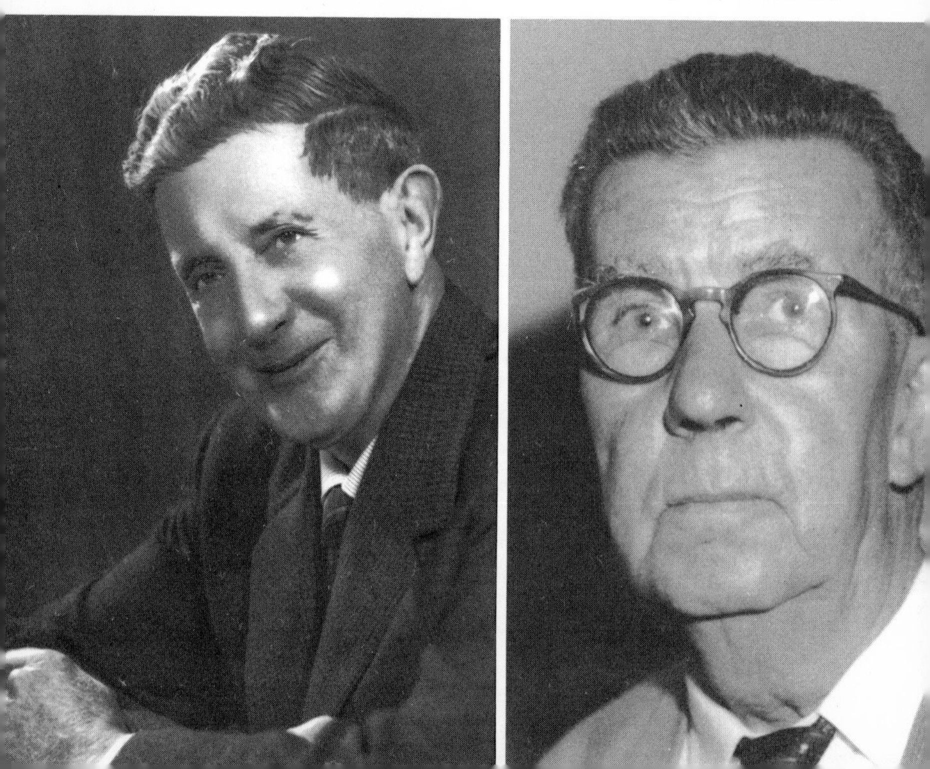

'I still enjoy writing,' he said, sitting in the living-room of his South Perth home, whose windows look across the Swan River to the city. 'I still do a fair amount of writing, but I'm not working on a book at present. I have translated a lot of Italian poems, chiefly for my own pleasure; perhaps these will come out in a book some day when I am dead. I might leave some notes on men I have known and admired, like Sir Robert Garran and Sir Frederic Eggleston, for later publication. I don't think I shall write an autobiography, though. I haven't the energy for it. I also feel the world has become a place with such issues at stake that anything one could write about himself would be trivial. And at my age one is justified in leaving the stage as gracefully as possible.' He has held to his decision not to write an autobiography, but a few months after I called he told me in a letter that he was in the middle of a small book, *Meanderings and Memories*, adding 'if I survive to finish it'. A more or less casual collection of personal reminiscences is perhaps the only book of the kind that Walter Murdoch could be expected to write. To him, an autobiography is probably a pompous work, even though he would not describe it so, for fear of hurting the feelings of those who round off their lives by writing autobiographies.

He was born at Pitsligo, Aberdeenshire, Scotland, the fourteenth child of a Free Church of Scotland minister. ('I've always believed in small families since then,' he says. 'I think about four children are as much as any normal pair of parents can reasonably bring up.' He and his wife had a son and two daughters.) He was ten when his parents came to Australia with their family, except for some of the older children who had already gone out to make their way in the world. He enrolled at Camberwell Grammar School, Melbourne, in 1887, then went on to Scotch College. When he finished his studies at the University of Melbourne, graduating M.A., with first-class honours in Logic and Philosophy, he had to begin earning a living at once, because the land boom had burst a year or so earlier, swallowing his parents' savings. He went first as tutor to a Beaufort squatter's children, for forty pounds a year and his keep. A year or so later he received a relatively dazzling offer from the principal of Hamilton Academy, a boys' boarding school; the remuneration was eighty pounds, with keep. 'The man who ran Hamilton Academy was an Australian edition of Squeers,' he recalls. 'He was a devoted believer in corporal punishment for boys. He was also an enemy of extravagance, and he'd shout across the table at any of us who seemed to be putting too much treacle or golden syrup on our bread. My duties did not end with teaching; I also had to help him with such non-academic tasks as killing sheep, and hanging their carcases beside the outhouse where we junior masters slept.'

Walter Murdoch endured life at Hamilton Academy for a year; then he went back to Melbourne, and started a boys' school at Camberwell, with his brother-in-law. They sold out after three years, and he took over a Warrnambool boys' school. 'I had only eight or nine boarders there,' he says, 'but a good big day-school. I liked the teaching, but running the school was a ghastly business; I had to be a kind of bagman, canvassing for pupils. What I most enjoyed at Warrnambool was fishing for bream at the mouth of the Hopkins River.'

He sold the Warrnambool school in 1903 and became Lecturer in English at the University of Melbourne. Melbourne had no Professor of English then, and when one was appointed in 1911 Walter Murdoch was passed over. He had been writing more or less regularly for the Melbourne *Argus* for some years, and he believes this weighed against him when the Chair was being filled; in those days academics looked askance at any man who wrote for a daily newspaper. He decided that, since the university had rejected him, he would reject the university; although he was married with two children, he resigned his lectureship and joined the *Argus* editorial staff. His chief task was to write one of the leading articles each day, usually something in a light and whimsical vein. 'The first leading article I was called on to write,' he says, 'was, however, neither light nor whimsical. It examined the question whether you should be allowed to take a bulldog into a railway compartment with you!' He liked journalism well enough, but when the University of Western Australia opened in 1912—it had a staff of eight then, and a hundred and eighty-three students—he was its first Professor of English. He retired from the Chair in 1939, but returned to academic life as Chancellor from 1943 to 1947.

Although Professor Murdoch is supreme among Australian essayists, he is irreverent about his essays; he calls them 'newspaper articles which I dignify by the name of essays'. Nor does he show any particular pride in his work as an anthologist—he has edited or co-edited six or seven verse and prose anthologies. The book of his own that most pleases him is his biography of Alfred Deakin, which he published in 1923. He does not call it a biography, but, modestly, 'a sketch'. 'Deakin was a many-sided man,' he says. 'I knew him well, and we used to exchange letters. I was very fond of him, and he was very good to me. I never knew anyone else I wanted to write a biography of.'

His most profitable books, however, were written when he was a young man; they were three school textbooks—a history of England, a manual of civics, and a short history of Australia—written for

Victorian State schools, and adopted also for schools in some other States. These textbooks have long been out of print, but the author draws some satisfaction from knowing that they helped to shape the thinking of tens of thousands of Australian boys and girls. One of these was a studious youth, born at Creswick, Victoria, who many years afterwards, when he was Prime Minister of Australia, told a Perth audience that he had been brought up on Walter Murdoch's history of England, *The Struggle for Freedom*. His name was John Curtin.

It is mildly surprising that a man of Walter Murdoch's broad literary sympathies should never have tried to write a novel. His only attempt at fiction was made twenty-odd years ago, when he wrote a chapter for *Murder Pie*, an experimental whodunit to which seventeen Australian writers contributed. 'It struck me from writing that chapter,' he says, 'that it would be fairly easy to write a detective story. My publishers once suggested I should write a detective story, but I never did.'

He continues to read the best work done by modern writers, as well as the classics, and his interest in the work of Australian writers, whether present or past, is as lively as ever. 'There have been marked changes in Australian writing,' he says. 'First it was crudely imitative of English writing. Then for a time it was dominated by *The Bulletin* school. Now it has caught up with modern culture; it has become civilized. Whether anything that is being written in Australia today will be more lasting than the best work of our earlier writers I don't know. We've had some good stuff. *Robbery Under Arms* should last a time yet. Some of 'Banjo' Paterson, and perhaps some of Lawson's short stories, will probably live. I don't know about Furphy. When *Tom Collins** first came out I was tremendously struck with it; it was so aggressively Australian. Perhaps that is the very quality that goes against it today.'

Some of Walter Murdoch's own writings also appear likely to live; they have qualities which time could neither diminish nor corrode. One of these is the constancy of the philosophy they express —for example, their author's attitude to the suburban spirit, of which he once wrote, 'The suburban spirit—that is, for me, the everlasting enemy.' Another is their fidelity to his own rule for anyone who would write good English: 'Say what you mean, and say it clearly, precisely, and unambiguously.' That is one thing he never fails to do.

* *Such is Life: Being Certain Extracts from the Life of Tom Collins* (Sydney, Bulletin Co.) 1903. Tom Collins was the pen-name of Joseph Furphy (1843-1912).

GENERAL

(Published by Angus & Robertson, Sydney, unless otherwise stated)

The Enemies of Literature (Melbourne, Lothian) 1907
Loose Leaves (Melbourne, G. Robertson) 1910
Alfred Deakin: A Sketch (London, Constable) 1923
Speaking Personally 1930
Saturday Mornings 1931
Moreover 1932
The Two Laughters (London, Dent) 1934
The Wild Planet 1934
Three Popular Prophets: H. G. Wells, Bernard Shaw, G. K. Chesterton (Sydney, Australian Broadcasting Commission) 1935
Some Fallacies (Sydney, Australian Broadcasting Commission) 1935
Lucid Intervals 1936
The Victorian Era: Its Strength and Weakness 1938
Collected Essays 1938
The Spur of the Moment 1939
Steadfast: A Commentary (Melbourne, Oxford University Press) 1941
Selections 1941
72 Essays: A Selection 1947
My 100 Answers (Adelaide, News Ltd.) 1953
Selected Essays 1956

VERSE

Anne's Animals, illustrated by Mrs Arthur Streeton (Melbourne, Endacott) 1921

Walter Murdoch is also the author of three school textbooks, *The Struggle for Freedom* (1903), *The Australian Citizen* (1912), and *The Making of Australia* (1915), all published by Whitcombe & Tombs, Melbourne.

Katharine Susannah Prichard

SO LITTLE TIME!

FIFTY-ODD years ago Alfred Deakin, then Prime Minister of Australia, gave a young Australian newspaper woman a letter of introduction to the English novelist George Meredith. Meredith was nearly eighty then, but his fine mind had lost none of its power. When the young woman, Katharine Susannah Prichard, visited Meredith at his home in the English countryside he asked her about her work. They discussed the techniques of story writing. She confessed to a tendency to revise too much. 'Throw it off ! Get rid of what there is in you,' Meredith advised her, meaning she should get down on paper whatever she had to say, without worrying too much about niceties of style and elegance of phrase. Meredith's advice stayed in her memory always, but it was many years before she brought herself to accept it without reservation. 'It's only lately, in fact,' she says, 'that I have realized it's more important for a writer to say whatever he has to say than to worry about form. It's what he says, not how he says it, that matters, although he must know the rules in order to break them effectively. Time is important to the writer. There's so much I want to do, so much I'll never have time to do now. I have an enormous amount of drafted stuff I'll never be able to finish. Life just isn't long enough!' Few serious Australian writers, however, have matched Katharine Susannah Prichard's output of published work—eleven novels, three volumes of short stories, a book-length children's tale, a travel book, two three-act plays, and two collections of verse. One novel, *The Pioneers*, was filmed in 1926, and the film shown throughout Australia.

Probably no Australian writer of this century has had more influence on Australia's literary development; many Australian writers of standing—and by no means all of them men or women who agree with her Left-wing political convictions—acknowledge a deep aesthetic debt to her. She is widely admired outside, as well as inside, Australia; after *The Roaring Nineties* was published in 1946, C. Hartley Grattan, the American critic, described her, in *The New York Times*, as 'unquestionably the most important living fiction writer of Australia'.

Although she is the widow of Captain Hugo Throssell, V.C., Katharine Susannah Prichard has retained her maiden name for literary work, and prefers to be referred to, as a writer, without the prefix Mrs or Miss. She published a collection of short stories, *N'Goola*, in 1959, but has not put out a new novel since 1950; this was *Winged Seeds*, the third novel in her goldfields trilogy. Now she is working on a novel, but heart trouble has broken the rhythm of her work in recent years, and progress has been slow. 'When finished—if ever—it's to be called *The Subtle Flame*,' she says. The title comes from a verse of Christopher Brennan.

Katharine Susannah Prichard was born in 1884, and is probably the oldest active novelist in Australia, and a living contradiction of a more or less popular theory that the creative instinct atrophies when a writer passes forty. She is a small woman, delicately boned, and perhaps five feet tall. Her bobbed hair is white, and the brown eyes behind her glasses have a kind of patient intentness; her nose and chin are strongly moulded, and the lines of her mouth are compassionate. The afternoon I called to see her at Greenmount, thirteen miles from Perth, she was wearing a brown corduroy tunic, slacks, and low-heeled brown shoes; when she moved it was with an air of almost girlish briskness.

Most of her writing has been done at Greenmount. She and her husband went to live in the old one-story house three years after they were married in 1919. It is a restful house, sheltered from the sun by trellised vines, and set in two and a half acres of wild garden. A detached workroom stands on the slope behind; her husband put it up for her many years ago, so she could shut herself away from interruptions. The workroom has timber walls lined with fibrous plaster, a great open fireplace, and cupboards packed with notes, manuscripts, and newspaper clippings. At her desk in this workroom she must have written well over a million words for publication, first drafting it in her small, pointed handwriting—which she unjustly calls an 'illegible scribble'—then typing it herself.

Many of her books have been translated for foreign publication. Her work appears in Russian, Armenian, Latvian, German, Polish, Czech, Slovak, Hungarian, Rumanian, Italian, French, and Chinese, and her first novel, *The Pioneers*, was translated into Afrikaans for radio broadcasting. These translations meant heavy work for her. She closely collaborated with the translators by letter; they sent her long lists of questions, seeking explanations of idiomatic terms, and she spent much time and thought in answering these. Many peculiarly

Australian words and phrases inevitably baffled the translators; these ranged from simple terms like 'billy', meaning the tin can the bushman uses to boil water for tea, to more complex expressions such as 'home and dried on the pig's back', which she defined as 'the successful conclusion of an enterprise: that a person will become wealthy and have no more financial worries'.

Although she has not published a novel since 1950, she has never stopped writing. In the last ten years she has written innumerable political articles, essays on literary subjects, and short stories for foreign and Australian publications. Her work for the World Peace movement has claimed a great deal of her time. She saw something of the battlefields in France and the terrible sufferings of wounded men during World War I; it was a great grief to her when her elder brother was killed in the fighting. The death of her husband, who died by his own hand in 1933, was an aftermath of war; and she suffered again the horror and anxiety of war when her son and only child, Ric, was on active service in New Guinea in World War II. Because she believes that to achieve a basis for the settlement of international disputes by negotiation, not war, is the most important objective of our generation, she has devoted energy to that purpose in practical activities, as well as in writing. Urged to write her reminiscences, she began on the story of her youth. But the reminiscences remain unfinished. 'I don't know,' she says, 'that the little incidents of one's life are worth remembering when so many big and important things are happening. There is so much to do, helping people to realize that another world war must not occur.'

Katharine Susannah Prichard, whose work is intensely Australian, was born, not in Australia, but in Levuka, Fiji, of mixed Irish, Scottish, Welsh and English ancestry. Her mother was born in Australia, and her father, Tom Henry Prichard, was for all practical purposes an Australian also; his Welsh parents brought him from England as an infant, and all his early life was spent here. He was editing *The Fiji Times* when Katharine Susannah was born; she was the eldest of his four children—two sons and two daughters. She remembers nothing of Fiji, because her parents came to live in Melbourne when she was three. Her father edited a Melbourne weekly, *The Sun*, for a while, then went to Tasmania as editor of the Launceston *Daily Telegraph*, which was then fighting hard to stay alive. *The Telegraph* closed in the end, and the Prichards returned to Melbourne, where Tom Prichard became editor of *The Mining Standard*; through its columns he played a significant part in influencing mining law reforms.

Katharine Susannah attended primary schools in Victoria and Tasmania, but the school she remembers best is South Melbourne

College. The headmaster, J. B. O'Hara, was not only an inspired teacher, but also a talented poet. He recognized her literary promise, and encouraged her. Her literary bent was part of her birthright; apart from journalistic articles, her father published much verse, and also a novel of early Melbourne, *Retaliation*, which came out in 1891.

Circumstances, notably an illness suffered by her mother, then lack of family means, prevented her from going to the university when she left school. So, after two or three years at home, she decided to see Australia. She went as governess to a doctor's family in South Gippsland; some years later she was to base her first novel, *The Pioneers*, on her experiences there. After a year she moved to a station beyond Broken Hill, still as a governess, and found herself in an environment utterly different from that of South Gippsland. She was writing steadily at that time, and publishing stories, sketches and factual articles in various newspapers and magazines; her first adult short story had been published some time before, when she was twenty, in the Melbourne magazine, *New Idea*, but she says it was 'very immature'.

In 1908, after seeing a good deal of Australia, she went to London and stayed a year or so, writing articles and interviewing people for the *New Idea* and the Melbourne *Herald*. On her return to Australia she was invited to become social editress of *The Herald*. Soon she was running her own page—the first woman's page, she says, in a Melbourne daily newspaper. She liked what she was doing, particularly the opportunities she had to study, and write articles about, the work of organizations such as the Anti-Sweating League which were attacking social abuses. 'What happened,' she says, 'was that my political consciousness began to wake.'

She left *The Herald* because her health broke down, and after a rest decided to go back to London. There, from a flat in Chelsea, she worked hard to break into print, at firs with no success. In Fleet Street one day she turned, on sudden impulse, into the office of *The Globe*, an evening newspaper, and asked to see the editor. To her astonishment, she was shown into his room after a few minutes. She handed him an article on osier harvesting and said, 'This has been returned from nearly every newspaper in London. Will you tell me what's wrong with it?' He read the article through and said, 'I like it.' He printed it, and asked her for more articles. Soon, her writings were appearing, not only in *The Globe*, but also in *The Star*, *Daily Chronicle*, *Daily Herald*, *Weekly Dispatch*, *English Review*, *Pall Mall Gazette*, and other English publications; she contributed also to French periodicals published in Paris.

After about two years she had enough money put by to keep

herself for six months without working, and she decided to write a novel and enter it in a competition organized by a London publisher. Her novel, *The Pioneers*, won the prize of a thousand pounds and was published in 1915. 'I wanted to come home then and write about Australia,' she says. 'It was to do creative work in Australia that I was in training. I didn't want to stay in London; I used to go round the cafés there and hear people talking of the wonderful things they were going to do, and I felt if I stayed I'd become like them, and talk instead of write.' She arrived home in 1916, and, although she has made one trip abroad since then, she has never wished to live outside Australia or write of any country but Australia.

'I like most of all,' she says, 'to write about the realities of life for men and women, in novels and short stories. It seems to me you get into closer sympathy with people by writing about human beings and interpreting, or trying to interpret, the depths of the human consciousness.' Apart from the large amount of her imaginative writing which has gone into books, she has also written plays, and most of these have been produced by amateur companies. The most effective of her plays is probably *Brumby Innes*, which in 1927 won the Sydney *Triad* prize for an Australian three-act play, but has never been produced—'Perhaps because it contains several aboriginal characters,' she says. As a writer for the theatre, she has been less successful than her son, Ric Throssell, an officer of the Australian External Affairs Department. Several of his plays have been produced in Australia by amateur or semi-professional groups; one, *The Day Before Tomorrow*, a three-act drama, was put on by a professional company at the 1960 Edinburgh Festival.

In her effort to do honest work, Katharine Susannah Prichard has specially prized two sentences of Auguste Rodin, the nineteenth century French sculptor. These, as she herself translates them, are: 'Art is the joy of the intelligence which sees the universe clearly and re-creates by illumination of the consciousness. Art is the most sublime mission of man, since it is the exercise of thought which seeks to understand the world and to make others understand it.' She believes those words will be valid for her as long as she goes on writing. That seems likely to be for as long as she goes on living.

So Little Time!

FICTION

The Pioneers (London, Hodder & Stoughton) 1915
Windlestraws (London, Holden & Hardingham) 1916
Black Opal (London, Heinemann) 1921
Working Bullocks (London, Cape) 1926
Coonardoo: The Well in the Shadow (London, Cape) 1929
Haxby's Circus (London, Cape) 1930
Kiss on the Lips and Other Stories (London, Cape) 1932
Intimate Strangers (London, Cape) 1937
Moon of Desire (London, Cape) 1941
Potch and Colour. Short stories (Sydney, Angus & Robertson) 1944
The Roaring Nineties (London, Cape) 1946
Golden Miles (Sydney, Australasian Publishing Co.) 1948
Winged Seeds (Sydney, Australasian Publishing Co.) 1950
N'Goola. Short stories (Melbourne, Australasian Publishing Co.) 1959

For Children

The Wild Oats of Han (Sydney, Angus & Robertson) 1928

VERSE

Clovelly Verses (London, McAllan) 1913
The Earth Lover and Other Verses (Sydney, Sunnybrook Press) 1932

GENERAL

The Real Russia (Sydney, Modern Publishing) 1934

DRAMA

Brumby Innes: A Play in Three Acts (Perth, Paterson's) 1940

Ion L. Idriess

BUSHMAN IN RETIREMENT

THE life of a popular writer is not all royalties and plaudits. It isn't for Ion L. Idriess at any rate. Not that Idriess dislikes being a popular writer or ever hankers to go back to the bush as a worker, instead of as a kind of privileged tourist who knows his way about. But now and then, when some fanatic tries to persuade him to use his influence and writing skill to advance one or another crack-pot scientific or political theory, he is tempted to head for the bush and go into hiding until the pressure is off. He suffers more than most writers do from such pests. This is not only because his books have made his name familiar to practically every Australian, but also because, being a kindly man who has known hard times himself, he can never bring himself to send importunate callers on their way. A man came to him not long ago with a scheme for simplifying travel between Australia and England which had a kind of heroic simplicity; it called for a shaft, with one end opening in Martin Place, Sydney, and the other in Trafalgar Square, London, to be driven through the centre of the earth. Idriess felt there were certain practical objections to the plan, but its author swept aside all argument; he had laboured for years to perfect it and it would, he insisted, work. He knew his tunnel would be costly to build, but he was confident that Idriess could fire Australians with enthusiasm for the idea and induce them to subscribe all the money required to turn the dream into an accomplished fact. He dogged his prey like a bloodhound; Idriess became nervous of answering the telephone, for fear the tunnel man would be on the other end, or to visit any of his accustomed haunts, lest the tunnel man should be lying in wait. 'I eventually foiled this bloke, though,' he says, in his lilting drawl. 'I took off for Queensland, going and returning the long way. But I still find myself peering over my shoulder at times, wondering if he'll drop on me again.'

Idriess, whose friends call him Jack, probably because Ion seems too grand a name for so simple a man, is now over seventy. His sparse hair is white and his mobile face and leathery neck are deeply lined, but his quick-moving slight figure and his bright and guileless grey eyes belong to a man twenty-five years younger. Every morning, unless he is on a professional walkabout in the bush, he catches a bus in Anzac Parade, near his home, in the Sydney suburb of Kingsford, and arrives at Angus and Robertson's in Castlereagh Street, by nine-thirty or ten; there, in a corner of an office on the first floor, he works at an old-fashioned wooden table, writing with a lead pencil in a sprawling hand, about thirty words to each quarto sheet of unlined white paper. He never works in the afternoon, and is always ready to push work aside in the morning for a yarn and two or three drinks with any friend who happens to call. Since a dozen or so of Idriess's outback friends are apt to be visiting Sydney at any given time, his morning's work is often interrupted. He likes it that way.

He can write a book easily in three months, and he never wishes now to write more than one book a year. Until 1953 he often wrote and published two books in a single year, and in each of three years—1932, 1940 and 1941—he put out three books. Then, finding that one book a year earned all the money he needed and that most of his royalties for extra books went in taxes, he decided to take life easily as a one-book-a-year author. He is no advocate of work merely for work's sake.

Practically everything Ion Idriess writes is based on experiences he had or stories he heard long ago in his bush days. Many, though not all, of his books are wholly reminiscent. He has always been an inveterate note-taker, and at his home he has enough unpublished stuff, scribbled in notebooks, to fill a book a year for the next twenty or thirty years. His 1960 book, *The Wild North*, is typical. It has twenty-four chapters, each a self-contained story; these bear such titles as The Slaying of Rungooma, The Big Toe of Wu-Roo-Moo, and The Lucky Opal. Apart from three stories, describing experiences Idriess had as a soldier in World War I, every story has the remote outback or the near Pacific islands for background. 'They were all written long ago,' he says. 'I put most of them down on paper about thirty years back, and stowed the manuscript away in a trunk when I came down from Thursday Island on holiday to Grafton many years ago. I did the same thing after World War I. I packed all my war diaries under my sister's house in Grafton. Years later, these became *The Desert Column*, which is still selling. I'd forgotten all about *The Wild North* stories until I lobbed on the notes of them while I was having a clean-up at my house one day. They seemed to me to give a reasonably true picture of aspects of Australian life which have vanished for ever. So I harnessed them together as a book.'

In 1961 he put out another book, *Tracks of Destiny*, based on things seen and notes taken in the early 1930s when he made a trip from Derby down through the Centre to the Tennant Creek goldfield.

Idriess, christened Ion Llewellyn, was born in 1890 in the Sydney suburb of Waverley, but by the time he was old enough to take notice of his surroundings he was far from any city. His father was a Welsh seaman who married an Australian girl, settled in Australia, and lived and worked almost entirely outside the cities. 'From six months of age, I was always travelling,' Idriess says. He decided to get away from his parents' home in Broken Hill when he was seventeen. In Sydney, he signed on the paddle steamer *Newcastle* as boatswain's mate. The ship, trading to Newcastle, and up the Hunter River to Morpeth, had more than her quota of bugs and fleas, but Idriess's berth was a good one by the standards of the time—thirty-five shillings a week and adequate tucker. He stood the bugs and fleas for about three months; then he paid off in Sydney and went back to the bush.

He knows most corners of Australia and the adjacent Pacific territories. He has worked as opal gouger, gold prospector, diver, station hand, miner, builder's labourer, wharf labourer, pearler, horse-tailer, horse-breaker, and many other things. He was one of the early miners at Lightning Ridge opal field in the Three Mile rush, over fifty years ago. He carried his swag there down the Barwon River from Collarenebri, where he had been working. Only a hundred and fifty men were on the field when he arrived, but within a few weeks the number had risen to fifteen hundred. Luck was against Idriess; he found no opal, and his money ran out, He left Lightning Ridge as he had arrived, carrying his swag, and took a job on Woorawadian station, outside Walgett. His pay there was a pound a week and keep, and as soon as he saved enough for a few weeks' tucker he went back to Lightning Ridge. He staked a new claim, started work, and struck good opal after six hours' digging; a few weeks' work gave him opal worth some hundreds of pounds.

'One of my friends at Lightning Ridge was a Sydney solicitor,' he says. 'Booze had got him, and his family had sent him there, with thirty shillings a week to live on, hoping he'd straighten up. He took a fancy to me. He said, "You're very observant of birds and nature in general. Why don't you write something for *The Bulletin*?"' Idriess wrote some paragraphs by the light of his slush lamp, and sent them to *The Bulletin*. They were acknowledged in the Answers to Correspondents column. The answer was: 'Stick to your pick and shovel; they're the pen that suits your style!' Undismayed, he kept writing paragraphs, and at last *The Bulletin* printed two or three, and paid him five shillings each for them. He found himself watching for curious incidents and listening for scraps of amusing conversation, and jotting the details of these down before he forgot them. Most of the paragraphs and sketches he sent to *The Bulletin* continued to be rejected, but his acceptance rate steadily rose. '*Bulletin* cheques often staked me to tucker in those days,' he says.

When war broke out in 1914 he was in Cape York Peninsula. He stowed away at Cooktown in the flag locker of a small steamer which took him as far as Cairns; there he again stowed away—this time in a lifeboat—in a steamer bound for Townsville, and there he enlisted. He served with the Light Horse on Gallipoli, on the Sinai Peninsula, and in Palestine, and was wounded three times. When he was invalided out of the AIF, a few months before the Armistice, the doctors told him he would never again walk unaided. He could not move without a crutch, but he would not accept the doctors' verdict. He put himself in the hands of the physical culturist brothers, Snowy and Harald Baker, and a few months later he was walking normally, without even a limp. He went back to the bush and started writing again for *The Bulletin*, which now occasionally printed one of his longer sketches, as well as many of his paragraphs. His name began to be known.

He does not recall when he first thought of writing a book, but the book itself, *Madman's Island*, came out in 1927. It was a failure. In the main it was a factual account of his own experiences on Howick Island, off the Queensland coast, but the publisher urged him to introduce a so-called love interest into it to 'broaden the appeal'. Against his own judgment, Idriess complied, and he feels the interpolation of that imaginary material made the story unconvincing. He is probably right; some years later he cut the love interest from *Madman's Island* for a revised edition which sold well and is still selling.

He did not dream of becoming a professional writer until 1931. That was soon after the economic depression began. Unable to find work in the bush, he went to Sydney and wore his boots out looking for a job. He was living in a five-shillings-a-week room—'a little dogbox under the stairs', he calls it—in a house in West Street, behind St Vincent's Hospital. One afternoon he was walking through Hyde Park, and an idea came to him. He went to Angus and Robertson's shop and offices, in Castlereagh Street, and asked for the boss. He was shown in to Walter Cousins's room; Cousins was then Angus and Robertson's manager and publishing director.

'Want a book?'

'What sort of book?'

'About looking for gold.'

'Sit down,' Cousins said. He sensed the possibilities of such a book, at a time when thousands of unemployed men were desperately seeking any way of earning a few shillings. He and Idriess talked for a while. Then Cousins rang for his secretary and said, 'Give this man a wad of paper and a dozen lead pencils. . . . Now,' he told Idriess, 'get to your room and get it down in a fortnight.'

A fortnight later Idriess's book *Prospecting for Gold* was not only written, but also printed, published, and on sale.

He has never stopped writing since then, and he never seems likely to stop now. His books have not given him affluence, but they have provided a comfortable living for him and his wife, whom he married soon after settling in Sydney, and their two daughters. He does not know how many books he has published. When I asked him he scratched his balding head, fingered his chin, and said, 'About fifty, or a few more perhaps. Anyway, they're all in print and go on selling, except about a dozen which were topical when they came out and weren't intended to last.'

What Idriess has done would be remarkable for a man who had devoted his whole life to building a writing career. For a bushman who was past forty before he considered writing to be anything more than a pastime, it is a phenomenal achievement.

GENERAL

(All published by Angus & Robertson, Sydney)

Madman's Island 1927
Prospecting for Gold 1931
Lasseter's Last Ride 1931
Flynn of the Inland 1932
The Desert Column 1932
Men of the Jungle 1932
Gold-Dust and Ashes 1933
The Drums of Mer 1933
The Yellow Joss 1934
Man Tracks 1935
The Cattle King 1936
Forty Fathoms Deep 1937

* *Madman's Island* was first published under the imprint of the Cornstalk Publishing Company, but this was merely a name used by Angus & Robertson for some books published in the 1920s; it was later dropped. A revised edition of *Madman's Island* was issued under Angus & Robertson's own imprint in 1938.

Bushman in Retirement

Over the Range 1937
Cyaniding for Gold 1939
Must Australia Fight? 1939
The Great Trek 1940
Headhunters of the Coral Sea 1940
Lightning Ridge 1940
Nemarluk 1941
The Great Boomerang 1941
Fortunes in Minerals 1941
Onward, Australia! 1944
The Silent Service (T. M. Jones & Ion L. Idriess) 1944
Horrie the Wog Dog 1945
In Crocodile Land 1946
Isles of Despair 1947
The Opium Smugglers 1948
Stone of Destiny 1948
One Wet Season 1949
The Wild White Man of Badu 1950
Across the Nullarbor 1951
Outlaws of the Leopolds 1952
The Red Chief 1953
The Nor'-Westers 1954
The Vanished People 1955
The Silver City 1956
Coral Sea Calling 1957
Back o' Cairns 1958
The Tin Scratchers 1959
The Wild North 1960
Tracks of Destiny 1961
My Mate Dick 1962

Six handbooks discussing different aspects of guerilla fighting, by Ion Idriess, were published in 1942 and 1943.

FRANK DALBY DAVISON

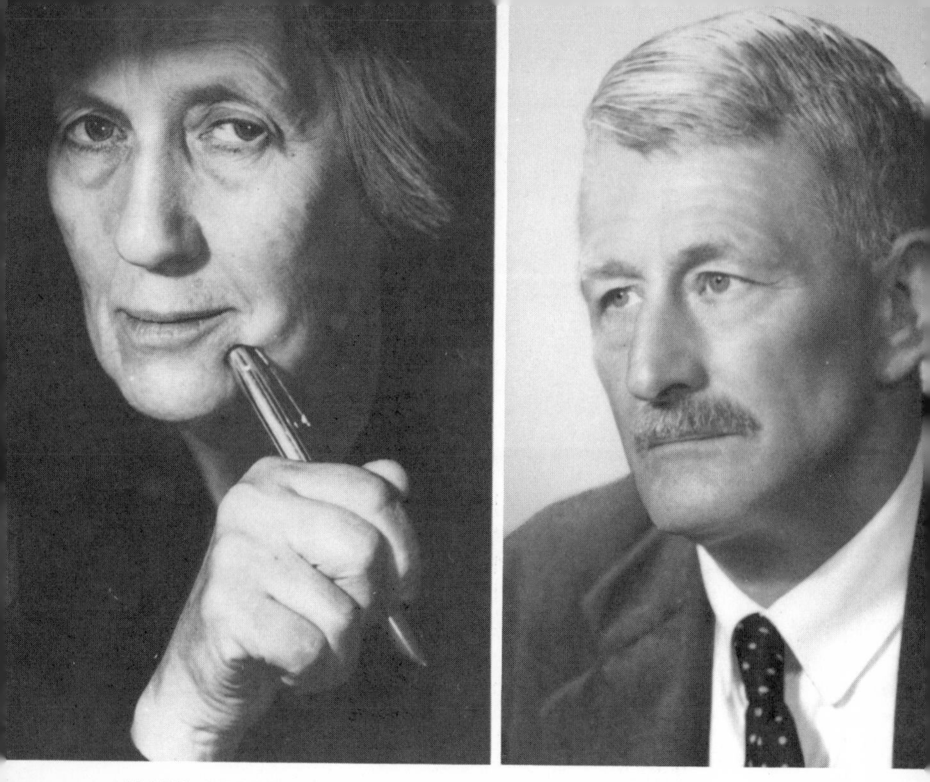

MARY MITCHELL LEONARD MANN

XAVIER HERBERT GAVIN LONG

Arthur Upfield

MURDER IS HIS BUSINESS

ONE literary critic or another every now and then tries to persuade Arthur Upfield to change his writing ways. Such advisers tell Upfield he is wasting his talents on mystery-detection stories and should abandon his half-caste aboriginal hero, Detective Inspector Napoleon Bonaparte, and write what are called 'straight' novels. Marshall Pugh, in the Scottish *Daily Mail*, Edinburgh, reviewing a novel by Upfield in 1957, said among other things: 'The great mystery to be solved is why so true a writer as Mr Upfield bothers to write crime fiction at all.' It is no mystery to Upfield. He says, 'I like writing what I write. There are only two subjects to write about—crime and sex. A good clean murder, no matter how badly written, is better than a sordid seduction, no matter how well written. That's my view, and I don't imagine I'll ever change it.' Upfield's admirers, not only in Australia, but also in the U.K., the U.S.A., Germany, South America, Italy, Denmark, Holland, Japan, and other countries where his books are read, doubtless hope he never will change it. In all these places Upfield's skill in depicting Australia and Australians has been noted and admired, but also in all these places it is chiefly for Bony that Upfield's books are avidly read. Nobody knows this better than Upfield. He knows he is an able craftsman, but gives himself no airs on that account; he sees no more reason for pride in being able to turn a good sentence than in being able to manage a fractious horse, which, as an old bushman, he can do equally well.

Now in the early seventies he bears few outward marks of his twenty years in the bush. His hands are those of a man who has done much rough work, and his hazel eyes, netted in fine wrinkles, are a bushman's eyes, but he dresses as conventionally as any retired bank manager or pharmacist. He is equable, tolerant in his judgments, easy in his speech. His nose is short and blunt, and his straight mouth good humoured. His strong dark hair, although greying, has not begun to thin.

Upfield's refusal to be jockeyed by critics into writing novels different from the kind with which he made his name does not mean he holds critics and their opinions in contempt. On the contrary, he believes he writes better books because he takes intelligent notice of critics. 'The great majority of critics have been kind to me,' he says. 'A book will bring anything from forty to a hundred serious reviews, and I always study the complete mass to see what I can learn from them. If three or more critics object to some particular point I avoid that point in the next book. If three or more stress the value of a book for, say, its background, I take note of that also for future use.' In short, Upfield is a thorough-going professional. He likes to read praise of his books. What author doesn't? But he does not automatically assume that adverse criticism is dictated by malice, envy, or the malfunctioning of the critic's liver.

Upfield has travelled from end to end of Australia, and has set novels in every State, but only in places he knows more or less intimately. He insists on being certain that his local colour is accurate down to the smallest detail; he likes to feel that not even the most carping veteran living in some town or district he writes about could fault him on the finest point of topography or idiom. He was delighted when his twenty-fifth Napoleon Bonaparte novel, *Bony and the Kelly Gang*,* roused approving interest in the solid New South Wales country town of Bowral, eighty miles from Sydney, where Upfield has lived for some years; for Bowral figures in the tale, which is largely set in the valleys honeycombing the nearby countryside. Nobody in Bowral challenged any of the local details in the novel; the principal of a large Roman Catholic school even bought twelve copies as prizes.

'In Bong Bong Street, Bowral's main street, on a Saturday morning,' Upfield says, 'you'll find all the types I've written about in *Bony and the Kelly Gang*. They're not figments of my imagination, but real people.' He wrote *Bony and the Kelly Gang* after making a long study of his characters (though none of the prototypes knew they were being studied, and would one day find themselves in a novel) and an equally long study of the valleys which provide the locale of the tale. These valleys, he says, were originally settled by Irish rebels, who made their own laws and handed their way of life down to their children and their children's children, generation after generation. They even distilled their own liquor in illicit stills, and continue to do so; for a hundred years, he discovered, one valley had a still hidden by the cataract of a waterfall. Even today policemen are anathema to

* *Bony and the Kelly Gang* is the title of the U.K. edition of the novel first published in the U.S.A. as *Valley of Smugglers*.

the valley people. Upfield says he knows of one policeman who was told by a valley-dweller only a few years ago, 'If you come into our valley you'll never get out!' It wasn't said as a joke. 'I've a great liking for the valley people,' Upfield says, 'and in *Bony and the Kelly Gang* I think I created great sympathy for them.'

It would be astonishing if Upfield did not admire rebels, because he is, by inclination, a rebel himself. If he were not, he would be a respectable suburbanite in his native England, not a novelist in Australia, the country he adopted fifty-odd years ago. His father was a draper, in the town of Gosport, on Portsmouth Harbour, and Upfield, the eldest of five brothers, was born in 1891. His people were strong non-conformists, but young Upfield would not conform even with non-conformity, and when he was nineteen his father summoned him and told him to pack his bags for Australia. 'I have come to look on Australia as the ideal country for you,' Upfield's father said. 'It is so far away that you will never save enough money to return.'

Arthur Upfield had twenty years in the bush. He worked at boundary riding, cattle droving, opal gouging, rabbit trapping, cooking, any and every kind of job, but in his early years here he had no time to write. While he was away with the AIF in World War I he sold to English magazines two or three short stories, set in the Australian outback, and when he came home to Australia in 1919 he went back to the bush, like a homing pigeon. He must have seemed, to people who did not know him, to be a drifter, a man without ambition. All the time, however, he was collecting material for novels, working toward the point where he would cease to be a bush-worker and become a writer.

He was stockmen's cook at a place called Wheeler's Well, in the Broken Hill region, when in the middle of the 1920s he wrote his first book; at least it was his first book since he had written three thrilling—and deservedly unpublished—novels as a youth in Gosport. It was some years before this book, twice rewritten and radically altered, was published, as *The Barrakee Mystery*. It came out in London in 1929, but not until a year after the appearance of Upfield's first published book, *The House of Cain*, a thriller which he wrote in between rewritings of *The Barrakee Mystery*.

The Barrakee Mystery really marked the beginning of his career as an author, for in it he created his now famous character, Napoleon Bonaparte, who has been the central figure in twenty-six of his thirty published novels. In the first draft of *The Barrakee Mystery* the murder of a full-blooded aborigine on a Darling River homestead was investigated by a white detective. Upfield liked the tale well enough, until one day an old bush friend called on him and spent the night yarning with him in his hut at Wheeler's Well. The caller was a half-caste aboriginal police tracker named Leon Wood, a man of high intelligence and some education combined with surpassing bush lore; and as Tracker Leon rode away the idea came to Upfield of scrapping his white detective in favour of a half-caste detective. At first he intended calling his detective Leon Wood, but some days later he was reading a life of Napoleon Bonaparte. Napoleon Bonaparte! It was perfect. And so Arthur Upfield's Napoleon Bonaparte was named.

Bony is now one of the world's most celebrated fictional detectives. Bony novels have sold well over a million copies in hard covers, and two million copies in paperbacks. *The Widows of Broome* is the biggest seller; in the U.S. alone, where it was a Mystery Guild of America selection, it sold two hundred and ten thousand copies in hard-cover editions. 'If I had achieved my success in the 1920s and early 1930s,' Upfield says, 'I'd have been able to afford a mansion and an ocean-going yacht. My books have earned big money only since 1943, however, and all I get out of them, taxation and costs being what they are, is a comfortable living.' But Bony will possibly yet make Upfield rich. Hollywood producers have nibbled two or three times, but Bony has not yet, like Perry Mason, Philip Marlowe, Nero Wolfe, Nick Charles and other celebrated detectives of fiction, gone into films. It hardly seems possible, though, that film-makers will neglect him for ever.

Upfield quit the outback in 1931, after his fourth book, *The Sands of Windee*, was published, and he was often on, and at times slightly under, the breadline in the next ten years or so. He kept on writing books all the time, and steadily building a reputation, but until 1943 he knew he was in a precarious business. Then a New York publisher 'discovered' Upfield and Napoleon Bonaparte. This publisher issued six Bony books in two years, and has gone on publishing Upfield ever since. The earnings of his books in the U.S.A., and in those other countries which took no notice of Bony until he was recognized in New York, have changed Upfield's life. 'Since the war,' he says, 'I've been able to get along without worrying about keeping the pot boiling. Now I turn out a book every nine or ten months—six months working on it, and three to four months loafing. Given a good run, I work easily enough, but an intrusion throws me for seven. First, I get the germ of an idea. Then I card-index all the characters, and live with them for some weeks before starting to write. After the first writing, I sleep well on it, then completely re-write the story. Whatever each of the characters has felt during the story, I have felt. I've experienced horror, narrow escapes, humorous interludes, sentiment, everything When it's ended I'm as empty mentally as a discarded bottle.'

At Bowral Upfield has an airy modern house, comfortably furnished in casual style, and he writes in a small study whose walls are hung with frames displaying dust-jackets of his books from publishing houses in nine or ten different countries. He works on a portable typewriter, at an austerely plain desk. On a handy shelf are the six or seven reference books he uses, including a two-volume edition of Taylor's *Principles and Practice of Medical Jurisprudence*, Spencer and Gillen's *Across Australia*, a Bible, a dictionary, and a volume of quotations. In this study Upfield also types answers to his heavy mail, which consists not only of queries touching his books, such as 'What became of the little dog in *Man of Two Tribes*?', but also of queries entirely unrelated to his work. Supposing him to be an authority on all things Australian, people throughout the world send him questions in a steady stream. A Chicago furniture manufacturer asked, 'What are the lasting qualities of red gum killed by water?'; a Finnish safety engineer, 'What openings are there in Australia for a safety engineer?'; a Harvard professor, 'What is the aboriginal meaning of the word Meenamurtee?' Upfield answered each of these inquiries to the best of his ability. He never ignores any question possibly because Napoleon Bonaparte's creator dare not admit himself to be less than omniscient.

From his Bowral study, he also personally answers occasional letters which come, addressed either to Detective Inspector Napoleon Bonaparte, Queensland, or to Upfield himself, written by people in different parts of the world who believe Bony to be a real person. 'It shows,' Upfield says, 'how many credulous folk there must be.' It doesn't. What it shows is that, in Detective Inspector Napoleon Bonaparte, Upfield has created a living, breathing man.

FICTION

The House of Cain (London, Hutchinson) 1928
The Barrakee Mystery (London, Hutchinson) 1929
The Beach of Atonement (London, Hutchinson) 1930
The Sands of Windee (London, Hutchinson) 1931
A Royal Abduction (London, Hutchinson) 1932
Gripped by Drought (London, Hutchinson) 1932
Wings Above the Diamantina (Sydney, Angus & Robertson) 1936
Mr Jelly's Business (Sydney, Angus & Robertson) 1937
Winds of Evil (Sydney, Angus & Robertson) 1937
The Bone is Pointed (Sydney, Angus & Robertson) 1938
The Mystery of Swordfish Reef (Sydney, Angus & Robertson) 1939
Bushrangers of the Skies (Sydney, Angus & Robertson) 1940
Death of a Swagman (New York, Doubleday) 1945
The Devil's Steps (New York, Doubleday) 1946
An Author Bites the Dust (New York, Doubleday) 1948
The Mountains Have a Secret (New York, Doubleday) 1948
The Widows of Broome (New York, Doubleday) 1949
The Bachelors of Broken Hill (New York, Doubleday) 1950
The New Shoe (New York, Doubleday) 1951
Venom House (New York, Doubleday) 1952
Murder Must Wait (New York, Doubleday) 1953
Death of a Lake (New York, Doubleday) 1954
Sinister Stones (New York, Doubleday) 1954
The Battling Prophet (London, Heinemann) 1956
Man of Two Tribes (New York, Doubleday) 1956
The Bushman Who Came Back (New York, Doubleday) 1957
Journey to the Hangman (New York, Doubleday) 1959
Bony and the Black Virgin (London, Heinemann) 1959
Valley of Smugglers (New York, Doubleday) 1960
The White Savage (New York, Doubleday) 1961
The Will of the Tribe (London, Heinemann) 1962

N.B. Many of Upfield's books appear under different titles in U.K.-Australian editions and U.S. editions. The title of any book listed here is that used in the first English-language edition, wherever published.

John Tierney

ON LAWSON'S HEELS

THE hamlet of Eurunderee, near Mudgee, N.S.W., was credited with a population of a hundred and one men, women and children when these words were written. Eurunderee was once much larger, notably in the district gold rushes of the 1870s, and later when intensive mixed farming lifted the population. But at best it was never anything more than a small town, so it is astonishing that from Eurunderee schoolhouse should have come two of Australia's most talented creative writers. One was Henry Lawson. The other, though less widely known, has of late years won a growing audience for his fiction; his name is Brian James. That at any rate is the name under which his short stories and the one novel he has yet published have been printed, but his legal name is John Tierney, schoolmaster by profession, farmer by preference, and writer by some kind of inner compulsion.

In writing of John Tierney it is necessary to decide whether to designate him by his true name or his pen-name; the choice is not really hard, for Brian James the writer cannot be adequately comprehended without examining John Tierney the man. He was a late starter as a writer. His first story appeared in print on June 17, 1942, which chanced to be the day he turned fifty—an age at which most writers have either published five or six books or abandoned altogether the struggle for literary fulfilment. (Students of coincidence might find it significant that he and Lawson were born on the same day of the year, June 17, although twenty-five years separated their birthdays.) In the next twenty years he published three volumes of short stories, *First Furrow*, *Cookabundy Bridge*, and *The Bunyip of Barney's Elbow*, and a novel, *The Advancement of Spencer Button*, as well as many other short stories which have yet to be collected into a book.

Tierney retired from school teaching in June, 1951, and he and his wife live in a pleasant one-story cottage at Beecroft, sixteen or seventeen miles from Sydney, on an edge of the 'green belt'. The immediate surroundings of the cottage testify to his love of the soil and his talent for wooing it; although he has well under half an acre of cultivable land he has girdled his house with about twenty-five orange and lemon trees, and a few peach and plum trees. A casual visitor could not spend ten minutes at the Tierneys' cottage without being aware that here is a man with a passion for making things grow in the earth. Yet the same visitor might well leave after staying all day without having discovered that John Tierney has ever written anything that has seen print. One of his closest friends says he is 'too modest for literary poses', and this is true. Not even a typewriter is visible. He writes all his fiction in his clear pointed handwriting, and his wife types the drafts which he submits to editors and publishers.

Critics have noted some external resemblance between the short stories of Lawson and Tierney, and this is not surprising, for Lawson's literary achievements almost inevitably influenced Tierney's outlook and aspirations. 'Lawson,' he says, 'filled a large part of my horizon as a child. I read everything he wrote. Also my family and Lawson's were intimately associated. Of course, I have never tried to imitate Lawson. Nor could I have done so—Lawson is inimitable. But the Eurunderee of my youth was still the Eurunderee that Lawson knew, and many of my stories are set in Eurunderee and Mudgee. Apart from that, there is little in common between us. Lawson's powers, though limited in many ways, were infinitely greater than mine.'

The first Eurunderee schoolhouse, built of bark, opened to pupils in 1876; John Tierney's father, a British army veteran who had come to Australia seeking gold, was the head (and at that time the only) teacher. Two years later a permanent schoolhouse, with a residence attached, was put up by Henry Lawson's father, Peter Lawson (or Larsen). This structure, built of hardwood slabs, served as a schoolhouse until the 1920s; then, the district population having diminished, the school was closed and the building dismantled. Young Henry Lawson, aged nine or ten, was an early pupil at Eurunderee, until his mother, a strong-minded woman, quarrelled with John Tierney's father and removed her son to a Catholic school at Mudgee. This was nearly fifteen years before John Tierney was born, in 1892. His father died some months before his birth, and he was the youngest of seven surviving children.

He was born on to a farm at Eurunderee which his father had been battling to develop for some years. As a farm, it was nothing wonderful, only a hundred and thirty acres, and much of the soil was rocky; but John Tierney's mother, who had been born on the Rhine of sturdy German peasant stock, continued working it, and somehow managed to wring a living for her family from that obdurate soil. Young John loved the farm, with all its shortcomings, and never wished to leave it. He wanted with all his being to become a farmer, and while he was getting his primary education at the Eurunderee schoolhouse he pictured himself running the farm; or, if not that farm, then another. Many of his short stories express his deep and abiding love of the soil, and in some ways his fiction has been a kind of substitute for the farmer's life which he missed. Although he did not wish to become a teacher, his mother felt that teaching offered a settled career; so when he finished school he became a pupil-teacher. At eighteen he went to Sydney and entered the teachers' training college. Then, after a spell as a primary school teacher, he took a B.A. degree and became a high school teacher in 1914. Eight years later he took an M.A. degree at Sydney and a year after that a Dip. Ed. at Oxford. For thirty-seven years his work took him to high schools in many parts of New South Wales, teaching English, history, geography, Latin, and mathematics; it also gave him the chance to acquire a deep knowledge of the ways of that strange, and often unpredictable animal, man.

He did not marry until he was forty, and at that time he was trying to combine teaching with farming. Two years or so earlier he had bought a smallholding of fifteen acres at Glenorie, N.S.W., and, having cleared much of it with his own hands, worked, mostly at weekends, to turn it into a productive farm. It was a wearing task, because he was teaching then at Fort Street Boys' High School, Sydney, and Glenorie lay about thirty miles from the city. In the end a combination of circumstances beat him, and he sold out. 'I made much more out of the farm by writing about it than by selling anything I ever grew on it,' he says. 'It gave me the characters and background for at least twenty stories.'

It was the Glenorie farm that launched him as a writer. His anecdotes about clearing the property entertained his wife, and she suggested he should write them into a connected narrative. He did so, then put the story away in a drawer and forgot it. Years later his wife mentioned the story to the Sydney novelist Marjorie Barnard, who asked if she might read it. She liked it, and John Tierney made some changes she suggested, and sent it to *The Bulletin*. To his astonishment, he says, *The Bulletin* published it. The story is called *Bungally*, the popular name of a species of low scrub which, sprawling all over the Glenorie property, seemed to be endowed with a kind of superhuman malevolence. John Tierney's first book of short stories, *First Furrow*, published in 1944, opens with *Bungally*; for a man's first story, like his first girl, has a special place in his affections. His Glenorie experiences inspired all the stories in *First Furrow*, as well as a dozen or so of the forty-two stories in a second book,

Cookabundy Bridge, a more ambitious volume which came out in 1946.

'The short story is my chief literary interest,' he says. 'To me, the writing of a short story poses more problems than the writing of a novel does.' Any man who has published as many short stories of high quality as John Tierney has done—his total, at latest count, runs between seventy and eighty, and he has another sixty or seventy in typescript—must be heeded on this point. Some of his friends, however, believe he would make a bigger literary name by concentrating on novels. *The Advancement of Spencer Button* indicated the range of his abilities as a novelist. In its ironic analysis of human behaviour, this novel recalls the work of the American Sinclair Lewis, who, John Tierney says, 'has made as deep an impression on me as any writer'. This does not mean that either Spencer Button or his story is an adaptation from Lewis. The novel is utterly Australian in atmosphere, sentiment and flavour, and Sinclair Lewis could no more have written it than John Tierney could have written, say, *Babbitt* or *Elmer Gantry*. Its theme, however, is universal. Spencer Button, although an Australian schoolmaster, is a type of man fairly common everywhere; a time-server, so calculatingly wooing success that he dies having missed everything which might have given his life meaning.

The Advancement of Spencer Button was published in 1950, and Tierney's admirers hoped it would be only the first of a sequence of novels by him. In 1956 he published a third book of short stories, *The Bunyip of Barney's Elbow*, but as the years passed and he did not put out another novel it began to appear that, like many a writer before him, he had grown weary of the lonely struggle. This was not so, however. Some years ago he finished a second novel, *Hopeton High*, and sent it to his publishers, but then withdrew it because he wished to do more work on it. Having modified it to his liking he resubmitted it for publication in 1963, and began work on a third novel, *The Swivel Chair*, while also getting together a collection of short stories and pushing on with the writing of a series of reminiscenses of Eurunderee and its people. Critics who have read *Hopeton High* in draft believe its publication will both enlarge John Tierney's reputation and add something to the stature of the Australian novel. He describes it as 'a satire on the illusion of progress, including the heaven the scientists promise us'. In elaboration of this theme he says: 'I don't believe the achievements of science—for all its wonders—are going to be the measure of human happiness. It seems to me there is, or should be, more in life than that. I have some close friends among Science men, some whom I both like and respect, but their general attitude that English is a pretty useless subject, and poetry a sheer waste of time—time, in their view, is evidently meant to be usefully employed in splitting atoms and extracting sunbeams from cucumbers—has always riled me.'

John Tierney is clearly one of those old-fashioned fellows who imagine a Shakespearean sonnet to be more important than a space capsule. He knows this view is hopelessly archaic, but he also knows he will never be able to change it now. As a matter of fact, he confesses that he wouldn't change it even if he could.

FICTION

As Brian James

First Furrow. Short stories (Sydney, Clarendon Press) 1944
Cookabundy Bridge. Short stories (Sydney, Angus & Robertson) 1946
The Advancement of Spencer Button (Sydney, Angus & Robertson) 1950
The Bunyip of Barney's Elbow. Short stories (Sydney, Angus & Robertson) 1956

Mary Mitchell

ONWARD FROM RURITANIA

THE popular notion dies hard that writing novels is a kind of innocent and genteel pastime, like tatting. Mary Mitchell was recently reminded of this truth. She lives at Kalorama, in the Dandenong Ranges, near Melbourne, and there one day she met an acquaintance she had not seen for some time. After courtesies had been exchanged, the acquaintance asked, with a bright smile: 'Still scribbling?' There is no record of the answer this question drew from Miss Mitchell, who has written twenty-odd serious novels (as well as three whodunits, which she published in the 1930s under the concealing pen-name of Josephine Plain). She probably let it pass; any established novelist learns to treat such things with civilized restraint, even though it is hard to do so.

Miss Mitchell, white-haired, tall, and as straight as a pine tree, has the composed face of a woman who has thought much about life and come to terms with it, yet yielded none of her principles in doing so. It is nearly thirty years since *A Warning to Wantons* was published in London and, having immediately captured the public fancy, made her name as a daring and accomplished novelist. English readers must have been astonished to learn that the author of *A Warning to Wantons*, a tale which has been described as 'a fantastic combination of ultra-sophisticated worldliness and romantic melodrama in a Ruritanian setting', was the work of an Australian. Many Australian readers of that novel, especially people who knew Mary Mitchell's parents, Sir Edward Mitchell, K.C., and Lady Mitchell, were also astonished, but for other reasons. 'I went through some embarrassing moments,' she says. 'There was a feeling of unbelief among my parents' friends that the daughter of such nice people could have written such a book.' One of her uncles, a man of fine literary taste, telephoned her and discussed the literary style of *A Warning to Wantons* at length, but studiously avoided any mention of the story itself; he could not have said more clearly that the novel was not, in his opinion, the kind a gently-bred woman should have written. She bore with fortitude all the censure, whether spoken or unspoken. She had merely written down, as effectively as she was able, a story which interested her, and she did not intend to apologize to anyone because it was a success. *A Warning to Wantons* is not her favourite among her own books, but she would be a queer writer if she did not have a fondness for it, both as her first published novel and as the most popular of all her novels.

The satisfaction she finds in writing novels has in no way diminished with the years. She would still rather write a novel than anything else, even though she lately gave much of her time and energy, for a year or more, to the writing of a non-fiction book. This is a book of a special kind. It is entitled *Uncharted Country*, and Miss Mitchell hopes it will improve practical relationships between sighted and blind people; she felt she must write it, because she herself is nearly blind, and has thought deeply about the problems of the blind. Her eyesight began deteriorating about the end of the war, and for some years she has been unable to read at all. She has to employ someone to read aloud to her everything essential to her work, including the typescript of her own books. Unable to draft her books by hand, before typing them, as she did for many years, she now speaks the first draft into a dictating machine, and later touch-types it, revising as she goes. In *Uncharted Country* she thus describes some of the handicaps imposed on her by the failure of her sight:

Hitherto all my writing had been done with the use of my eyes. I had used them to check what I was writing, either in longhand or on the typewriter. I had used them to reread what I had written and make the necessary corrections. I had used them to verify facts in dictionaries, encyclopaedias and other books of reference—and more of this has to be done even when writing a novel than most people imagine. And always they had been on the job, collecting material, noting some bit of scenery, some facial expression, some figure, some gesture, some colour, a new fashion in dress or hair-do, street scenes, buildings old and new—all of which got themselves stored away in my mind to be brought out when needed. I realized in fact that at least half the material on which I drew for my writing had come to me through sight. . . . .

. . . more than once the germ of a novel, the thing which had set my imagination working had been something that I had seen. There had been that time just before the outbreak of the last war when on a holiday in Brittany I had sat in a train opposite a Breton woman and watched her face as she talked to a companion. Her face was so alive and animated, so full of humour, intelligence and that kindly tolerance which comes from the wise assimilation of experience, that it was impossible not to wonder what had been those experiences when, instead of her wrinkled brownness, there had been the freshness of youth. Watching her and thinking of her set my mind on the track which eventually produced *Stupidity's Harvest*. It is beside the point that the heroine of that novel ultimately turned out to be quite different from that Breton peasant. The point I want to make is that looking at that woman gave my imagination the necessary stimulus.

No decline is apparent in the number or quality of the novels Miss Mitchell has published since her sight failed, however. In 1948 she put out her fourteenth novel, *The Pilgrimage of Mrs Destinn*, and since then new novels by her have appeared at regular intervals. Nothing in the character of her work in this period suggests that she is writing under physical disability of any kind.

Mary Mitchell was born in East Melbourne, in 1892, in an old red brick mansion in Gipps Street, opposite Bishopscourt. Her father was for many years leader of the Victorian Bar; her mother was a daughter of Dr Alexander Morrison, headmaster of Scotch College from 1857 to 1903. She and her three sisters were educated by governesses until they were old enough to go on a finishing trip to Europe, and nobody could have foreseen that one of them would later startle the virtuous by writing such a novel as *A Warning to Wantons*.

When the first war ended, Miss Mitchell, looking at the new world born of that conflict, knew she could not go drifting through life as an unemployed gentlewoman. She therefore went to England and took a secretarial course at the Women's Institute, London. Back in Australia, she joined the paid staff of the Red Cross Society in Melbourne, working first as assistant secretary, then as secretary of the Victorian Junior Red Cross. She had no thought of becoming a writer then. Some years before she had tried to write a short story, but the story she produced did not please her; she remembers it as 'sprightly'—in the derogatory sense of that word. 'My own judgment,' she says, 'told me to leave writing alone.' It was well on in the 1920s before she reversed this judgment.

One of her mental pastimes had always been the devising of stories for her own amusement; what she did, she says, was to indulge in an adult version of the romantic imaginings often practised by children, with the difference that she carried her stories to a conclusion. Her brain was particularly fertile when she lay in the dark at night, before going to sleep, and at last one set of characters whom she imagined in a series of situations took possession of her mind. She decided to put the story on paper, and by the time she had done so she had a manuscript about the length of a conventional novel. She sent it to England. Nine publishers rejected it, but because she had enjoyed writing it she spent her spare time writing a second novel. Every publisher again said no.

She began to doubt that she would ever see one of her novels in print, but she was not unduly depressed. After all, she liked dreaming up these stories, then writing them down. She could not shackle her imagination, anyway; it still went sweeping off on flights of its own, with or without her consent. And that was how *A Warning to Wantons* began. All she knows of the genesis of that novel is that, one day, she discovered the theme and the central scene fixed in her mind, vivid and complete. She took it from there. She began by writing the middle part—that is, the abduction scene, and the section of the story immediately surrounding it—and leaving the opening, as well as the closing, section until later. 'It isn't a method I recommend,' she says. 'But, having written the middle part, I began wondering what circumstances would have produced that situation and what the results would be. Then I had my novel.'

The first publisher who saw *A Warning to Wantons* rejected it. Two readers for the next publisher it was offered to reported against it, but the firm's managing director read it, liked it, and accepted it. The English critics gave it a mixed reception, but it was a Book Society Choice, and the public seized upon it and quickly made a best-seller of it. 'There was a strong element of luck in its success,' Miss Mitchell says. 'It came out in 1934 just when people were fed up with war books and wanted something different. If it had appeared at any other time, the chances are it would have made nothing like the hit it did make.' For no obvious reason, it flopped in America, but as some kind of consolation it was translated into Swedish, Hungarian, French and German. *A Warning to Wantons* was filmed in 1948, and its author was fairly well pleased with the film 'considering the way some books get bashed up.' In Melbourne, however, the film was screened in a city theatre usually reserved for Westerns and, not surprisingly, ran for only a week.

Miss Mitchell feels that first success, however pleasing at the time, was a dubious blessing; it tended to obscure her later work, including several novels which she considers to be substantially better than *A Warning to Wantons*. She believes *One More Flame*, published in 1942, which she wrote during the early part of the war, to be at least the equal of anything else she has done. Few Australians have read it, because the ship bringing supplies to Australia was sunk by enemy action. *One More Flame* follows the fortunes of one family, and it explores the theme that, in Australia, the land is stronger than the people, and exercises an unescapable influence on everybody's life, whether the individual lives in the country or the city. 'It's my own favourite among my novels,' she says, 'even though I had to hurry the writing of it. I was finishing it when the Japs were coming, and I wanted to say what I had to say before we all went up in smoke.'

She does not usually know where her ideas for novels come from; they come, they grow, and presently she finds herself with a theme, a story, and a set of characters, demanding to be written about. One of her novels whose origin she can pinpoint is *Prelude to Jesting*, which is set in the sixteenth century. A Melbourne women's club she belongs to has a faithful reproduction of a painting of a dwarf by Velasquez, the seventeenth century Spanish artist. Studying this print one day, she asked herself, 'What kind of experiences could have produced a face like that?' The question nagged at her mind until she set to and wrote a novel about it.

She is realistic about her work, and discusses her novels with complete detachment. Of *Maidens Beware* (1936), she says, 'A romantic story and a poor one'; of *Dark Tapestry* (1942), 'I have always thought it was pretty good'; of *Simon Learns to Live* (1945), 'I have never thought highly of it'. As might be expected of any woman capable of such self-criticism, Mary Mitchell has never accepted the belief held by some writers that the writer is entitled to claim special privileges from society, any more than she has ever been able to see herself as a divinely gifted genius. 'The trouble I've always been up against,' she says, 'is that my books are so much better before they're written!' Most honest writers would endorse that finding on their own account; but only one in a hundred or more would say it out loud.

FICTION

(Published by Heinemann, London)

A Warning to Wantons 1934
Pendulum Swing 1935
Maidens Beware 1936
Decline and Fall of a British Matron 1937
Meat for Mammon 1938

(Published by Methuen, London)

Who Pays? 1939
Viper's Progress 1939
Stupidity's Harvest 1941
Dark Tapestry 1942
One More Flame 1942
The Wood and the Trees 1944
Simon Learns to Live 1945
Servants of the Future 1946
The Pilgrimage of Mrs Destinn 1948
Black Crusade 1949
Prelude to Jesting 1950
Prisoner's Base 1951
Simple Simon 1952
Proof of Victory 1954
The Undefeated 1955
Birth of a Legend 1956

Under the pseudonym of Josephine Plain, Mary Mitchell published three whodunits in the 1930s. Entitled *The Secret of the Sandbank*, *The Secret of the Snows*, and *The Pazenger Problem*, these were issued by Thornton Butterworth, London.

Frank Dalby Davison

A SEAT IN THE KITCHEN

MANY successful authors do their writing at mahogany, oak or walnut desks. It is an expression of Frank Dalby Davison's nature that he should prefer to write, and usually does write, at the kitchen table. On most days you could find him in the kitchen of his Arthur's Creek farmhouse, twenty-five miles from Melbourne, bent over his typewriter and working away at a novel—latterly *The White Thorntree*, the second of two novels which represent about fifteen years' work and, together, will constitute, in Davison's words, 'a fictional investigation of our sex culture'. He finished the first of these novels, *Land of Blue Horses*, in 1961, but then felt he might do better to go on and complete the entire work, perhaps by the end of 1962, before seriously seeking publication, either in Australia or overseas. 'In these novels,' he says, 'I'm trying to say something about the boy-girl and man-woman relationship which, as far as I know, has never been said before; or at least not in the same way. These books are my attempt at major fiction.' From many writers this estimate would deserve no more than polite acknowledgment, because nearly every writer is convinced that whatever book he happens to be working on at any given time is an attempt at major fiction. From Frank Dalby Davison it compels attention; for, though a generous critic of other writers, he is an almost tyrannical critic of his own work. For example, of *Forever Morning*, his first published book, which had many admirers when it came out in 1931 and has many admirers still, he says: 'It's the book of a man who had never thought much about the novel as a medium. It has a hackneyed theme, and I want it charitably overlooked. Every writer is entitled to write at least one book like that.'

Although Davison's clipped moustache, and the hair fringing his high-domed bald head, are grey, his voice is strong and untiring, and the eyes behind his glasses are bright, alert, young. When the strain of putting the finishing touches to *Land of Blue Horses* was over, he was found to be suffering with a tired heart. His doctor ordered him to go slow for a time, and he quickly recovered and was soon working again at his accustomed pace. He has a ready smile, and seems to find reason for amusement with much in life, including, quite often, himself. 'A man,' he says, 'needs a thin skin to be a writer, and mostly needs a thick skin to put up with the consequences.' His good humour and lack of self-importance are part of the reason why he is liked by an extraordinary range of people. He has even achieved the more or less unprecedented feat of being a best-selling novelist—*Man-Shy* is in its twenty-sixth edition, *Dusty* in its seventeenth—and yet retaining the approval of the most exclusive Australian literary sects, which habitually consider that any writer whose books sell well is artistically damned.

He has taken advancing years in his stride, but this does not mean he imagines he could repeat today either his physical or literary deeds of thirty years ago. 'There's a time in one's life to do things,' he says. 'I couldn't write now the books I made my reputation with, books like *Man-Shy* and *The Wells of Beersheba* and *The Woman at the Mill*. The time for me to write those books was when I did write them, and I could no more do it today than that young man could do the two-novel job I'm working on now.'

Not all his books will outlive him, but several of them will probably do so. He believes *Land of Blue Horses* and *The White Thorntree* will be among them. These are novels about city life; or, rather, about human beings in a city environment. The city is Sydney, and the two central characters—a man and wife, nearing middle age when the critical action of the story takes place—live in a socially irreproachable suburb. In the original conception this work was to have been one massive book, probably as long as the three volumes of *The Fortunes of Richard Mahony*. Then, when he was rather more than half-way through it, he found it divided naturally into two volumes, which would between them make perhaps a thousand printed pages. Whether his hopes of this pair of novels will be fulfilled remains to be seen, but on his earlier books alone Davison stands among the foremost Australian writers of his time.

Those earlier novels and short stories, which exhibit his profound knowledge of life in the bush, have encouraged an idea that he was born and bred in the outback and spent most of his life as a bushman. This is not so; he has probably lived no less of his life in cities than in the bush. He was born at Glenferrie, a Melbourne suburb, in 1893, and soon afterwards the family moved to Gardenvale. He remembers it as 'a place of wide paddocks, Chinese market gardens, old orchards, extensive heath country with plenty of rabbits, plantations of old pines, and the beach little more than a mile off'. Five days a week for years, he walked a mile each way across paddocks to and from Caulfield State school. His passionate love of Australia took root in him and flowered then, and it has never wilted. His father, a master printer, was active in the Australian Natives' Association, at that time an organization of young Australians determined to assert themselves in the running of Australian public affairs. The son naturally absorbed many of the father's ideas, and, stimulated by reading poets like Kendall and Gordon, developed many ideas of his own.

By the time he was twelve he had reached the top class at Caulfield State school, and felt he had enough education and wanted to live a freer life. His father, an understanding man, yielded to the boy's persuasions, and let him go to the bush to work out a life of his own. He spent the next three years on the land. He had a spell on a farm belonging to family friends in the Kinglake Ranges, then moved on to a small cattle station at Bulumwaal, in the mountains about twenty miles north of Bairnsdale. His stay at Kinglake was the basis of one of the best—and one of the longest—of his short stories, *The Road to Yesterday*, and his experiences, both at Kinglake and Bulumwaal, helped to shape his philosophy of life. For one thing, his Australianism received a new stimulus at Bulumwaal; the boss's son, a man about thirty, was well versed in the Australian balladists, and while he and young Davison were tailing cattle through the hills he would ride along reciting the swinging ballads of 'Banjo' Paterson* at the top of his voice.

The boy might well have become a bushman for life, but when he was fifteen his father gathered up the family and took them to the United States of America. They lived in Chicago, and there Frank Davison learned his father's trade of printer. He was in America when World War I broke out, and he got himself to England and enlisted in a British cavalry regiment; he ended the war as an infantry subaltern, but his cavalry experiences were the ones that bit deep. One of his best books—for many Australians, his best-loved book—is *The Wells of Beersheba*, which is only about one-tenth the length of the average novel. Davison called it 'a Light Horse legend', and it aimed, in his words, 'to clothe literal fact with those imaginative truths of which historians do not speak'. The narrative is built around the exploits of the Australian Light Horse in the attack on Beersheba in World War I, but his own cavalry experiences gave him the expert knowledge he used in the story.

Davison came back to Australia after the war, with his first wife, whom he had married in England. He tried farming in western Queensland, and went broke after four years. His father was running

* Andrew Barton Paterson (1864-1941).

a monthly magazine, *The Australian*, in Sydney, so Davison moved to the city and joined the magazine staff, doubling as advertising canvasser and fiction writer. That was how he came to write *Man-Shy*; he turned the tale out as part of his job, and it was published in instalments. Then the magazine went bung, as magazines have a habit of doing, and he was at a loose end again. He wasn't worried, even though he had a young family to keep; no fit and willing young man had much need to worry in the 1920s. After due consideration, he opened a real estate office in a Sydney suburb, and set out to make a fortune. He was doing nicely until the economic depression arrived at the beginning of the 1930s. Nobody wanted to buy real estate, and, without a job or prospects, he went to the back files of *The Australian*, clipped out the instalments of *Man-Shy*, and tried to find a publisher for that story. Failing to do so, he paid a local suburban printer to print *Man-Shy*, took the printed sheets home to fold and stitch, then bound them into books with wallpaper bought cheaply at Anthony Hordern's. He hawked his do-it-yourself book from door to door through the Sydney suburbs. Even at sixpence a copy, the public did not rush it, but it sold steadily, if slowly. Then an astonishing thing happened: *Man-Shy* was awarded the Australian Literature Society's medal for the best novel of the year. 'This made me a bit sorry for myself,' Davison recalls. 'I had become an author, but I was still hawking my book and being chivvied by other people's dogs.'

But gradually the clouds thinned. Angus and Robertson, the Sydney publishers, offered to issue *Man-Shy* as a commercial book, and about the same time Davison began getting an occasional commission as a book reviewer. He was still living hand-to-mouth, however, and he could feel the pavement through holes in the soles of his shoes on the day *The Bulletin*, through Cecil Mann, its associate editor, invited him to become a 'preferred contributor' at seven pounds a week—real money in the depressed 1930s. For some years he was the mainstay of the Red Page, under Mann's general editorship. He was writing books, too. *The Wells of Beersheba* came in 1933, then followed *Blue Coast Caravan*, *Caribbean Interlude*, and *Children of the Dark People*. War was looming when differences of political views led to the end of his association with *The Bulletin*, and, aided by a Commonwealth Literary Fund Fellowship, he settled down and produced a book of short stories, *The Woman at the Mill*, and did some preliminary work on his later novel, *Dusty*.

He worked in Sydney for the Commonwealth Aircraft Department in the early years of the war, then moved to the publishing section of Labour and National Service, which transferred him to Melbourne late in 1944. There, with a steady salary coming in, and probably more settled than he had ever been in his life, he wrote *Dusty*, working at evenings and weekends to do so. The book at once justified his efforts—financially at any rate—by winning a prize of five hundred pounds for a novel offered by the Melbourne *Argus*.

Seeking a permanent home, he and his second wife, Marie, found themselves, two or three years after the war, looking at a house standing in sixty-odd acres of scrub and gravel at Arthur's Creek, in the Plenty Ranges, about twenty-five miles north of Melbourne. They bought it, and settled down there, on the dairy and pig farm they call Folding Hills, which their loving husbandry, aided by science, transformed into sixty-odd acres of sleek green paddocks. 'The trouble about a farm,' Frank Davison says, standing on top of one of his hills and looking away over the tranquil valleys, 'is that it can satisfy a man's creative instinct on a simple level. I could easily spend the rest of my life doing things on the farm, and never writing a line.' It seems improbable, however, that he will ever stray far from his typewriter for long. His wife, although not country-bred, likes farming, and she willingly does much of the work of Folding Hills that he would normally do, freeing him to write. More often than not, he gets to his typewriter—on the kitchen table, of course—about nine o'clock of a morning and works until he is tired; but on days when he has to start by doing four or five hours' farm work he probably doesn't write at all. 'If I come in tired,' he says, 'I want to lean on some other writer's book, not sweat over my own.'

Like nearly every writer of serious intent he finds it hard to set down on paper precisely what he wishes to say, but he says he has never had a better place for writing than the kitchen of Folding Hills. The kitchen has two windows looking out across the hills, and outside one of them is a tall apple tree which kindly drops its apples on the roof. He has ample room at Folding Hills for a study, furnished with a desk, shelves of reference books and other literary paraphernalia, but he believes that in such a room he would feel painfully self-conscious and would probably write stilted prose. So he gladly settles for the kitchen, where he can hear his wife moving about, and where his red setter bitch Shiela can come indoors at will and lie at his feet in mute sociability. That he feels this way will surprise nobody who has read his books. They could have been written only by the kind of man who prizes the simple things.

FICTION

* *Forever Morning* (Sydney, Australian Authors' Publishing Co.) 1931

* *Man-Shy* (Sydney, Australian Authors' Publishing Co.) 1931

The Wells of Beersheba (Sydney, Angus & Robertson) 1933

The Woman at the Mill Short stories (Sydney, Angus & Robertson) 1940

Dusty (Sydney, Angus & Robertson) 1946

For Children

Children of the Dark People (Sydney, Angus & Robertson) 1936

GENERAL

Blue Coast Caravan, with Brooke Nicholls (Sydney, Angus & Robertson) 1935

Caribbean Interlude (Sydney, Angus & Robertson) 1936

* Both *Man-Shy* and *Forever Morning* were first published privately, under the imprint of the Australian Authors' Publishing Co., but were re-issued in the same year by Angus & Robertson, of Sydney.

Davison is also the author of a 24-page pamphlet, *While Freedom Lives*, which was privately published in Sydney in 1938.

Leonard Mann

FOR RICHER OR POORER

ALL down-to-earth practical men agree that anyone who persists in writing novels which earn little money is a fool. If the down-to-earth practical men are right, then Leonard Mann is a fool. He began writing novels about thirty years ago, and has published six all told. Only one of his novels, *A Murder in Sydney*, published in 1937, has scored a good commercial success. The reason why Mann, or any novelist whose books are modest earners, goes on driving himself to write, instead of spending his free time, like any sensible fellow, watching television or playing bowls, is too complex to be stated in a few sentences. It is partly explained in Mann's case by a conviction that the novel is important to the social and cultural development of any country, including Australia; or perhaps particularly Australia. 'There is, I believe,' he says, 'a largely increased and increasing acceptance by Australians of creative works produced by Australians—and even a desire for them, because from them may be got the true values of a civilization suitable to ourselves. Having said that, I have sometimes wondered whether there is not a diminishing demand for the novel, as distinct from other creative works. I don't know. If there is, it may be only temporary. But any serious decline in the number of novels of quality might have ill-effects not readily foreseen; for the novel is the source of ideas, and indeed the main substance, for cinema, radio, television, and the stage. So a decline in the quantity of good novels could easily lead to a decline in the quality of those other media.'

Mann's realization of the novel's usefulness, apart from any other worth it might have, does not wholly explain his determination to go on writing when he might devote his spare time to doing what many people consider to be more profitable things. The real explanation is that he is simply one of those men who, for better or worse—and certainly for richer or poorer—are born to write. 'I had to come to it,' he says. 'And, once started, it became the only work that mattered to me.' Although his most implacable enemies would not accuse him of having scamped any job he ever did, for many years his salaried work was, to him, primarily a means of feeding, clothing and housing himself and his family and giving him a few hours a week for writing.

Leonard Mann's thick and somewhat untidy hair is grey, and fine lines have multiplied on his face, especially round the perpetually questing blue eyes. His manner of talking with a stranger is almost diffident, though never indecisive. One of his closest friends says of him: 'He has a habit, following a remark addressed to him in conversation, of falling into abstraction for a period of a minute or more. Just about the time you have forgotten what you said last and are wondering if you had not better take a walk round the block to relieve your embarrassment, he comes up from the depths of his cogitations and replies to your words. He has been neglecting the small social courtesy of remaining aware of your physical presence while paying you the higher social courtesy of carefully considering what you said and giving equal care to the terms of his reply. This habit, rather disconcerting in early acquaintanceship, becomes, on better knowledge of him, an amusing and very lovable idiosyncrasy.'

He must have needed all his determination to keep on writing. When he was working in city jobs, much of his writing was done in crowded suburban trains between his home and office, or in trains and planes between Australian capital cities. He seems to have the ability to withdraw mentally from his surroundings and lock himself away in a room whose walls are no less solid for being intangible; lacking this ability, he could not have produced any substantial volume of published work. He does not remember when he first tried to write, but he knows the itch began when he was young. His earliest attempts were with verse, which still fascinates him. Australians know him chiefly as a novelist, but he has published much verse also. The best of this is collected in four volumes; a 1941 collection won the Crouch prize for poetry, and a 1957 collection the Grace Leven prize.

He was born in Toorak, in 1895, and lived much of his youth in Brunswick. His father kept a draper's and men's wear shop in Sydney Road, and Mann and his younger brother, Jack, who retired in 1952 as Engineer-in-Chief of the Australian Army, attended Moreland State school. Each won a scholarship to Wesley College, and there Leonard Mann first heard his writing praised by a man qualified to express an expert opinion. The man was Frank Shann, then English master at Wesley, and later headmaster—from 1917 to 1943—of Trinity Grammar School. One day Mann wrote an essay about Sydney Road on Saturday night, which in those days before

World War I, with pedestrians thronging the sidewalks and drunks roistering about, friendly or aggressive, morose or rowdy, cheerful or obscene, was vital, vulgar, and, to him, fascinating. He knew it well; he always lent a hand in the shop on Saturday nights, and he and his father, after locking up, would walk home at eleven o'clock or later, through the gaudy and boisterous clamour. He sketched the scene in words, and turned in his essay, half-wondering if he was making a fool of himself. Mr Shann cornered him in the school yard a few days later. 'You know, Mann,' he said, 'I was surprised by that sketch you wrote. I never expected that from a schoolboy!' Mann does not know if Mr Shann realized what those words meant to him. He has never forgotten them. Another member of that particular Wesley College English class was a tall dark youth named Bob Menzies. Menzies and Mann sometimes shared a desk, but what subject Australia's future Prime Minister wrote on when Mann submitted his essay on Sydney Road is not known.

He had no privileged boyhood. His father's shop, which was never highly profitable, went broke, and when Leonard Mann, aged sixteen, left Wesley he had to earn a living at once. He became a clerk in the Defence Department, and, having a hankering for the Bar, studied law in his spare time. War service interrupted his studies when he had done two years of the course. He volunteered for the AIF in 1915, but the department would not release him. He kept pestering his superiors, however, and at last they capitulated, and in 1917 he was in France. He was lucky to come back. As Corporal Mann, 39th Battalion, AIF, he was one of half a dozen men defending a post near Passchendaele in October, 1917. In the early-morning darkness a heavy-calibre German shell buried three of the Australians under some tons of Flanders mud. Mann, who was one of the three, lost consciousness after a short unequal struggle for air. Nobody would have given much for his chance of seeing another dawn, but that was his lucky day, little though it appeared so at the time. His two mates were less deeply buried in the slime than he was, and when they had freed themselves they dug for him, and presently he was dragged clear, unconscious, but still able to breathe. He was outwardly little the worse, although the experience did lasting injury to his nervous system—a more or less invisible wound of war which has plagued him ever since.

He finished his law studies after the war, and, having graduated, read with his old schoolfellow, Menzies, by then a rising figure at the Victorian Bar. The 1920s were hard for young Australian barristers and Mann, who married in 1926, had to battle for a bare living. He served for two years or so as associate to Judge L. O. Lukin, of the

Commonwealth Arbitration Court; then in 1930 he became secretary of the Employers' Federation.

It was in this period that he launched himself as a writer by publishing *Flesh in Armour*, based on his own experiences and observations in World War I. He began writing that novel in 1929 and published it in 1932, and many critics still consider it the best novel of any war yet written by any Australian. When Mann finished writing *Flesh in Armour* he sent it to England. It went the round of publishers and came back, unwanted. So, feeling it said something he must say, he decided to publish it himself. Australia was then deep in an economic depression, and Australians were not rushing to buy books —Australian books least of all in those days. But *Flesh in Armour* appeared; and, astonishingly, it sold. Most of the critics liked it, and gradually the whole edition of a thousand copies was cleared. This was a modest birth for a novel of high quality, but Mann's judgment in publishing *Flesh in Armour* at his own expense was vindicated. It was later successfully issued by Robertson & Mullens, of Melbourne. The first edition is now, ironically, a collector's piece, and one collector or another occasionally asks the author if he has a spare copy of it to sell. To his regret, the author hasn't.

Flesh in Armour won him a solid reputation with publishers, as well as readers, and Angus and Robertson, of Sydney, published his second novel, *Human Drift*, in 1935, and Jonathan Cape, of London, his third, *A Murder in Sydney*, in 1937. *A Murder in Sydney*, which was an English Book of the Month Club selection, remains his best popular success. Mann, who shows little interest in sales figures of his books, thinks it sold perhaps fifteen thousand or twenty thousand copies, but he is not sure of the total.

He left the Employers' Federation early in World War II and joined the Department of Aircraft Production; one of his reasons for making the change was that his social philosophy had, as he himself puts it, 'ceased to be appropriate for a paid officer of the Employers' Federation'. This terse explanation needs no elaboration for anyone who has read Mann's second book of verse, *Poems from the Mask*, which was published about 1941; this is laden with trenchant social criticism of a kind which must have caused consternation to many of the industrial magnates who were members of the Employers' Federation. He stayed in aircraft production throughout the war, then went to Labour and National Service.

In 1945 Mann and his wife bought a property of a hundred and sixty-seven acres at Macclesfield, in the Dandenong Ranges, thirty-odd miles from Melbourne, and went to live there. For five years he travelled to and from his job in the city every day, five days a week.

Then he decided to turn the property into a poultry farm and quit the city 'for independence and freedom'. At Macclesfield he worked on his farm seven days and sixty hours a week, rising at four in summer and five-thirty in winter. But he still managed to write. He sold the farm to his son Dick in 1960, and he and his wife moved into a cottage at Olinda. There he put the last touches to a novel, tentatively entitled *Venus Half-caste*, which is listed for publication in 1963.

Having long ago learned to take life as it comes, Leonard Mann makes no complaint that he has had to do all his writing in what spare time he could find from the task of earning a living. He believes, however, that Australian governments, especially the Federal Government, should do more to enable the Australian creative writer to do 'his real work'. 'Political fear seems to be the obstacle,' he says. 'All creative writing, by the very fact of its creativeness, is more or less subversive of something or other. Our governments are evidently not civilized enough to do what many European governments, including the British Government, do by giving incomes, for life if need be, to writers, and not merely old ones, who have produced works of quality. In France, once and perhaps still, writers have been given jobs in the public service which, if not entirely sinecures, did allow time and energy for writing. Wasn't there a Minister of the Third Republic who complained, "Of course, they can do their writing in the office. What I object to is their entertaining their girls there"?' Leonard Mann is not pleading his own personal cause when he urges more government support for Australian writers; anything of the kind would be too late to help him much. But he hopes it will come one day. He believes the investment would return handsome national dividends—not necessarily in cash, but probably in more valuable form.

FICTION

Flesh in Armour (Melbourne, Phaedrus) 1932
Human Drift (Sydney, Angus & Robertson) 1935
A Murder in Sydney (London, Jonathan Cape) 1937
Mountain Flat (London, Jonathan Cape) 1939
The Go-Getter (Sydney, Angus & Robertson) 1942
Andrea Caslin (London, Jonathan Cape) 1959

VERSE

The Plumed Voice (Sydney, Angus & Robertson) 1938
Poems from the Mask (Melbourne, The Hawthorn Press) 1941
The Delectable Mountains (Sydney, Angus & Robertson) 1944
Elegiac and Other Poems (Melbourne, Cheshire) 1957

Xavier Herbert

COTTAGE AT REDLYNCH

'ANY fool,' said Xavier Herbert, 'can write one good book. It takes a good man to write two good books.' We lay among rank grass, on the side of a mountain (Xavier Herbert calls it his mountain), looking down on Redlynch, the North Queensland township in which he lives. The humid afternoon was still, and the coastal plain, stretching away to Cairns and the Coral Sea, was a chequerboard of tropic greens. I was thinking that Xavier Herbert had yet written—or any rate published—only one good book, *Capricornia*, and that his admirers were still waiting for his second good book. What he was thinking I have no idea, but I am sure doubt of his ability to fulfil himself was not troubling him. For Xavier Herbert has abiding faith in himself.

At that time, early in 1961, he had finished work on a novel which, he hoped, would be his 'second good book'. This novel, *Soldiers' Women*, was published a few months later with a flourish of publicity; Herbert even broke his self-imposed exile in North Queensland and visited Sydney and Melbourne for the launching. The public and critical reception given to *Soldiers' Women* will be discussed in more detail on a later page. At this point it is only necessary to say that this novel seems more likely to be remembered as a courageous, but unsuccessful, attempt by Herbert to deal with a massive theme than for any other reason. Unless posterity reverses the judgment of his own time, *Soldiers' Women* will not add anything to the name he made with *Capricornia*.

Herbert is perhaps the most psychologically complex Australian novelist of the day, a blend of humility and self-assurance, iconoclasm and idealism, simplicity and sophistication, boyishness and maturity, gentleness and passion. He has two convictions which cannot be separated from any consideration of his work. One of these, in his own words, is that 'genius is first of all a great capacity for loving', the other that a writer must be prepared to give up everything for writing. 'I don't mean most of everything,' he says. 'I mean everything. You mustn't worry about getting published. You mustn't even worry about making a living. It's the only way you can hope to write about the terrible, beautiful and painful thing that life is.'

He and his wife Sadie live—or lived at the time of this writing—on the outskirts of Redlynch, which is seven miles from Cairns in rich sugar-country. His friends there are not literary people but men like Percy Trezise, a commercial airline pilot who is also an artist and potter, Max Gorman, a former AIF paratrooper who runs the pub, and some of the railway gang. Herbert, superficially, looks his age, but his mind and body are both apparently as flexible, as resilient, and as durable as a young man's. Nearly every day he climbs a thousand feet or so up his mountain, which has no name as far as he knows but is part of the Coast Range, extending from Townsville to Cooktown. When he is alone, as he usually is on this climb, he runs much of the way at a seemingly tireless trot. A one-track railway line scars the face of the mountain perhaps five hundred feet up, and Herbert's route crosses the line at a point where a ganger's disused trolley stands under a crude shelter, consisting of a corrugated-iron roof supported on cornerposts of bush timber. There he takes a breather, and, sweating, seats himself on the trolley and does some writing on special cards he always carries. For some reason the physical effort of the climb stimulates the creative part of his brain, and he finds his thoughts run free, clear and strong on his quiet mountainside, with no other human being near.

Herbert has dark hair, which is greying and receding from his high sloping forehead. His brows bristle above light blue eyes, and he has a clipped moustache, a laughing mouth, and a jaw with a strong thrust. His nose was for many years badly deformed after having been broken in a riot in which he went to the aid of overwhelmed police. Now the bridge of the nose carries only a small scar left by the plastic surgeon who repaired it some years ago, using a piece of cartilage from Herbert's hip. 'I'm not sorry I had the nose mended, because it interfered with my breathing,' he says, 'but it had its points. Coves looking for a fight hesitated to pick me when they saw my nose. They thought I was an ex-pug and probably dangerous. That's all I got out of that riot. I got no thanks from the police.'

Even with a remodelled nose, Herbert has kept his reputation of being an awkward man in a brawl. Although little above medium height, he is muscular, lithe, and quick on his feet, and he knows the tricks of roughhouse fighting. He has many other physical accomplishments, including horse-breaking, but he says he was always afraid of horses, and that horses sensed his hidden fear of them. Seeking a substitute for horses, he decided to learn to fly some years ago. He started when far past the age at which most pilots retire, but qualified for his licence without difficulty.

He is an extraordinary mixture of man of action and man of mind. All his life these two opposites have struggled inside him, and they will probably go on struggling inside him for as long as he lives. Out of this conflict came his first novel, *Capricornia*, big, powerful, irreverent, ugly and beautiful, deliberately rough-hewn in places and lyrically exquisite in others, as timeless as the stars, as Australian as spinifex. Herbert spent six years writing it, and Australian publishers started by sniffing at it but it became a best-seller when it was published in 1938, and won the Commonwealth sesquicentenary prize and the Australian Literature Society's gold medal. It was later published and acclaimed in Britain, the U.S.A., and many other countries.

Capricornia earned Herbert a lot of money, and its success persuaded publishers, critics and booksellers, that, having launched himself, he would settle down to a major novelist's life, putting out a new book every eighteen months or two years and living graciously on his royalties. He disappointed these expectations. He talked of other novels which he wished to write, and he also wrote prolifically but published nothing. He finished one long novel, *Yellow Fellow*, but would not let it be published. '*Yellow Fellow*,' he says, 'would probably have sold well and made money, but it was just *Capricornia* over again on a grander scale. It would have enlarged me as a novelist, but it wouldn't have enlarged me as a human being.'

For fifteen years he talked persistently of *Soldiers' Women*. The idea for it came to him in the war, while he was an AIF sergeant at Darwin. He wanted to write on the theme that women are always under men's domination except in wartime, when their men are away, but it took him years to get started. First, he discovered he did not understand women, so he systematically studied them. He watched them, listened to their talk, probed their minds; he clipped hundreds of items about women from newspapers, especially sensational newspapers, and pored over these, seeking enlightenment. For the first two years of that period he and Sadie lived on the Daintree River, south of Cooktown, in North Queensland. Later they moved to Cairns, and then to Redlynch; or, more accurately, Sadie did. Her husband visited her every few weeks, but he lived like a hermit in a hut on Black Mountain, twenty-seven miles north of Redlynch. He often went as much as three weeks without seeing another human being. 'If anyone spoke to me when I made one of my occasional descents from Black Mountain my heart would hammer and I couldn't answer them,' he says. 'I'd hide when Sunday visitors came to Black Mountain, because I was scared of them and because they'd ask me where the game was and I wouldn't tell them. The animals and birds were my friends.'

After putting about ten years' work into *Soldiers' Women*, he believed himself beaten and decided to abandon writing altogether. Writing would not abandon him, however, and presently he wrote a short novel, *Seven Emus*. This was published in 1959—his first published novel since *Capricornia*. It raised little enthusiasm, but to Herbert it was a milestone. Seeing *Seven Emus* in print, he realized, he says, how *Soldiers' Women* should be written, and at Redlynch he went to work and rewrote it in three and a half months.

Some people who read *Soldiers' Women* before publication predicted that it would, with *Capricornia*, establish Herbert as a great Australian novelist. These forecasts appear to have been wildly over-optimistic. Most Australian literary critics found grave faults in *Soldiers' Women*, although two or three gave it high praise. Gavin Casey, himself a competent novelist and a brilliant short story writer, reviewed it in the Perth *Weekend News* under a four-column headline: 'Here's a landmark in Australian literature.' Casey wrote: 'Though scene and theme are very different, it is very much and obviously the work of the author of *Capricornia*, not of some older, less vigorous man into which he has changed. . . . His humour and his tragedy bite just as hard, his torrents of words gush out just as freely, his contempt and his pity are just as moving, and his strength as rugged.' In a no less responsible review in the Sydney fortnightly, *Nation*, Geoffrey Dutton, poet, biographer, and novelist, wrote: 'The theme is worthy of the author of *Capricornia*, with its huge possibilities of tragedy and comedy; likewise the book itself is big enough, and has had enough time and work spent on it, to be a major novel. It is not. It is an appalling and embarrassing flop.' Like Casey and Dutton, every critic was positively for or positively against *Soldiers' Women*; none was neutral. And most of them saw the novel as a failure, even if a brave one.

Herbert could hardly have had a less literary background. His father was a locomotive engine-driver in Western Australia, and Xavier Herbert, whose blood is a mixture of Irish, English and Welsh, was born in 1901 at Port Hedland, and brought up in the north-west. He learned then how to face the wilderness, but he is not a conventional bushman, although a great part of his life has been lived in the bush, which he prefers to the city. 'If I have any control over my death-time,' he says, 'I'll die in the wilderness.'

There were four Herbert children—a stepbrother and stepsister, older than Xavier, and a younger brother—and their parents took them to live in Fremantle when Xavier was twelve. After leaving Fremantle Christian Brothers' College at seventeen, he studied to be a pharmacist and qualified, but soon discovered he did not wish to spend his life behind a chemist's counter. In 1923 he went to Melbourne, and studied medicine, while earning his living as a pharmacist and in other jobs having some kinship with medicine. He did his first professional writing at this time, and his first short stories appeared, under the name of Herbert Astor, in *The Australian Journal*. Then suddenly he knew that his true calling was writing, and he abandoned medicine and went roving. In 1927, in Queensland, he discovered Redlynch, at the back of Cairns. He was carrying the swag over to the Gulf Country at the time. 'I thought Redlynch the most beautiful place I ever saw,' he says, 'and that if I ever settled anywhere it would be there.'

Over the years his nomadic instinct was to steer him into most of Australia's primitive corners, and to other parts of the world also, because he took to sailoring. Abroad, he lived chiefly in London, writing, but earning little. An important thing happened to him there, however. He met Sadie Norden who was to become his wife, and she inspired him to write *Capricornia*. Sadie, a Jewish milliner, with all the astutemess and deep maternal quality found in many women of her race, divined the talent in the young Australian and set herself to nurture it. She maintained him while he wrote the first draft of *Capricornia* in a garret in North London. He returned to Australia with that first draft, and, as an exercise in preparation for finishing it, set himself to write short stories for a living for a year. Sadie soon came out from London to join him. He could have turned his hand to many lucrative jobs, but preferred to go short of money and concentrate on writing. Sadie also preferred him to do so. Whenever he has worked at anything other than writing it has been to earn a holiday for both of them. He has made his living in many ways, as pharmacist, bacteriologist, union organizer, stockrider, sailor, miner, railwayman, airman. Sadie says their life is never dull.

Whether Herbert will yet write a novel which will confirm, beyond all argument, the reputation he made with *Capricornia* is a large question. Unless the weight of first judgment was entirely wrong, *Soldiers' Women* is not that novel. Perhaps it does not matter anyway; perhaps *Capricornia* is a big enough achievement alone for any novelist. One thing is pretty well beyond doubt; even if Herbert should achieve great commercial success with later novels he and Sadie would not change to an urban and expensive way of life. Sadie, the Londoner born, is as much a bushie as he is now. They are happy at Redlynch, with their tropical garden, full of bananas, papaws, custard apples, coconuts. Herbert has found Redlynch a good place for his writing, and he will go on writing. What he will write in the end is less certain, although he has talked of another novel, *Winged Horses*, whose theme owes something to his discovery of the poetry and wonder of flight. Herbert cannot be pushed, cajoled, coaxed or bullied into going at a different pace. Whether as man or writer, he has always travelled by his own route and at his own speed.

FICTION

Capricornia (Sydney, Publicist) 1938
Seven Emus (Sydney, Angus & Robertson) 1959
Soldiers' Women (Sydney, Angus & Robertson) 1961

Gavin Long

HISTORY FOR THE PEOPLE

AUSTRALIANS interested in military history had a standing lament in World War II. 'Australia will never,' they used to say, 'find another Charlie Bean to write the history of this war!' Time proved them wrong. C. E. W. Bean's official history of Australia's part in World War I is a formidable work, but it is not superior to Gavin Long's history of Australia's part in World War II. Neither Bean's nor Long's history is perfect, in the sense that nobody finds fault with it; no work of military history ever has been or ever will be perfect in that sense. But people who wish to know in reasonable detail what Australia did in the two world wars need not look much beyond Bean and Long. Long's history is not yet complete; when this profile was published six volumes had still to come. But on the evidence of the sixteen published up to the time of this writing, the quality of the work is beyond challenge. It is also—and this is important for a people's history—wonderfully readable.

Gavin Long, a tall, slender man, with thoughtful brown eyes, black hair, a thin line of moustache, and a slow smile, was born in 1901. From 1943 he gave all his energies to studying, writing and editing the war history, and over the years his shoulders acquired a scholarly stoop, which matched his air of rather professorial vagueness. He personally wrote two of the first volumes to be published, *To Benghazi* and *Greece, Crete and Syria*. He also wrote *The Final Campaigns*, finishing it in 1959; he held *The Final Campaigns* for later publication, however, since some other writers' volumes, describing earlier operations, were not ready to go to the printer at that time. Long is also preparing a one-volume history of Australia's part in World War II. This is to be a concise version of the full history written by himself and his team of twelve writers, as Bean's *Anzac to Amiens* was of the first war history. 'I hoped to do it in three hundred and fifty pages,' he says, 'but it is about five hundred pages now, and I don't see much chance of shortening it.'

The official history will contain about seven million words, and Long's own four volumes about one million two hundred thousand words, and every volume will bear the imprint of his editorial guidance. Gavin Long still hesitates, however, to class himself as an author. Some years ago he was invited to join the Canberra branch of the Fellowship of Australian Writers. 'Do you think I'm eligible?' he asked the Fellowship secretary, who had approached him. 'Perhaps I should be just an associate member.' Other Fellowship members had no reservations about him, and he was elected a full member, in face of his own sincere misgivings. This does not mean that he doubts the value of his own major life's work. He expressed his view on that point thus, in an article for the March-April, 1955, issue of *Stand-To*, official organ of the Australian Capital Territory branch of the Returned Sailors', Soldiers' and Airmen's Imperial League of Australia: 'The smaller partners in alliances can be sure that if they do not write their own histories their individual experiences will be written very small in the pages of recorded history, if only because it is not easy for the historians of the larger partners to find out much about that experience, and they are to chronicle it only in a broad and general way. For example, in many books written in Britain and the United States and touching on the South-West Pacific campaigns of 1942, 1943, and early 1944, those campaigns are recorded in so brief and shadowy a fashion that the reader might well be hardly aware that anything of great significance happened in this theatre until the last eighteen months of the Japanese war.'

Long made his home in Canberra while working on the war history. He travelled widely throughout Australia in the course of his work, but could not have done justice to it if he had lived in any city except Canberra. He likes Canberra anyway; the Federal capital's urbane placidity is more to his taste than the clamorous bustle of Sydney or Melbourne. For a number of reasons, however, he intends to settle in Sydney on his retirement from the post of Australia's chief war historian. As the prospect of retirement drew nearer, he began to think what work he might do once he had seen the last volume of the war history to press, but he did not worry about it overmuch. 'I've considered writing biographies of a couple of Australian literary figures,' he says. 'Beyond that, I have nothing in mind.'

There is a strong general resemblance between Gavin Long and Australia's 1914-18 war historian, Dr Bean. Both are tall and unusually lean; until he was past middle-age Long never weighed much more than eleven stone for his six feet two and a half inches, and even in his sixties is only twelve stone. The mental resemblance between Bean and Long is also striking. Each man has a passion for detail, combined with oriental patience and calm. Both were newspapermen before they became historians, but perhaps the oddest coincidence is that both are old boys of All Saints' College, Bathurst, N.S.W. Bean's father was headmaster of All Saints', and Bean attended the school as a small boy; Arthur Jose, who was later to write the RAN volume of the 1914-18 history under Bean's editorship, was an assistant master at the school then. Thirty years later Gavin Long had some years at All Saints' before going on to the University of Sydney.

Gavin Long, the first of three sons and three daughters of George Merrick Long, who was to become one of Australia's most eminent prelates, was born at Foster, Gippsland, Victoria, while his father, then a young Anglican priest, was in charge of the parish. He was still an infant when his father went, as curate, to Holy Trinity, Kew. When a group of citizens of the growing suburb of Kew decided to establish a full-size grammar school Mr Long was chosen as headmaster. That was the start of Trinity Grammar School. Gavin Long was at Trinity until his father became Bishop of Bathurst in 1911; there the boy was sent to All Saints' College.

He believes his lifelong absorption in military affairs began with his acute interest in the first war; he was thirteen when it began and seventeen when it ended. While it lasted he, like other boys of his age, more or less avidly read every scrap of war news, and pored over photographs, artists' sketches and battle maps published in such periodicals as *The Illustrated London News*, *London Sphere* and *Sydney Mail*. The war came nearer in 1917 when his father went overseas as an AIF chaplain. After a few months in France Bishop Long was appointed AIF Director of Education, with the task of organizing an ambitious soldiers' education plan.

Right through the adolescence of boys born in 1900 and 1902, the war was in the near background. If their eagerness to be in it was tempered by increasing apprehension, the war was yet always close to them. Gavin Long was still six months under eighteen when the Armistice came. He was to have begun sitting for his Leaving Certificate on November 11, 1918; the N.S.W. Education Department postponed the examination for a day because of the public excitement. Peace having returned, he had to forget about enlisting and content himself by studying Arts at the University of Sydney. He was a resident of St Paul's College. 'When I reached the university,' he recalls, 'about half the residents of every college were young returned soldiers who had seen hard fighting. The rest of us looked up to them. We felt we lacked something they had. We belonged to a lesser breed.'

Long graduated, and went as an assistant housemaster to The King's School, Parramatta; he claims he was chosen less for scholastic ability than because, as a handy oarsman who had rowed for his university college, he was qualified to coach the school's second four. Two years later, having saved some money, he went back to the university, gained a Diploma of Education, and was still able to afford a one-way ticket to London, with a few pounds over. In his first fortnight in London he found a job at Australia House, interviewing prospective immigrants. After nearly a year, he spent some months travelling on the continent of Europe, then came home as welfare officer in a migrant ship. Back in Sydney, he decided to try journalism. He had published occasional articles in his teaching days, and from London had sent theatre notes and a little verse to the Sydney magazine, *Triad*, now defunct. The Sydney *Daily Guardian* gave him a general reporter's job at five pounds a week. He learned quickly, and within a year the Melbourne *Argus* offered him a reporting job at six pounds twelve and sixpence a week. 'After I had been in Melbourne a few weeks this six pounds twelve and six went to my head,' he says, 'and I got married.' He stayed four years with *The Argus*, doing a wide variety of work, including a column of film reviews for the weekly *Australasian*; this is claimed to have been the first serious film reviewing ever attempted in Australia.

In 1930 he went back to Sydney and joined *The Sydney Morning Herald*, as an assistant sub-editor. After a year he was devoting himself chiefly to art, theatre and film writing, but also writing occasional articles about foreign affairs and defence. 'These subjects had always been my chief private interest,' he says. 'In 1936 I was appointed chief cable sub-editor, and the amount of my writings on defence increased: the idea that war was coming had begun to penetrate.' Lord Gowrie, then Governor-General of Australia, paid a goodwill visit to Java in 1938, and Long went with him to write articles about East Indies defence and the Singapore base. Those articles foretold pretty well how Singapore was to fall in 1942, predicting that the naval base would be taken from the landward side, as it was taken; and although he was not the first Australian to publish this warning he was the first journalist to do so in a daily newspaper.

War was less than a year off when Long's newspaper sent him to join its London staff. In England he met an English writer on sea warfare, Russell Grenfell, a retired RN officer, whose writings he had read and admired. They discovered their views on Singapore's vulnerability to be almost identical, and decided to collaborate on a book, envisaging an attack on Singapore by Japan. They called the book *Defence Against Japan*, and it was practically finished when war broke out in Europe and caused them to abandon it. 'As I remember it,' Long says, 'it was a reasonably accurate forecast of what happened when the Pacific war came.' Grenfell returned to the wartime Royal Navy. He later increased his fame as an author with books about naval operations in the last war, notably *The Bismarck Episode* and *Main Fleet to Singapore*.

Long was one of the first three Australian correspondents accredited to cover British operations in France in the last war. He saw enough of the 'phony war', and more than enough of the blitzkrieg, before getting away from France through Boulogne, and crossing the Channel in a small and heavily overcrowded steamer. He went to the Middle East later that year, arriving in time to report the first Western Desert campaign in the 1940-41 winter, and the later operations in Greece and Crete. Then his newspaper recalled him to Sydney. He had a full hand in Australia, especially after the Pacific war began, until his future was settled by his appointment, early in 1943, as general editor of the war history. 'I didn't know when I started how unfitted I was for the job,' Long says. 'I went into it with a fairly light heart and great enthusiasm, because I was Bean's nominee; I thought, "If Bean says I can do it, then I can do it." It wasn't long before my temerity began to appal me.'

From the time of his appointment until the war ended, Long spent about half his time on Pacific battlefronts, including a valuable period with the U.S. Sixth Army, and the other half in Australia organizing for the task ahead. He was never able to be near the fighting for more than three months at a time, but he saw something of the Sattelberg, Bougainville, Aitape and Wewak operations, and the later phases in Borneo. He was in the air between Morotai and Balikpapan when he heard the news of Japan's surrender. He knew then that his work as official historian was really beginning.

'I originated little in the technique of writing the war history,' Long says. 'I merely followed Bean's principles, modifying these to meet the special requirements of the World War II history.' Long even adopted Bean's method in writing his own volumes. He writes everything by hand, about nine lines to a foolscap page, with wide spaces between each line to give room for the insertion of afterthoughts and corrections. He rarely writes more than two thousand to three thousand words in an uninterrupted day's writing. He believes high-grade historical writing cannot be done except at deliberate speed. When the official history team was still incomplete, someone suggested that a newspaperman who had written several popular war books, rattling off each of them in four or five weeks, should be appointed to write a certain volume of the war history. Long pondered the suggestion with crinkled brow. Then his slow smile came. 'Well,' he said gently, 'he'd certainly write it very fast!' The nomination lapsed.

GAVIN LONG

GENERAL

To Benghazi (Canberra, Australian War Memorial) 1952. Vol. I of Series One of Australia in the War of 1939–1945

Greece, Crete and Syria (Canberra, Australian War Memorial) 1953. Vol. II of Series One of Australia in the War of 1939–1945

Henrietta Drake-Brockman

THE NORTH WAS BLUE

FOR a woman who did not see the outback until she was twenty, Henrietta Drake-Brockman has some astonishing skills. Among other things, she can roll a swag as expertly as any bushman. She learned how to do this on a journey in 1922 from Wyndham to Carnarvon via Hall's Creek, and she believes she could still roll a swag with anyone, although it is many years since she needed to do so. Talking with Mrs Drake-Brockman in the living-room of her flat, near the top of one of Perth's tallest buildings, it is hard to realize that her knowledge of bushmanship is actual, not theoretical. Outwardly, she is a city woman to her fingertips, and you would not be surprised to hear that her personal acquaintanceship with the bush had been limited to the drinking of billy-tea at country picnics. Anyone familiar with her novels, plays or short stories would not be deluded, however; few of her writings could have come from anyone lacking deep practical experience of the outback and the way outback people live, speak, act, and think.

In her novel, *The Wicked and the Fair*, published in 1957, she broke away from the outback as such, and built her story round the characters and events of an episode of Australia's early history—the wreck in 1629 of Francisco Pelsaert's ship *Batavia* on the Abrolhos Islands, off the Western Australian coast. 'From the viewpoint of my abiding interest in human courage, resilience and endeavour,' she says, 'I said more of what I wanted to say in that novel than in any other of my books.' But, whatever the excellence of *The Wicked and the Fair*, which many people consider her best novel, Mrs Drake-Brockman has probably made her most lasting impression on Australians with her twentieth century novels, such as *Younger Sons*, and her outback short stories, particularly those concerning aborigines.

In 1963 she hopes to publish a biography of Francisco Pelsaert, *Voyage to Disaster*. This will be a substantial work, and will include a history of the wreck of the *Batavia*, and a translation of Pelsaert's journals by Evert Drok, a Dutch friend of Mrs Drake-Brockman.

But when she talks of *Voyage to Disaster* you feel that, having learned more than any other living man or woman knew of Pelsaert and the Abrolhos episode while gathering material for *The Wicked and the Fair*, she wrote the book from a sense of duty to Australian history, rather than because, as with her novels, she felt an inner compulsion to write it. 'It will probably be my most important book, in the Australian sense,' she says. 'It explores a historical field hitherto neglected. For myself, though, I find my creative works more satisfying, especially my plays—*Men Without Wives* in particular—and some of my short stories.'

Mrs. Drake-Brockman, a tall woman, with arresting eyes and a gently ironic mouth, is forceful without being aggressive, talkative without being garrulous, courteous without ever retreating from any opinion she has formulated after mature thought. She began to make her name between the two world wars when Australian writers were caught in, as she puts it, 'a deadly doldrums'. At that time hardly anybody cared whether they wrote or ran hot-dog stands. 'Then the doldrums broke,' she says, 'and it's been wonderfully exhilarating. The war did it. The war moved young people all round Australia and got them interested in their own country, and it brought the Americans here asking questions and making us look for the answers.'

She was born in Perth in 1901, the only child of Martin Edward Jull, an Englishman who became Western Australia's first Public Service Commissioner; her mother, a Scotswoman, had been Perth's first woman medical practitioner, before marriage. The earliest home Mrs Drake-Brockman remembers was in orchard country at Armadale, about twenty miles from the city. She learned to swim there, in a dam on the property. There also she listened, entranced, to her father's tales of his South Sea island experiences on a trading schooner. She was a lonely child, and had to look inside herself for amusement and companionship; the only friend she had near her own age at Armadale was a girl five years older than herself.

When she was nine, her mother took her to Scotland, where she went to boarding school. She was often acutely homesick for Australia, and found her best consolation in reading and re-reading the only Australian book she had in Scotland, *The Lady of the Blue Beads*, by Ida Rentoul Outhwaite. Her writing ambition had not stirred then, and while she was away she decided to become a painter—of people, because landscape did not greatly interest her. At twelve, she came back to Australia. Her mother intended sending her back to Scotland in two or three years to finish her education; World War I put an end to that plan, but it was understood she would go to Paris to study art when peace came. Meanwhile, she was sent to boarding school in New South Wales.

Mr Jull died when his daughter was fifteen, and Dr Jull, who had never let her medical knowledge become rusty, took a job as first medical inspector of Western Australian State schools. There was no more school for Henrietta; she matriculated with the aid of a tutor. Their home was sold, and mother and daughter moved to a flat. Henrietta did the housekeeping, and took English and French literature at the university. She also began working five days a week in the studios of Henri van Raalte, a Dutch artist trained in Holland and London, who came to Australia for his health and taught in Perth; he later went to South Australia, and at the time of his death was director of the National Gallery of South Australia, Adelaide.

When the war ended Henrietta saw Paris within her reach at last. But in 1919 a young Western Australian, Major Geoffrey Drake-Brockman, came home with the AIF; he had served on Gallipoli and in France, winning his commission—and a Military Cross—in the field. He and Henrietta Jull became engaged, and were married in August, 1921. 'I said, "Well, I won't be just an amateur, so that's the end of painting!" ' says Mrs Drake-Brockman. It was. Her husband, a civil engineer, was appointed Western Australia's Commissioner for the North. For the next five years they were constantly on the move, roughing it, living hard, sleeping out as often as not. They never stayed more than a few weeks in one place, rarely saw a town larger than Broome or Wyndham.

Mrs Drake-Brockman's ideas of the outback and its people were nebulous until she went North. This was not only because she had lived most of her life in a city environment, but also because her mother, a strong-minded woman, filled with nostalgia for Scotland, had little interest in Australian literature. 'I had read practically nothing about Australia,' Mrs Drake-Brockman says. 'My mother wouldn't even have the Sydney *Bulletin* in the house. But I was allowed—and greatly influenced by—Syd Ure Smith's magazine, *Art in Australia*.' She was utterly unprepared for what she found; and, not knowing there was already an impressive literature of the outback, she thought, 'Isn't it shocking that people don't seem to realize how exciting Australia and Australians can be!', and wished she could tell them.

The idea of herself writing about the outback dawned one day on the wharf at Cossack, one of the old ghost towns on the Australian continent's north-west shoulder. 'Fred Teesdale, the State M.P. for that area, a great raconteur, was telling me how the pearlers used to play ninepins with bottles of champagne, and often enough bring the natives in on chains to be used as naked divers,' she recalls. 'Both fascinated and horrified, I made up my mind to write.' She started by writing newspaper articles about the North; feeling it was a man's country, but grim from a woman's point of view, she published these under the name of Henry Drake. She had never lost her desire to paint, but now she sublimated it in writing. Travelling by car, as she and her husband did, with only a swag and a small suitcase, she could not carry painting equipment, but she could carry a fountain pen and two or three exercise books, even through country so rough that twelve or fifteen miles was a good day's journey. (Her husband tells of these adventures in his autobiography, *The Turning Wheel*.) Finding 'his' articles read well in *The West Australian*, Henry Drake wrote some short stories. The first of these to be published—'It was something about pearls,' Henry Drake's *alter ego* remembers—appeared in the Melbourne *Australasian* in 1925, in the same week that 'his' first baby was born.

Henry Drake must have had a personality of his own; and a masculine personality at that. Two commercial travellers, seasoned men who knew the north, were overheard talking in a Western Australian country train one day.

'Who's this bloke Henry Drake?' one asked.

'In my opinion,' the other said sagely, 'he's a middle-aged man who knows life.'

Mrs Drake-Brockman, who at that time was about twenty-five, treasures that tribute.

In the middle 1920s she finished writing a novel she had started some years earlier. It was called *The Disquieting Sex*, and described the emotional eruptions caused by a young woman's arrival in the cattle country. She was persuaded to enter *The Disquieting Sex* in the Sydney *Bulletin*'s 1928 novel competition—of course, under Henry Drake's name; to her surpiise the judges highly commended it. She wrote a second novel, *Blue North*, and entered this for *The Bulletin*'s 1929 competition; it ran fifth, was serialized in *The Bulletin* and later published as a book. 'From then,' she says, 'I set to work seriously.' And she has never stopped. *Blue North*, a novel of the pearling coast, saw the painless extinction of Henry Drake; Mrs Drake-Brockman's husband convinced her she should henceforward publish her writings under her own name.

Being self-critical, she is not a prolific writer; self-critical people working in any creative field tend to have a small high-grade output rather than a large f.a.q. output. She has also had to adjust her writing desires to her domesitc obligations; she has a daughter and a son, both married now, and seven grandchildren. She has published five novels, a collection of her best short stories, and several plays. Her three-act play, *Men Without Wives*, won the drama section of the Commonwealth sesquicentenary competitions in 1938. Immediately produced in Sydney, this play has been a favourite with little theatres, and is known in many parts of Australia. In 1939 she won the *Bulletin* short story prize.

'As a writer,' she says, 'I'd rather have been a playwright than anything else, but the opportunities for Australian playwrights until lately were practically nil. The theatre has always fascinated me, from the age of seven or eight, when I saw a performance of *Peter Pan* in Perth. Like Strindberg, I can truthfully say I have enjoyed writing plays better than all else I have done. I think it is the marvellous combination of creative arts—writing, acting, producing, design, music, colour, everything—and everyone working together to produce a living whole that makes theatre so satisfying to me. But when I wrote *Men Without Wives* in 1933 I don't believe I had even heard of any Australian play—I know for certain I had neither read nor seen one. Western Australia was like that, then. That play was concerned with human courage—the everyday, underestimated courage of the women who at that time lived in the North.'

She has edited several successful short story anthologies. Of these, *West Coast Stories*, published in 1959, is specially near her heart, because every story in it is by a Western Australian, and also because royalties go toward the maintenance of Tom Collins House, the Joseph Furphy memorial in Perth.

Except for one longish World War II break in Melbourne, when her husband was recalled to the Army, she has lived in Perth since 1927, with occasional trips away to study backgrounds for her writings. The Drake-Brockmans' flat looks down on Perth's Esplanade, with the river beyond, and in Mrs Drake-Brockman's words, 'Everything happens there, from the Queen's reviews, and Anzac services, to helicopter landings, to marching girls, to sports, to metho addicts at night. And we see it all!' As a background for a novel—in this instance, a modern city novel about life in Perth which Mrs Drake-Brockman has always wanted to write—it seems to have no less exciting possibilities than the pearling coast, the cattle country, or the Abrolhos Islands. Her friends hope she will write that novel some day.

HENRIETTA DRAKE-BROCKMAN

FICTION

Blue North (Sydney, Endeavour Press) 1934
Sheba Lane (Sydney, Angus & Robertson) 1936
Younger Sons (Sydney, Angus & Robertson) 1937
The Fatal Days (Sydney, Angus & Robertson) 1947
Sydney or the Bush. Short stories (Sydney, Angus & Robertson) 1948
The Wicked and the Fair (Sydney, Angus & Robertson) 1957

GENERAL

On the North-West Skyline (Perth, Paterson) 1946

DRAMA

Men Without Wives: A North Australian play in three acts (Perth, Paterson) 1938
Men Without Wives and Other Plays. Including *Hot Gold* (three acts), *Dampier's Ghost* (one act), *The Blister* (one act), (Sydney, Angus & Robertson) 1955

Alan Marshall

THE SINGING MAN

ONLY time will tell whether Alan Marshall is more successful at writing of life or living it. Marshall is not the kind of writer who shuts himself away from the world and writes of life with scientific detachment; as his books and stories show, he lives, and always has lived, every minute of every day. 'I feel it is more important to make a success of living than of writing,' he says. 'The two don't always coincide. As a writer, I want to record my experiences, or rather to record what I have learnt from them, but to do this truthfully and courageously one must first of all establish himself as a man. That is the most difficult task of all.' These words imply that Alan Marshall has found difficulty in establishing himself as a man; if so, his closest friends are not aware of it. He seems to have an unexcelled talent for going anywhere and making himself acceptable in any company.

Although he was crippled by polio when he was six, his capacity for getting about, often in rough places, is prodigious. His legs are useless, and his back is cruelly twisted; he cannot move a yard, standing upright, without his crutches. Yet, driving his own caravan, he has travelled, unaccompanied, to most parts of the Australian outback. He has even penetrated to some of the remotest corners of Arnhem Land, where primitive tribesmen welcomed him, listened to his stories, told him their own stories in return, and dubbed him Gurrawilla, which means 'the Singing Man'. In Australia he is one of the most widely known of all Australians. Many people who have never read one of his books, and a few people who don't even know he writes books, are his friends. They don't pity him; nobody pities Alan Marshall. He has a kind of inner magic which makes people, five or ten minutes after meeting him, forget he is a man labouring under an immense physical disability.

Although Marshall was born in 1902, and is bald except for a fringe of greying hair, he radiates youthfulness; the tumbling speed of his conversation, his quick spontaneous laugh, the dancing of his

ENRIETTA DRAKE-BROCKMAN

ALAN MARSHALL

ROBERT CLOSE

JOHN MORRISON

JOHN K. EWERS

CYRIL PEARL

JOHN O'GRADY

GAVIN CASEY

pale blue eyes suggest the boy he must have been, rather than the man he is. His head, strong-boned and aggressive, and the set of his prominent nose indicate, however, that Marshall has done whatever he has done in life, not by accident, but by design.

When he is not roaming Australia—and at the time of writing it is some years since he made an extended trip—he lives at Eltham, in a roomy self-contained bungalow behind his mother's house. The bungalow suits Marshall to perfection, whether as a workshop or a place to meet his friends. It has many shelves packed with his own and other writers' books, a few souvenirs of his travels such as a collection of bullock-bells, and a bed in which he wakes in the morning to look out over a tranquil valley. He does his writing at a built-in desk under the window—not only his writing for publication, but also the fifty or so letters he writes every week to people who have written to him because they are interested in his work or, often, simply because they feel he can given them spiritual help. Most of his replies are only a few lines on a card, but sometimes, perhaps to a crippled child, or a man or woman lying in hospital, he writes two or three pages; for Marshall has a knack of becoming emotionally involved in other people's problems.

To his bungalow come children, writers, artists, old bushmen, bodgies, beats, university professors, and many unclassifiable folk whom Marshall likes and who like him. The casual visitor is as likely as not to find himself introduced to a man who turns out to be an ex-housebreaker. Marshall is a popular lecturer at Pentridge—he is a popular lecturer wherever he goes, if it comes to that, for he is perhaps an even better raconteur than a writer—and every now and then some ex-prisoner visits him and spends a couple of hours yarning with him. Such callers don't go to him for wise counsel or moral uplift; they can find plenty of wise counsel and moral uplift elsewhere. What they want of Marshall, and what they get, is the feeling that he is interested in them and their affairs. His interest in people, all kinds of people from nuclear physicists to illegal car users, is no pretence. A Czech professor said of Marshall, after reading some of his books, 'He loves everything that lives, from a blade of grass to a human being.' Every man, woman and child he meets senses that quality in him.

Marshall's first book, *These Are My People*, was published in 1944. He has published nine books since then, with varying success; some have been reprinted several times, others have just about paid their way. In 1961 he put out a book of a type he had never before attempted. This is *The Gay Provider*, a history of the first fifty years of the Myer Emporium, Melbourne, from the time of its foundation in 1911.

Marshall was commissioned to write the history, and spent three years on it. He says his biggest difficulty in writing it was the need to turn his back on 'the development of the characters of all those men who made Myers what it is today, and concentrate on the history of an organization in which people are dwarfed by its very size and complexity'. To do this must have been agony for Marshall to whom people are always paramount. He once said, 'Literature must be based on the lives of people, revealing all their weaknesses and strengths.'

He found deeper satisfaction in writing a book, *This is the Grass*, published late in 1962. This is the sequel to his autobiographical novel, *I Can Jump Puddles*, which sold sixty thousand copies in Australia and about one hundred thousand copies in oversea editions. He did most of the work on *This is the Grass* after finishing *The Gay Provider*, and when he wrote the closing words he believed it to be the best book he had written. He hid himself in the bush in his caravan for some months because *This is the Grass* is a book, he says, that had to be written 'at a high emotional level which it was necessary to retain until the very end'. *This is the Grass* carries the story of Marshall's life up to 1926, and he plans another book—or, more than likely, other books—to complete his personal story. The title is drawn from Walt Whitman's poem 'Song of Myself', in *Leaves of Grass*.

Recognition comes easily to some writers, though not many, but few writers have had to fight harder for recognition than Alan Marshall did. He was well past thirty before he seemed likely to make any kind of literary name. He was born in Noorat, in the Western District of Victoria, where his father, a bushman to the fingertips, who had in his time been a horse-breaker, drover and outback hawker, ran the general store. Alan had his early education at Terang State school.

He always knew what he wished to do with his life, even though many years were to pass before he was able to do it. When he was eight he told his thirteen-year-old sister Elsie, 'I'm going to write books when I grow up like Kingston and Ballantyne.' At that time he was an avid reader of boys' adventure tales by W. H. G. Kingston, R. M. Ballantyne and similar authors; to him, as to most boys of that period, these books were the flower of literature. 'You'll write books,' said his sister, with uncanny sagacity, 'but different ones.'

The years Alan Marshall lived at Noorat, until his father moved the family to Melbourne in 1918, were probably the most valuable of his life in giving him material for his later writings. Although he has occasionally written a story set in the city, his overriding interest has always been in the bush, which he first came to love in childhood, and in bush people whom he first came to understand at the same time. He probably learned more of the bush and its people from his father than from anyone else. He learned other things from his father also, including a principle he has always tried to honour in his work. 'I like books that tell the truth,' his father used to say. 'I'd sooner be sad with the truth than happy with a lie, blowed if I wouldn't.' The memory of those words played a big part in making Alan Marshall the kind of writer he is.

The Marshalls came to Melbourne so that Alan, then sixteen, could study at a city business college; he had won a scholarship which gave him a free course in accountancy at this college. His difficulties began when, having graduated, he looked for a job; no employer seemed anxious to engage a cripple, even one with a bright brain and a distinguished record as a business college student. Marshall kept trying, and at last he found a temporary job in the shire office at Kangaroo Ground, some twenty miles from Melbourne. The wage was only twenty-five shillings a week, but it was a start. When that job ended, he took anything that offered. Some of his jobs lasted a month or two, some only a few weeks. Probably the cushiest of them was in a Brunswick coffin factory, where Marshall doubled as a clerk by day and a watchman by night, drawing two weekly pay envelopes, and living, sleeping and eating in a room on the premises, surrounded by coffins.

And he was constantly writing. He destroyed most of what he wrote, but occasionally he sent out a story or a sketch to some magazine or newspaper; it always came back, but he kept on, struggling to express himself, slaving to learn the writer's craft. At thirty, he was still unknown, outside a small circle who believed his writing had possibilities. He was working then as accountant for a struggling Clifton Hill shoe company, and nobody would have given much for either his business or literary future. He scored a few small successes. His short story, *A Little Son*, won the Australian Literature Society's prize for the best short story of 1933, and two or three of his other stories were published; but when the shoe company closed down in December, 1935, nobody would have supposed he had done enough to warrant a belief that he would ever be able to earn a living as a writer. Nobody, that is, except Alan Marshall. He had some time earlier concluded that he was not temperamentally fitted to be a business man; if he could not have economic security except by working as an accountant, he reflected, then he would sacrifice economic security.

He had a grim battle for the next five or six years, and sometimes his room-rent was in arrears, sometimes he was hungry, but he never seriously contemplated surrender. He sold a short story here, a newspaper article there, and cheques for such work helped him to keep going until the tide turned. He did not, like some writers of talent, scorn journalism in his struggling days. In 1938 he launched, of all things, a newspaper column of advice to the lovelorn. This continued to be published, with some interruptions, for nearly twenty years. It drew many thousands of letters, and gained Marshall a large following among women. He also wrote hundreds of whimsical sketches for different Australian magazines and newspapers; the best of these have been collected and published in books, under the titles *Bumping Into Friends* and *Pull Down the Blind*. But it is as a serious writer, with his short stories and his autobiographical novel, *I Can Jump Puddles*, and with his books describing his personal wanderings, *These Are My People*, *Ourselves Writ Strange* and *People of the Dream-time*, that he has made his deepest mark. Marshall has often had periods of financial worry, but since his early battling years he has never been utterly broke. He was even prosperous enough to marry in 1941; his marriage, of which there are two daughters, ended in divorce some years ago.

His serious books are Australian to the last syllable. Nobody but an Australian with a consuming love of his own country and its people—the dark-skinned, as well as the light-skinned people—could have written them. The astonishing thing is that a man crippled as Marshall is crippled should have been able to acquire so vast a knowledge of the bush, bush people, and bush traditions. It is astonishing at any rate to people who don't know Alan Marshall. He has never admitted that his physical disabilities constitute any kind of handicap. He has never pitied himself, and any hint of self-pity in another physically disabled man or woman shocks him. 'He asks no quarter on account of being a cripple,' one of his friends says. 'We were out walking one day, and we came to a small paddock-flower of some interest. Alan dropped his crutches, and lay on his belly to examine it, discussing it with me over his shoulder. I went to help him up. He explained to me—in all good nature—that to help a cripple rise by taking hold of his arm is the same as trying to help an ordinary man by taking hold of his legs. Your greatest kindness to a fallen cripple is to leave him alone—he knows how to get up! We came to a broadish gully with a tangle of undergrowth that looked to me rather difficult for a man on crutches. I was needlessly anxious. Alan tossed his crutches, one by one, over the gully, dragged himself across to them on his belly, recovered them, and then went on as if his action had been the most natural thing in the world. To him, it was.'

Alan Marshall himself said the last word about his crippled body at the very end of *I Can Jump Puddles*. Recording a conversation he had with his boyhood friend Joe, when the Marshalls were leaving Noorat to live in the city, he wrote:

'I wonder how you'll get on with your crutches down there?' Joe mused. 'The crowds an' that . . . ?'

'Crutches!' I exclaimed, dismissing the inference contemptuously. 'Crutches are nothing . . .'

What Alan Marshall the man has done seems to prove that Alan Marshall the boy was right that day. To him, crutches are nothing; to him, they always will be nothing. They do not, as they so easily might, govern his life. He governs them.

FICTION

Tell Us About the Turkey, Jo. Short stories (Sydney, Angus & Robertson) 1946
How Beautiful Are Thy Feet (Melbourne, Chesterhill Press) 1949
**I Can Jump Puddles* (Melbourne, Cheshire) 1955
How's Andy Going? Short stories (Melbourne, Cheshire) 1956
**This is the Grass* (Melbourne, Cheshire) 1962

GENERAL

These Are My People (Melbourne, Cheshire) 1944
Ourselves Writ Strange (Melbourne, Cheshire) 1948
Pull Down the Blind (Melbourne, Cheshire) 1949
Bumping Into Friends (Melbourne, Cheshire) 1950
People of the Dreamtime (Melbourne, Cheshire) 1952
The Gay Provider (Melbourne, Cheshire) 1961

* *I Can Jump Puddles* and *This is the Grass* are listed as fiction because, although they are largely autobiographical, the author has, on his own statement, 'gone beyond the facts to get at the truth'.

Robert Close

SAILOR ASHORE

A SMALL, swarthy, hook-nosed man accosted a surgeon striding down Collins Street, Melbourne, some years ago. He seized the surgeon's hand and shook it with fervour. 'You wouldn't remember me, doctor,' he said, 'but I'm the one that got away.' The surgeon's name doesn't matter, but the small man was Robert Shaw Close, the merest mention of whose novel, *Love Me, Sailor*, still makes Australian literary censors automatically reach for their blue pencils. Until that day in Collins Street he and the surgeon had not met for ten years or so, at which time Close had been languishing with a supposedly mysterious illness, which was later diagnosed as tuberculosis. 'I agreed,' Close says, 'to let this surgeon make a twenty-inch slit in my abdomen, have a look round inside, and pluck out anything he was suspicious about. He did me no good, and for quite a while afterwards I could find nothing in the experience to laugh about, but I'd recovered my sense of humour when I saw him in Collins Street. The memory of the look on his face the day I accosted him still makes me laugh. It's all I recall now of an otherwise unpleasant affair.'

Close has always been able, after a decent lapse of time, to wring humour from his own worst misfortunes, including his trial in the Melbourne Criminal Court in 1948 for having published an obscene libel in *Love Me, Sailor*. He admits he was not amused when he was found guilty, and sentenced to serve three months in gaol and pay a fine of a hundred pounds; an appeal court later quashed the gaol sentence but increased the amount of the fine to a hundred and fifty pounds. Now he can see the funny side of the episode, and can even give an irresistibly droll description of the nine days he spent in Pentridge, although at the time prison seemed to him a grimly humourless place. 'Gaiety, rather than grog,' he says, 'is my great unwinder, and when I'm not working I'm always looking for an opportunity to make people laugh, not so much to amuse others, as to amuse myself. I can always make jokes against myself from the fund of stupid things I've done, and I laugh as loudly as anyone else does at my own jokes. I've always thought the rule that one shouldn't laugh at his own jokes is both selfish and illogical; it's like telling the host he shouldn't be drinking—it's only for the guests!'

At the time of writing, Close has lived mainly in Paris ever since he left Australia in October, 1950. He says he went away because he was 'tired of living in an atmosphere of parochial suburbanism'. He would like to visit Australia, but is emphatic that he will never come back to stay. 'I have never missed Australia since I left,' he says, 'except occasionally friends, the bush and birds. I have no plans to return. It would be like trying to get back into short pants that never really fitted me anyhow. It wouldn't work out.'

He and his second wife, Francette, whom he married in 1954, have a small apartment, not far from the Eiffel Tower, but Close spends much time outside France. In 1961 he bought a stone villa 'with balconies and a big cellar that will hold enough wine to float a ship' in Moncalvo, a village on a hill in the north of Italy, in beautiful country, with no tourists to disturb the peace. He had several times gone to Moncalvo, sometimes for periods of months, and found it an ideal place for writing, and he hopes he and his wife will be able to live there for about five months of every summer. When he is writing, he must have tranquillity all the time, and absolute solitude for most of the time, because, once started on a book, he writes every day until he has finished. He wrote his novel, *With Hooves of Brass*, in Moncalvo, while living in a balcony room at an inn. The surroundings could not have been bettered, but the struggle to get down on paper what he wished to say was as desperate as it has always been for him—in his own words, 'the straining stare at the sheet of paper, the mounting tension, sinus headaches, pallid face, sweating hands'. For his novel, *She's My Lovely*, which he calls 'a social fantasy, of international significance (if it has any), or perhaps a social satire', he went to the south of Spain, but found himself drawn back to Moncalvo and finished the book there. He wrote *She's My Lovely* with the idea in the forefront of his mind that it might become a stage musical, but by the time he finished it that idea had, he says, 'drifted over the horizon', and he was more interested in seeing it appear as a book.

Acquaintances of Close in pre-war days when he sold electrical appliances for the Victorian State Electricity Commission, worked for a Melbourne newspaper as an account-collector and later a reporter, and did a wide range of other jobs to earn a weekly wage, would still know him at a glance. His small, but tough, body—he is only five feet five inches tall—has thickened a little, and his naturally dark hair is grey-white and his moustache is greying, although his eyebrows remain obstinately black; but otherwise his appearance has undergone little change. For some years in Paris he wore a small beard, but eventually shaved it off.

When he went to live in France he had published three books; these were *Love Me, Sailor*, a second novel, *The Dupe*, and an autobiographical account of his seafaring days, *Morn of Youth*. Year followed year, and fragments of news about him filtered back and appeared in Australian newspapers from time to time, but he wrote nothing new, and even some of his admirers began to think he was finished, a writer with nothing more to say. After reaching Europe he spent months writing an autobiographical novel, *Not of Salt Nor Earth*. A London publisher accepted it with enthusiasm, but when Close reread it he withdrew it, because, he says, it 'lacked objectivity'. He also wrote a play, but scrapped that before offering it for production. He must have wondered at times whether he would ever again see in print a new book bearing his name. Perhaps he would never have done so if he had not met and married his present elegant and attractive wife. He was first married at Malvern Presbyterian Church in 1927, but for many years that marriage was rocky, and it ended when his wife divorced him in 1950; there are two grown sons. His second wife, who comes from Martinique, in the West Indies, has lived in Paris for over twenty years. It was after Close and she married that he got down to serious writing again. Until then he had appeared more or less content to drift along on royalties earned by overseas editions of his books; his income from this source was modest, but it paid his rent and bought his food, wine and clothing.

Francette had faith in his talent and urged him to start writing again, and he, having found in Francette the sounding-board and point of return he needed, went to work. His talent was rusty, but at last he struck form, and in 1957 published *Eliza Callaghan*. This novel is based on the co-founder of Melbourne John Batman's courtship and marriage of a young Irish girl, who was transported to Tasmania for forgery. The *New York Times* called it a 'realistic historical story, replete with sex, booze, violence and malevolence', and, although descendants of Batman living in Australia did not like it, and said so, it showed Close had lost none of his narrative skill. Since then, having published two more novels, and with work mapped out to keep him busy for some years, Close seems to be in the midst of the richest creative period of his life.

He had evidently written himself into a satirical frame of mind by the time he completed *She's My Lovely*, and he toyed with the idea then of writing another satire 'taking the micky out of the U.S.

scene'. He decided to defer that project, because to do it justice he would have had to pay a more or less extended visit to America, which he did not wish to do at that time. Instead he began thinking hard about a novel which has the tentative title *From a Fountain Boiling*. The theme and characters of this novel had haunted Close for years, and he had long before prepared a full synopsis of it and drafted perhaps one-third of the narrative. 'It will be my most ambitious book yet,' he says, 'and probably the last novel I'll write to be set in Australia, unless I go back to replenish my reservoir of Australian experiences, which I don't see myself doing at present.'

For a man who did not know until he was past thirty that he had any talent at all for writing fiction, much less that he would one day make his living by writing it, Close has travelled a long way. He came to writing by a circuitous route, and, from choice, he would probably have been a seafarer. A physical defect compelled him to relinquish that ambition; when he sat for his second mate's ticket at Hull, England, in 1923, after six years at sea, he was found to have faulty colour vision, and this meant the end of his sea career. Back in Victoria, where he was born in 1903, he tried many kinds of work. For three years he was a labourer; then he had five years running Ford's shipping department at Geelong, and he might have settled for business life if the economic depression had not closed his job down. With a wife and two young sons to keep, he weathered the depression better than most other men did who lacked any particular skills; this was because he discovered a gift of salesmanship, and was doing nicely until tuberculosis knocked him off his feet. He went into Gresswell sanatorium in 1936, and while there sold his first short story to a Melbourne newspaper. He worked hard at writing while convalescing, and gave every spare second to it after going back to a daily job in 1937. His short stories began winning notice, so, as a test of his intellectual stamina, he tried a novelette, called *The Dope Peddler*. It was published, and was also serialized on the air by the Australian Broadcasting Commission.

Close talked himself into a reporter's job on Melbourne *Truth*, the newspaper he had been working for as an account-collector, but he knew he would not stay in journalism; he had decided he was going to be a novelist, and that nothing would stop him. He finished *Love Me, Sailor* in 1945, after working at it for eighteen months. The first publisher he offered it to, Georgian House, of Melbourne, took it at once. The subsequent prosecution of Close and Georgian House for having published an obscene libel turned the spotlight on him, but he denies that it helped his career. 'It made the road tougher, not easier,' he says. 'With one exception, none of the overseas publishers who later issued *Love Me, Sailor* exploited my gaoling or the banning of the book to push sales. France was the exception, but although the French edition was a best-seller the publisher went into liquidation, and I got only part of the million-odd francs owing me, and that in dribs and drabs.' The overseas editions of *Love Me, Sailor* laid the foundation of Close's international reputation. *Eliza Callaghan* and *With Hooves of Brass* enlarged it, and he believes his 1962 novel, *She's My Lovely*, will add to it. His books have sold best in the U.S.A., England, Australia and Germany, but, rather surprisingly, none of them has been filmed.

Close says fiction is the only literary medium which entirely suits his ideas, and he adds to this: 'I like writing satire best. It gives me an opportunity to lampoon modern stupidities and illusions, and also to make my comments. I have a lot still to say, and I intend to say it.'

He has no difficulty in finding agreeable ways of passing the time when he isn't writing. He likes to relax over a few drinks, but is a less ardent drinker than he was before leaving Australia. Whether France, and a French wife, have taught him the art of civilized drinking or advancing years have taught him alcoholic caution is not clear. He also likes listening to good music (he once trained to become a professional singer, but tuberculosis disqualified him), studying international affairs and politics in authoritative newspapers and magazines, and exploring the French countryside in search of out-of-the-way villages. 'I also,' he says, 'still find fun in puncturing the pompous and the prudish, and those warped types who try so hard to put sin into sex, and in ridiculing such absurdities as Australian literary censorship, which bans books freely available to readers in England and most other countries of the world. Some people influencing censorship in Australia would put trousers on table legs.' At fifty-eight, when he said that, Close's zest for life was manifestly unimpaired. It will probably be unimpaired if he is still round at eighty-eight.

FICTION

Love Me, Sailor (Melbourne, Georgian House) 1945
The Dupe (Melbourne, Georgian House) 1948
Eliza Callaghan (London, W. H. Allen) 1957
With Hooves of Brass (London, W. H. Allen) 1961
She's My Lovely (London, W. H. Allen) 1962

GENERAL

Morn of Youth (Melbourne, Georgian House) 1949

John Morrison

FLOWERS AND FICTION

JOHN MORRISON was going home to Mt Evelyn, in the Dandenong Ranges, one evening in the train from Melbourne. He had finished his day's work as gardener at Caulfield Grammar School about half an hour earlier and was dressed accordingly. At Box Hill a man entered the compartment, and, after a few moments, Morrison recognized him as an acquaintance he had met now and then at literary functions. They exchanged greetings and fell to yarning while the train climbed into the Dandenongs.

'Where are you working now?' the other man asked.

'Caulfield Grammar School,' Morrison said.

'Oh, what are you teaching there?'

Morrison glanced down at his gardener's overalls and heavy boots. His acquaintance's face testified to the honesty of the question, but the temptation was too strong for Morrison's quiet, but unsleeping, sense of humour.

'Botany,' he replied.

The episode, unimportant in itself, suggests the effect John Morrison's personality is apt to have on people he meets; they are conscious, not of what he is wearing nor of his surroundings, but only of the man himself. In the late fifties, he is dark and balding, with a strong blunt nose, gently appraising eyes behind the lenses of his glasses, and a sensitive mouth with full underlip. If his parents had been better off, and could have given him a higher education, there is a strong likelihood that he would in fact have earned a living by teaching botany, instead of by gardening; natural history was always his favourite subject. Or, more probably, being the kind of man he is, he would not be teaching botany to classes, in pedagogic style, but writing books about it, along with his novels and short stories. For Morrison is a man who must write. 'The writing disease,' he says, 'took me while I was in my teens. I began with essays on natural history. All I have ever wanted to do has been to earn enough to keep my head above water so I could write. I've never considered abandoning writing, and I can't imagine I ever shall. I suspect I'll always go on trying to say, in readable fiction, something nice about things I like or something nasty about things I don't like. On those terms a man should never go short of something to write about in these lively days.'

It is not altogether easy to comprehend why a man who was born in Sunderland, County Durham, in north-east England, and lived all his early life there should have become one of the most effective writers about Australia. That phrase 'one of the most effective writers' does not mean Morrison's books have been big sellers or that his short stories command glittering fees. What it does mean is that his writings are more widely published, and are read in the long run by more people, than are many books and stories which earn their authors more money. Most of his short stories appear first in Australian literary quarterlies, which cannot pay much but have a longer life and penetrate deeper than mass-circulation magazines that nominally reach larger numbers of readers. His stories have a broad human quality, owing nothing to their Australian locale, which makes them understandable to people abroad who have barely heard of Australia, and his work has been published in England, Soviet Russia, Germany, Hungary, Rumania, Czechoslovakia, Yugoslavia, Poland, Red China and Italy. A small collection of his stories came out in Moscow in 1961 and a much larger collection in 1962.

Even the most carping critics admit that in his two novels, *The Creeping City* and *Port of Call* (both written under Commonwealth Literary Fund Fellowships) and in some of his seventy or eighty published short stories, John Morrison has expressed something of the spirit of Australia and Australians which is as authentic as a gum tree. His writing output has never been large, because he has always had to earn a living and only his hands to earn it with, but his stature has grown, unspectacularly but steadily, ever since he first published a short story, *Night Shift*, when he was nearing forty.

When Morrison was born in 1904, in Sunderland—'a dreary town', he calls it—it was odds-on that he would become a marine engineer. Sunderland lies at the mouth of the River Wear, and draws its economic life-blood from shipbuilding and coal-mining. In Morrison's youth Sunderland boys never asked one another, 'What are you going to be when you leave school?', but 'What shop are you going into?'—'shop' meaning the marine engine-works in which an apprentice engineer was grounded before going to sea. Morrison was one of four children and the eldest of three brothers, and his father, a Scotsman from Inverness, who was a head foreman in the telegraphs construction branch of the British Post Office, believed he would become a marine engineer, in the Sunderland tradition. But John Morrison did not want to become an engineer of any kind; he left school when World War I was in its last year, and, hearing the Sunderland museum required a boy assistant, applied for the job and got it.

The Museum is one of the few things about Sunderland that he remembers with pleasure. Plants, flowers, seashells, butterflies and birds have always fascinated him, and at the museum he was able to immerse himself in a natural history atmosphere, and draw a weekly wage for doing it. He always knew this walk in paradise must end, because his parents could not afford to give him the advanced education which would have equipped him to make a career of it and perhaps become a museum director. And so, when he was nearing seventeen, he found himself out of work. Too old to become an apprentice engineer, he got a job working in the garden of a big private home in Sunderland. He also applied for appointment as a student gardener at the Royal Botanic Gardens, Kew. His application was accepted, but he was told he would have a long wait before Kew could take him on its strength; as one of the world's great botanic gardens, it always had many more young men seeking studentship than it could place at once, even when all but the best had been rejected.

After two years John Morrison was still a gardener in Sunderland, awaiting his call to Kew. So one day he decided to come to Australia. He knew nothing about Australia, except what he had read and heard, but at that time the between-wars immigration boom was at its height and, to him, Australia represented a wider, freer, better world. He sailed from Liverpool as an assisted immigrant, one of eighty or ninety single young men, in the steamship *Suffolk*. He admits he not only had the vaguest idea what kind of country Australia was; he was even vague how long it would take to get there. 'Just before I sailed,' he says, 'I was talking with a Sunderland friend who was a marine engineer and knew a little of the outside world. I was staggered—and thrilled also—when he told me it would take five weeks to get to Melbourne. I had expected the trip to take a few days.' He landed in Melbourne, and, from a selection of jobs offered to him at the immigration bureau, chose one as a gardener at Zara station, New South Wales. Zara was a family station, thirty-three miles from Deniliquin, run by the Officers, and the other men working there accepted John Morrison from the first. He learned to do things, like riding horses and milking cows, which he had never dreamed of doing in Sunderland. 'To come straight from the drizzly, windy north-east coast of England to the Riverina, with its long sunny days, was like walking into another world,' he says. 'I fell in love with Australia from the beginning.'

He stayed nine months at Zara; then, having thousands of miles to roam in, he moved on, going wherever his legs and his fancy carried him. After some months wandering he took a rouseabout's job at 'Grendon', a guest-house at Sherbrooke, in the Dandenong Ranges, near Melbourne. He went from Melbourne by train to Ferntree Gully, then by service car; arriving at night, and in darkness, he had no idea what kind of country he was passing through. Getting up next morning to milk the cows, he walked through the dawn and saw the valley at his feet, brimming with mist, and great mountain ash trees towering all about him. He had never lived in hills before, had never really seen hills before, and at that moment the Dandenongs laid a spell on him which has remained unbroken. He knew that, of all places, this was the place he wanted to be. In one of Morrison's earliest published stories, *All I Ask*, he described the central character's first sight of the hills from a service car in words which recapture his own wonder: 'And this was it—this lofty timber, these hairpin bends in the high-banked road, these cosy doorways beaming amongst the leaves every time they stopped to set someone down. These black abysses rimmed with polished blackbutt spars. There came over him a soothing sense of remoteness, of flight fulfilled.'

At 'Grendon'—burned down in the 1930s, and since replaced by another guest-house, 'Marybrooke'—Morrison began writing seriously for the first time. He had much to learn; he was to write and destroy scores of thousands of words before ever a line was printed. But, labouring with pencil and paper when he was not labouring at his rouseabout's job, he began to lay the foundations of his deceptively simple literary style. Since those days he has gone away from the Dandenongs for periods both long and short, to work in Queensland, in New South Wales, in other parts of Victoria; from 1940 to 1954, he and his wife—in 1928 he married an Irish girl from Newry in Melbourne—lived in Mentone. But he has always returned to the hills in the end; and now, having been settled for some years in his own place at Mt Evelyn, he seems likely to stay in the hills.

His longest absence for some years came late in 1961 when, as a member of a two-man delegation from the Fellowship of Australian Writers, he visited Soviet Russia for three weeks. 'It was,' he says, 'by far the greatest experience of my life, and I came back confirmed in everything I had believed in for over twenty years. Political interest and convictions apart, it was a cultural injection that will benefit me to the end of my days. Tolstoy has been a magic name for me all my life—I cut my reading teeth on him as a teenager—and it was something to stand looking at the desk he wrote at, and walk through the big room where he debated with Turgenev and Gorki, and where all three of them listened to Chaliapin singing. . . . I was staggered to see, alongside all the new work going on in Soviet Russia, the immense and painstaking reconstruction and restoration of the old and historic.'

The impact on his mind of the Soviet Union did not, however, cause his love of the Dandenongs to diminish. He has freely expressed that love particularly in his first novel, *The Creeping City*, published in 1949, and in a number of his short stories, but he does not write only of the hills and the people he knows there; his knowledge of Australia and Australians is far deeper than that of most men born here, and his fiction reflects it. He calls himself 'a realist writer'. This phrase is as accurate as any ready-made label pinned to John Morrison could be, but at its best his work has an imaginative sweep which places him above and outside any recognized literary school or coterie. Many of his readers imagine him to have been a seaman, because his stories often concern ships, sailors, and the sea, but he was never really a seafarer; his marine knowledge was acquired in his native Sunderland and while, for most of the war and some years afterwards, he was a wharfie on Melbourne's waterfront.

He is still, as these words are written in 1962, a working man and likely to remain one for the rest of his active life. He does a four-day week as gardener at Caulfield Grammar School, rising at five o'clock in the morning of every working day, catching a train to the city at six and getting home about seven in the evening. Yet he manages to go on writing. There is rarely a time when he is not working on a short story. He said some years ago that he doubted if he would ever write another novel, not because he found novels harder work than short stories, but because he believed he could say more in twenty-five or thirty short stories than in one novel. He has since qualified those words, however. 'I said that,' he confesses, 'only to console myself, because I didn't expect ever to have enough time to tackle another novel. The full truth is that I'd dearly like to have a go at another novel, and will do so if sales of my collections of short stories provide the means.' The story collections Morrison had in mind when he said this were one put out in the U.S.S.R. in 1961, and a second projected there, and a new volume, published in 1962 by the Australasian Book Society, under the title *Twenty-Three* (the number of stories in it).

A man of simple tastes, his chief pleasure is still, as it was when he was a boy in north-east England, wandering in the open, observing the way wild things grow and wild creatures act. Whether he has a

COLIN SIMPSON

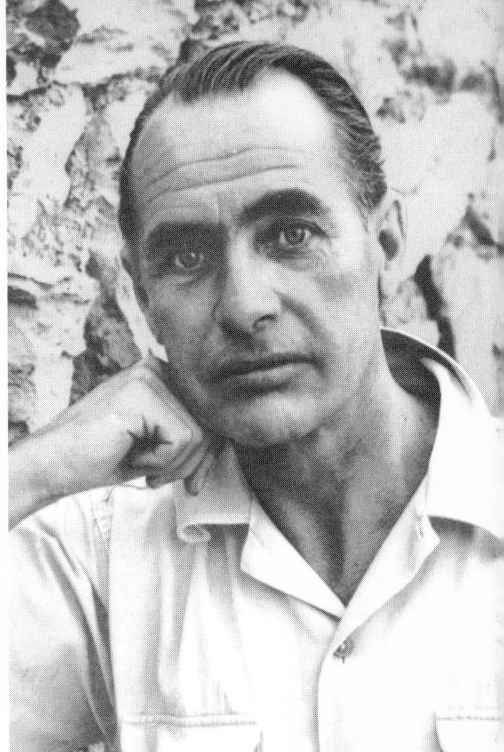

ALAN MOOREHEAD

OLAF RUHEN

JUDAH WATEN

KYLIE TENNANT

PATRICK WHITE

MARY DURACK

DAVID MARTIN

keener eye for wild creatures' behaviour than for the behaviour of that theoretically domesticated creature, man, is an interesting question. Judging by his writings, he doesn't miss much about either the one or the other.

FICTION

Sailors Belong Ships. Short stories (Melbourne, Dolphin Publications) 1947

The Creeping City (Melbourne, Cassell) 1949

Port of Call (Melbourne, Cassell) 1950

Black Cargo. Short stories (Melbourne, Australasian Book Society) 1955

Twenty-Three. Short stories (Sydney, Australasian Book Society) 1962

Volumes of short stories by John Morrison have been published also in Warsaw (1955), Bucharest (1957), Budapest (1959), and Moscow (1961).

John K. Ewers

JOURNEY FROM MONEY STREET

EVERY now and then John K. Ewers meets someone for the first time who says: 'Ewers, eh! You write, don't you? . . . I've read your novel, *Money Street*. When are you going to write something else?' Such remarks no longer irritate him. He is an equable man, who does not easily lose his temper or raise his voice. But he hopes a time will come when his first novel, *Money Street*, originally published twenty-eight years ago, will cease to be the only one of his books many people seem to remember. 'They talk of *Money Street*,' he says, 'as though I had been living in a vacuum ever since. In fact, since *Money Street*, I have published thirteen books, not counting school textbooks, half of them fiction. Several of the novels are better than *Money Street* ever looked like being.'

Not that Ewers despises *Money Street*. On the contrary, that novel has a special place in his affection. It takes its title from the name of a real street, flanked by splendid plane trees and small unpretentious houses, which lies on the northern fringes of Perth. In the early 1930s, Ewers used to walk through Money Street at least twice a week to call on Jean McIntyre, the girl he married in 1936. Something about it fired his imagination, and almost before he knew what was happening he built a story about it. Looking back now on that story, which explored the lives of a group of people living in Money Street, Ewers feels it has no particular distinction; he has moved from the romantic to a more realistic style of writing. Though never a big seller, *Money Street* has always commanded admirers. The first Australian edition was published in 1948, fifteen years after the book came out in London, and its sales indicated its enduring popularity.

From the time he wrote *Money Street*, the novel and the short story have been his major literary interest. He has written much non-fiction, but it is with novels such as *Men Against the Earth* and *For Heroes to Live In*—those two depict life in the Western Australian wheat country—that he has made his deepest mark; he has also found more satisfaction in writing fiction than anything else. His fiction output is not heavy, because he likes to work deliberately, and *The Monkey Puzzle Tree*, a novel he was still writing when this profile went to the printer, was his first for six years. He gave most of his writing time for three years to it and it was simmering in his mind for some years before he began putting it down on paper. It has a city setting, and is his only novel since *Money Street* with an urban background.

John K. Ewers, most of whose friends know him by his second name, Keith, belongs to a generation of Australian writers who had a hard struggle to get their work printed, or noticed once it was printed. Only the determined kept going, and Ewers was one. He did so for two reasons. First, writing was the thing he really ached to do. Second, he believed Australia must create its own literature. 'My attitude,' he says, 'has always been that Australian literature is a new literature, not a branch of English literature. Many critics disagree with me, but I am convinced I am right.' Ewers has never wavered from this view. He seized every opportunity to express it when he became first president of the Western Australian branch of the Fellowship of Australian Writers, in 1938-39, and in his three later terms as president. He expresses it also in his critical work, *Creative Writing in Australia*, first published in 1945, and revised and enlarged in 1956, and again in 1962 for publication in 1963. *Creative Writing in Australia* is widely used as a textbook in Australian teachers' training colleges.

Ewers has emphatic views on the shape and pattern of the work Australian novelists are doing, and also on the identity of the writer who, he believes, is the most important creative writer in Australia today. 'Patrick White undoubtedly,' he says. 'He showed extraordinary development, from his first two novels, *Happy Valley* and *The Living and the Dead*, to his latest novels. If continued, that development will make him a writer of such power that he must be seriously considered for the Nobel Prize. So many modern novels are merely reportage. White's novels are major essays of the imagination. He has a talent for penetrating into people's secret lives, and revealing the uttermost depths of their minds and hearts.' Ewers has always been generous in assessing other writers' work. For many years he has helped to enlarge the reputation of those Australian writers he admires, through public lectures, broadcasts, and readings. This is unusual among writers, most of whom are more concerned to boost themselves than their rivals.

He lives at Cottesloe, a Perth suburb, in a pleasant rambling house which is a workshop as well as a home. He does all his writing there, and his wife, a potter, has her own kiln in the garden. They find the house rather more than large enough for their needs, since their daughter, Patricia, married in 1961. Ewers is a short man, compactly built, and perhaps twelve or fourteen pounds heavier than he was thirty-odd years ago when, weighing nine stone seven pounds, he played football on the centre wing or at half-back, in various Australian Rules country teams. He is practically bald, and lines are plentiful around the thinking blue eyes behind the heavy horn-rimmed glasses. He wears a clipped grey moustache, and his mouth suggests extraordinary determination.

'I have sometimes been attacked by politically-minded critics who say I know nothing of the hardships of life,' he says. 'Well, I saw plenty of hardships when I was a kid.' He was born in 1904, in a little wooden house in the Perth suburb of Subiaco, three months after his parents arrived in Western Australia from Victoria. Reared on a small berry farm in Gippsland, Ewers senior had no trade. In the West he worked at a number of unskilled jobs, and Keith Ewers remembers that sometimes his father's earnings were inadequate. By considerable self-sacrifice on his parents' part, the boy had five years at Perth Modern School. Then, at seventeen, he joined the Western Australian Education Department, as a trainee teacher, and, at nineteen, went to the country. In the next five years he was in charge of three one-teacher country schools.

He had written a few short stories while studying at the teachers' training college, in Perth, but until going to the country he thought of writing only as an agreeable hobby. Then, at South Tammin, his first country school, he formed a friendship with an old farmhand, named George Walker, who had left Victoria for Western Australia, as a boy of sixteen, to seek gold. Having failed to find gold, Walker had stayed in Western Australia, and had an apparently inexhaustible fund of stories about his adventures. While ploughing he would think up yarns and at night tell these to Ewers, who then went away and wrote them down. Ewers sent one of these tales to *The Australian Journal*, in Melbourne, which published it. So he sent more, and these also were published. He shared the reward with George Walker; whenever a story was paid for he bought the old man a pound of tobacco. It was a strange literary collaboration, but valuable to Ewers; it gave him confidence and helped him to build a literary style.

He has always been a versatile writer. As well as novels, short stories, and newspaper articles, he has written literary criticisms, plays, verse, and four book-length regional histories. He has also written textbooks on English for primary schools. These are widely used in Western Australia, and some other States also prescribe them. In fact, with a total sale of well above three hundred thousand, his textbooks are easily his biggest sellers.

He wrote his first novel while teaching in country schools, but could not get it published. He was transferred to Perth in 1929, and arrived there bringing the manuscript of a book-length story in verse, *Boy and Silver*, in which the central characters were an adolescent boy and a kangaroo. He quickly discovered that no publisher would gamble on a story in verse by an unknown writer, so he scraped together thirty pounds and put out an edition of *Boy and Silver* at his own expense. It was a modest seller, but Ewers cleared costs and made a small profit. No mentally balanced writer ever expects to make more than pocket-money by writing verse, and Ewers had no illusions on that point. He has, however, written one unusually profitable set of verses, *The Red Road*. These, which originally appeared in print in 1932, were later set to music by the Perth composer, Edward Black, and for years *The Red Road* has been a popular ballad with concert and radio singers. It brings Ewers about a pound a year in royalties, and he says, 'Considering the standard fees for verse, I hit the jackpot with that one!'

Ewers taught in Western Australian schools for twenty-five years, except for a year abroad, in the U.S.A., Britain and Europe, on a working honeymoon in 1936-37. He did not seek promotion beyond first assistant because this would have interfered with his writing. In 1947 he resigned from the Education Department, in spite of the head-shaking of friends who said, 'Do you think you're doing a wise thing? What about security?', and for the next five years gave all his time to writing. In that period, he gathered material for his non-fiction book, *With the Sun on My Back*, describing three outback walkabouts, which won the 1951 Commonwealth Jubilee five hundred pounds prize for non-fiction. This was published in 1953 and went into three editions. 'It's the only book I have written straight on to the typewriter,' he says, 'I began writing it in February, and raced against the clock to finish it by September, in time for the competition. I usually write a book first in longhand, then type it, chapter by chapter, revising heavily as I go, but that time I could not loiter.'

He never intended returning to a settled job, but in 1952 took a six months' appointment to the teacher training section of Western Australia's technical correspondence school. He stayed, and is now editor of courses on a part-time basis which frees him to write for about half the normal working week.

Ewers admits his philosophy of life has radically changed since he first began writing, but one conviction he held then remains unaltered; that is, he still insists that Australia must go on building its own literature. He remains unshaken about this, even when he discovers, as he does every now and then, that a surprising number of intelligent

Australians don't care about, or perhaps are merely unaware of, the work of Australia's creative writers. He has found that even many Australians who should know better are indifferent to their literary heritage. He once had a boy in his class who was a grandson of Joseph Furphy, the author of *Such is Life*. One day he told the class—fourteen-year-olds—to write an essay on 'a famous Australian'. They fell to it and Ewers, moving among the desks like any watchful teacher, found himself looking down at the head of Furphy's grandson, bent over his exercise book, intent on his task. Ewers stole a glance over the boy's shoulder to see what subject he had chosen. He was writing about Ned Kelly. 'When something like that happens it almost makes you wonder why you keep on writing,' Ewers says. 'Perhaps the answer is that you don't keep on to please anyone else, but, like the old prospector who dies looking for gold, to please yourself.'

FICTION

Money Street (London, Hodder & Stoughton) 1933
Fire on the Wind (London, Hodder & Stoughton) 1935
Men Against the Earth (Melbourne, Georgian House) 1946
For Heroes to Live In (Melbourne, Georgian House) 1948
Harvest. Short stories (Sydney, Angus & Robertson) 1949
Who Rides on the River? (Sydney, Angus & Robertson) 1956

For Children

Tales from the Dead Heart (Sydney, Currawong) 1944

VERSE

Boy and Silver (Fremantle, Porter & Salmon) 1929

GENERAL

Tell the People! (Sydney, Currawong) 1943
Creative Writing in Australia (Melbourne, Georgian House) 1945
With the Sun on My Back (Sydney, Angus & Robertson) 1953

Ewers is also the author of a number of school textbooks, and of four regional histories; these are: *The Story of the Pipeline* (Perth, Carroll's: 1935); *Perth Boys' School*, 1847-1947 (Perth, Government Printer: 1947); *The Western Gateway* (Fremantle City Council: 1948); and *Bruce Rock: The Story of a District* (Bruce Rock District Road Board: 1959).

Cyril Pearl

BRICKBATS GALORE

ON November 22, 1960, Senator J. E. Marriott, a Tasmanian Liberal, rose in the Senate Chamber, Australian Parliament House, Canberra, to ask a question. Let Commonwealth Hansard take up the story:

Senator Marriott.—My question is addressed to the Leader of the Government in the Senate as the representative of the Prime Minister, who administers the Commonwealth Public Service. Has he seen an advertisement in the publication *This Week in Melbourne* of 18th November, concerning the book *So You Want to be an Australian*, in which it is alleged that the author of that book, Cyril Pearl, has written *inter alia*—

A powerful virus called myxomatosis is keeping the rabbit menace in check.

And then later—

No way has yet been discovered of keeping the public service menace in check.

Is it to be taken that Mr Pearl believes that public servants who are employed in the defence departments, the defence services and the Social Services, Repatriation, Health, Education and other departments, are a menace? If not, does the Minister not believe that public servants employed in revenue raising departments are very necessary and therefore they cannot be classified as a menace? Is there any way of preventing or toning down such insulting and erroneous statements, which are apparently written by some authors and writers for publicity purposes and which can only do harm to the morale of a fine and loyal body of Australian men and women in the Commonwealth and State Public Services?

Senator Spooner.—I have not read the publication; I have not heard of it. I do not know the author; I have never heard of him. All I am intent on doing is completely dissociating myself from the sentiments he has expressed.

No record exists of the response, if any, that this senatorial defence of public servants drew from Cyril Pearl, but it must have filled him with a rich unholy joy. For Pearl is a social historian, and any social historian, especially one who writes books about his own time, must either go out of business or learn early to catch brickbats aimed at him by angry hands and hurl these back at the throwers before they have time to duck. Pearl discovered his throwing muscles while still at school, tested them at the University of Melbourne, strengthened them as editor of a Sydney Sunday newspaper, and has kept them in constant trim since publishing, in 1955, his first substantial essay in social history, *The Girl with the Swansdown Seat.* Each of his books, with the exception of *Always Morning*, a biography of the poet 'Orion' Horne, in which he displayed unwonted restraint, has contained material calculated to inflame the ill-will of persons offended on their own account, on account of the community's moral health, or, like Senator Marriott, on account of some 'fine and loyal body of Australian men and women' who deem themselves to have been spotted with ink from Pearl's pen.

Pearl, who always goes hatless regardless of the weather, has lank dark hair touched with grey but looks less than his age, possibly because he moves briskly, with an air of set purpose. He is five feet ten and a half inches tall, and not fat, although he takes no organized exercise and likes good food and good wine; he does not, however, either eat or drink immoderately. He is a fluent talker with a talent for hyperbole, and his brown eyes examine persons he dislikes with unconcealed hostility and those he thinks fatuous with a kind of calculating irony. He was born in 1906, in the Melbourne inner suburb of Fitzroy—'on the firing-line', he says, for in those days the predominantly hard-working population of Fitzroy was laced with criminals whose rivalries exploded now and then in shooting, stabbing and razor-slashing affrays which kept the district fairly well spattered with the blood of the lawless and of such innocent bystanders as were not spry enough to jump clear when trouble started.

Of all his books none has stirred so much anger in some quarters and so much exuberant admiration in others as *Wild Men of Sydney*, which centres upon the escapades of 'three remarkable rogues—John Norton, William Patrick Crick and William Nicholas Willis', who were prominent, if hardly distinguished, figures of New South Wales political and public life in the closing years of the nineteenth century and the early years of the twentieth. All three, and many of their associates, are examined in *Wild Men of Sydney*, but none so searchingly as Norton, the founder of *Truth* newspaper, who emerges from Pearl's pages as a hypocritical, an unscrupulous and a brutal megalomaniac. 'My interest in the Norton story,' says Pearl, 'began when I encountered many of his former associates in Sydney, and realized that the spirit of the Wild Men still survived in many aspects of Sydney life'. When *Wild Men of Sydney* was published in England, John Norton's son, Ezra, still controlled the *Truth* newspaper chain, and about the time supplies of the book reached Australia, hurriedly-prepared legislation widening the libel law to protect dead men against defamation was steamrollered through the New South Wales Parliament. Suggestions that the Defamation Act was specifically designed to block the distribution of *Wild Men of Sydney* were denied by spokesmen of the Government, but the legislation achieved that result in part. As soon as the controversy over the Bill started, several big Sydney bookshops withdrew the book from sale, and it stayed out (or under the counter at any rate) until a year or so after the Act was passed, though small shops continued to sell it without suffering legal consequences. Since then the existence of the Defamation Act is believed to have caused Australian publishers to reject more than one book containing statements which might have invited legal action in N.S.W. The slender body of Australia's published social history has thus been subjected to a process of emaciation it cannot afford.

The indignation his books have generated does not appear to have persuaded Pearl that he should seek some more tranquil field for the exercise of his talents. After having forsaken salaried journalism for five years in favour of authorship, he went back to it late in 1960, as editor of the Sydney *Sunday Mirror*, but this could hardly have been in pursuit of tranquillity; at any rate after less than a year he retired once more to write books, in a house in the elegant Sydney suburb of Hunter's Hill. From that retreat he said of his literary genesis and aims: 'I think, like many Australians of my generation, I was influenced by Mencken* as a satirist, by Bertrand Russell* as a thinker, by Herbert Asbury* as a social historian (non-academic and therefore readable). I think Australia needs a Mencken today, as much as America needed one in the 1920s. This doesn't mean, of course, that I am trying to be one. But I have certainly been influenced by Mencken's passion for clarity, and long ago I took Walter Savage Landor's† precept to heart—I hope with some effect: "Keep always to the point, or with an eye upon it, and instead of saying things to make people stare and wonder, say what will withhold them from wondering and staring." Russell's simple prose has also influenced me—I hope. Asbury first made me realize how social history had been ignored in Australia and neglected in England.'

Pearl claims to have learned little at the four schools he attended—

* H. L. Mencken, American critic (1880-1956); Bertrand Russell, English philosopher, critic and author (b. 1872); Herbert Asbury, American social historian (b. 1891).

† Walter Savage Landor, English poet and writer (1775-1864).

a Carlton State school and a Carlton Roman Catholic primary school, then Scotch College, Melbourne, and Hale College, Perth—but somewhere on his scholastic journey he discovered the Melbourne Public Library, and there, he says, got most of his education. After doing little to qualify himself for a money-earning career, he went to the University of Melbourne early in the 1930s on what he justly describes as 'a very mixed ticket'. He did Russian, the History of Philosophy, and Metaphysics, and, for reasons of whimsy clear to himself at any rate, Neurology. Neurology was a second-year medical subject, and the Registrar of the University told Pearl, in effect, that it was not open to any but medical students. Pearl appealed to the Professor of Anatomy, F. Wood Jones,* who listened to this turbulent student's statement of his claim to a seat in the Neurology class, then asked:

'What the devil are you?'

'A whiffler,' replied Pearl, who had just discovered the old Saxon world 'whiffle' and was enamoured of it and all it stood for.

'What's a whiffler?'

Pearl explained that a whiffler was someone blown around by the wind.

'That's a very good word,' said Professor Wood Jones. 'Well, you go and tell the Registrar that you can whiffle in my class to your heart's content.'

Those were exciting days at the University of Melbourne. The student body had not then discovered a veneration for conformity, and the talented eccentric, the witty screwball, or the entertaining ratbag was apt to be cherished, rather than viewed as a thorn in society's ample side. Pearl qualified under any and all of those three heads, as well as under a good many others. His journalistic knack first became evident when for a period he was editor of the students' newspaper, *Farrago*. His editorials won special, if not always approving, notice. One called forth a rebuke from the Melbourne morning newspaper, *Argus*, now defunct, but at that time the acknowledged, though unofficial, organ of the Establishment. Another caused *Farrago's* sporting editor to protest to Pearl that no one knew what it meant. The sporting editor, Alan Moorehead, who was later to become one of the world's largest-selling authors, sought to prove his point by conducting a one-man Gallup Poll at the University gates. He asked every student who passed what the editorial meant. No one knew. About the same time Pearl, having energy to spare, launched an

* Wood Jones was Professor of Anatomy at Melbourne, 1930-37, and later Professor of Anatomy at Manchester, and Sir William Collins Professor of Human and Comparative Anatomy at the Royal College of Surgeons. He died in 1954.

avant-garde monthly magazine called *Stream*. He and his associates started with a capital of forty pounds, and *Stream* had three issues. These are prized by collectors interested in the sad and gallant history of Australian literary magazines.

Pearl, in short, became a kind of literary man-about-town at a time when such a figure in Melbourne was nearly as conspicuous as a mad dog and, in the view of solid and respectable citizens, rather less desirable. Faced at last with the need to find gainful employment, he joined the Melbourne evening newspaper, *Star*, before it was launched in 1933, and stayed with it until shortly before it ceased publication in 1936. In all, he was to spend twenty-odd years in journalism, notably as the first editor of the Sydney *Sunday Telegraph*, which he edited for ten years. His period in journalism hardly matters, except as it deferred his emergence as a writer. He must look back ruefully on those locust-eaten years. While working in journalism, he was always plagued by the true writer's hankering to write something less ephemeral than newspaper articles, but the demands of journalism prevented him from doing much about it. In 1944 he put out a book of comic verse, *Going Jeep*, under the pen-name of Tom Ugly, and in 1954, with his wife Irma, published *Our Yesterdays*, which is a social history of Australia from 1853 to 1919 in photographs and expository captions. But Pearl the writer did not really emerge until *The Girl with the Swansdown Seat* came out. The quality of that book removed any doubt that, whatever Australia had gained from his exertions as a journalist, it had lost rather more by the delay in his appearance as a writer. His retirement from regular journalism at any rate, though not as a contributor to periodicals, now appears to be permanent.

As a full-time writer, Pearl works no less systematically, and perhaps rather harder, than he ever worked as a journalist. On books demanding research he tries to spend the morning writing and the afternoon devilling. He writes with least effort in the day, and says he cannot write at night. He considers himself to be primarily a social historian (which he defines as 'a bloke who believes that how a lot of people lived is more important than how a few people reigned or ruled'); he also considers social history and social criticism to be the most neglected of all fields in Australian literature, and the bush novel to be the most overworked. 'Almost nothing,' he says, 'has been written about life in Sydney in the middle of the nineteenth century. And the enormous overlay of humbug, conformity, hypocrisy, obscurantism, backslapping and stupidity that stifles Australia today surely needs blasting away.'

Whether Pearl's purposes could be best achieved by essays in factual social history, such as *Wild Men of Sydney*, or by medium of the novel is a matter of conjecture. He says he is more interested in factual than imaginative writing, but he has done some work on a novel—the first novel he has attempted—of which he will say no more than that it is satirical in manner and theme. *The Girl with the Swansdown Seat* is his favourite among his own books, and he admits to an astonished kind of gratification with the success of two short books, *So You Want to be an Australian* and *So You Want to Buy a House*; these are essays in knockabout satire inspired by certain aspects of Australian manners and taste in the years that followed World War II.

Pearl is one of those writers who are doomed to be widely misunderstood, in their own time anyway. His habitual manner, whether he writes or talks, is cynical, irreverent, derisive and iconoclastic, and literal-minded people, confusing manner with purpose, are apt to dismiss him as an entertaining fellow but nothing more. While something of the undergraduate persists in Pearl—for example, he has never quite outgrown a liking for startling his immediate listeners with utterances of calculated outrageousness—this is merely one small facet of the man. Although his enemies would deny the notion, he is intensely serious in his ultimate aims. Like every social historian, he is a missionary, but clearly believes himself more likely to influence his hearers by making them laugh than by thundering at them to save their souls while there is yet time. Whether he is right or wrong about this is anybody's guess, but a country in which many serious writers are as solemn as mourners at a wake cannot afford to see him change.

VERSE

Going Jeep. Under pseudonym Tom Ugly (Sydney, Pinnacle Press) 1944

GENERAL

Our Yesterdays—Australian Life Since 1853 *in Photographs*, with Irma Pearl (Sydney, Angus & Robertson) 1954
The Girl with the Swansdown Seat (London, Frederick Muller) 1955
Bawdy Burns—The Christian Rebel (London, Frederick Muller) 1958
Wild Men of Sydney (London, W. H. Allen) 1958
So You Want to be an Australian (Sydney, Ure Smith) 1959
Always Morning (Melbourne, Cheshire) 1960
So You Want to Buy a House! (Melbourne, Cheshire) 1961
Anzac Newsreel Photographs and explanatory text (Sydney, Ure Smith) 1962

John O'Grady

NINO CULOTTA'S PRISONER

WHEN John O'Grady began writing *They're a Weird Mob* in 1955 he had no way of knowing what the consequences were to be. He did not dream then that his story was to have bigger sales than any novel ever before written by an Australian, and still less that he was to become the helpless prisoner of the fictional Italian immigrant, Nino Culotta, whom he created as the ostensible author of *They're a Weird Mob*. O'Grady has since said that he invented Nino because he wanted to pull Australians' legs. 'I had no idea,' he confesses, 'it would come off as well as it did.' Nino Culotta however rouses conflicting emotions in John O'Grady. On the one hand, O'Grady is gratified that a character who refuses to die should have sprung from his imagination. On the other hand, he cannot quite forgive Nino Culotta for having submerged his creator in his own identity and personality, as he unquestionably has done.

O'Grady is by no means the first writer to have become the prisoner of some character he created. Literary history offers several instances of authors forced by public demand to go on writing about a character they had come to detest. One of the conspicuous examples was Sir Arthur Conan Doyle who, having grown tired of his fictional detective, Sherlock Holmes, brusquely killed him off but had to resurrect him, and then went on to write five further volumes describing his exploits. John O'Grady did not liquidate Culotta, but after publishing a second novel, *Cop This Lot*, also ostensibly written by the indestructible Culotta, he announced, in effect, that in future he intended to write as John O'Grady. What he said was, 'I'll have to be hungry to use Culotta again.' The brisk economy of that sentence is typical of John O'Grady's style of speech; although a picturesque talker, he always makes his point without wasting words. He could hardly have said more clearly that he was done with Nino Culotta, for any possibility that in the foreseeable future John O'Grady would be hungry, except by his own choice, was remote. So it seemed then that Nino's brilliant—and, for O'Grady, highly profitable—career had ended when Nino returned to Australia, from visiting his native Italy, in the last pages of *Cop This Lot.*

Like the report of Sherlock Holmes's death, however, the announcement of Nino Culotta's retirement was premature. A year after *Cop This Lot* appeared, John O'Grady published another novel, *No Kava for Johnny*; this was his third novel, and the first to be issued under his own name. It sold well, as Australian novels go, but modestly by comparison with *They're a Weird Mob* and *Cop This Lot.* The unescapable conclusion was that, while some Australians were interested in John O'Grady, they were outnumbered perhaps ten to one by those interested in Nino Culotta. O'Grady's publisher felt the lesson could not be ignored, but O'Grady himself, a determined man of independent spirit, was unpersuaded. He had banished Culotta from his life, and would not recant. In 1961 he began writing a humorous novel about fishing—not about amateur anglers but about professional fishermen who live by their skill. He spent many months gathering material for this novel; to ensure that the background would be authentic, he even took out a professional fisherman's licence and worked in the industry. Then, with the outline of his story clear in his mind, he sat down at his typewriter. 'I wrote thirty thousand words as John O'Grady,' he says. 'It was terrible. I tore it up, and wrote another ten thousand words as an out-of-work boilermaker who takes up professional fishing. This was even worse. I then agreed to my publisher's request that I should resurrect Culotta. What else could I do?' That was the manner in which Nino Culotta came out of his brief retirement. And John O'Grady, whatever his mortification at having to realize that he is never likely to escape Nino Culotta now—or at any rate never for long—could hardly fail to be gratified with the Australian public's response to pre-publication announcements of that novel, *Gone Fishin'*. For O'Grady is, above all things, a man with his feet on the ground, and too realistic to try to persuade himself now that he is not a more effective writer as Nino Culotta than as John O'Grady.

He is a thoroughly relaxed man as, dressed in slacks and a green open-necked shirt, he wanders, talking, about the unpretentiously comfortable living-room of his house in Oatley, a Sydney suburb. The house, which stands on a narrow point of high land, two hundred feet or so above George's River, is, no less than Nino Culotta, a testimony to O'Grady's imaginativeness. Architects told him he'd never build a house on that site, so he went to work with pencil and paper and designed the house he wanted. It is a longish narrow house, built on three levels, and O'Grady and his second wife, Molly, who have lived in it since it was finished just before Christmas, 1959, say it is ideal for their needs.

O'Grady had a stroke in August, 1958, and this made him temporarily speechless, and for three months he had no power of co-ordination. He made an excellent recovery, but after working hard on *Cop This Lot*, which was published in June, 1960, he decided to do no major writing for a year. He was determined to make a full recovery—or as full a recovery as the man who has suffered a stroke can ever hope to make. Nobody meeting him casually would suspect he had ever had any illness worse than a common cold. Chunky, with a thickening torso and powerful shoulders, he moves with a boxer's lightness. He wears a square-cut beard, which is greying fast, and below his dark hair, also greying and brushed straight back, his brow is broad and smooth, and his blue eyes are direct, almost guileless. He was born in 1907, and looks it, but as he talks, in swift flowing sentences, he displays a mind as flexible and adventurous as that of a man in the twenties. 'I'd hate to think I was going to spend the rest of my life writing,' he says. 'There are so many things I haven't done yet. Life's too short, of course. It would be nice if a man could live to be about three hundred.'

His literary success was late in coming; nobody, unless perhaps a handful of his intimates, thought of him as a potential writer of best-selling novels before *They're a Weird Mob* began breaking sales records. At that time he had been writing for about thirty years, and before inventing Nino Culotta he wrote and published many short stories and articles, and some verse; he also wrote—and acted in and produced—several one-act plays, which were staged by Sydney theatre groups. But until *They're a Weird Mob* appeared, none of his writings yielded him more than pocket-money; like many another Australian who dabbles in writing, he discovered that, as he puts it, 'In Australia you can't eat on short stories. On verse, you can't even buy a beer.' It is certainly improbable that he ever expected to make a living, let alone a handsome living, as a writer.

He was born, the eldest of eight children, in O'Brien Street, Bondi, Sydney. Soon afterwards his father quit his job as editor of the N.S.W. *Agricultural Gazette* and moved himself and his family on to a farm in a remote corner of New England. The nearest school was at Tamworth, about ten miles away, and John O'Grady had no formal schooling until he was twelve, and could be trusted to drive to and from school in the family sulky. He went later as a boarder to St Stanislaus College, at Bathurst, N.S.W., and while there determined to become a doctor. His luck was out; when he was about to leave school and begin studying medicine, drought drove his father off the New England property. Since there was no money to pay the cost of a medical course, young O'Grady, still fired with an ambition to heal the sick, decided to become a pharmacist. 'I was wrong,' be says. 'Pharmacy is purely commercial. It gave me a living for much of my life, but I found the work utterly frustrating.'

He worked in Sydney pharmacies, then took a job managing a pharmacy at Ballina, on the north coast of N.S.W. It was a good business, and after a year or two he bought it. He had a wife and a young family then, and it looked for a time as if he would settle down at Ballina, and become a pillar of the place. He didn't. John O'Grady's spirit is too restless to let him be chained to any one spot for too long. 'I decided there must be more interesting things to do than run a pharmacy in Ballina,' he says, 'and I sold out.' That was in 1936. At that time the ages of his children—John, Denis and Frank—ranged from four and a half years down to nine months, but he has never been nervous of his ability to earn a living, and he wasn't nervous about it then. He took a job travelling for an American firm selling medical goods. His territory was Western Australia, South Australia, and the Northern Territory, and he was continually on the move, calling on doctors, chemists, stores. After two or three years of this, he began to wonder. His sales figures were steadily rising, and his employers were well pleased with him. But where, he kept asking himself, was it all leading?

The war solved his uncertainties—temporarily, at least. He joined the AIF soon after Pearl Harbour, and served in New Guinea and Borneo, as a medical corps pharmacist. After the war he stayed in the army, and had a tour of duty in Japan. Then in 1950 he shed his captain's uniform and returned to civilian life, a fit, but no longer young, man, who had seen much of the world and met a large assortment of people, yet seemed to be going nowhere in particular, and, if it came to that, to have nowhere in particular that he wished to go. One of his first acts was to take a job with a Sydney pharmacy chain; one of the next was to grow a beard, possibly as a thanks-offering for his escape from military discipline after eight years. But a pharmacist's life quickly palled, and in 1954 John O'Grady went out and found a job as a bricklayer's labourer. He had never worked for wages with his hands, and he felt he should do so before he was too old to try. The 'brickie' he applied to eyed him dubiously and said, 'Look here, mate, you're a bit old for this caper. I'll have to see how you go before I decide what to pay you.' That was on a Monday morning. On the Wednesday the boss said, 'You're doing all right. I'll put you on a second-class labourer's rate.' On the Friday O'Grady was paid the first-class labourer's rate—sixteen pounds and ten pence a week at that time. Few things in his life, including his success as a novelist, have given him more satisfaction.

John O'Grady's hobby throughout his adult life has been the study of people and languages. He speaks Malay, Japanese, Samoan, Italian, French, and Spanish reasonably well, and reads, but does not speak, German. It was his interest in the Samoan language, and a desire to know something about Polynesians, which took him to Samoa. He had a few hundred pounds and a wife who, accustomed to her husband's horror of cosy suburban ruts, was willing to go along with him. So late in 1955 they headed for New Zealand. The New Zealand Government, which is the protecting power controlling Samoa, could not make up its mind about O'Grady. Time ran on, his money ran low. Feeling he must work at something, he started writing a novel, ostensibly written by an Italian immigrant to Australia. And so Nino Culotta and *They're a Weird Mob* was born. 'It'll sell about five thousand copies,' he told his wife, as he hammered out the story on his portable typewriter in their Auckland flat, 'and make a few hundred pounds.' (At latest report, *They're a Weird Mob* had earned O'Grady well over thirty thousand pounds, including tax. And it hasn't finished earning money for him yet, even though, for some reason, the immense charm Culotta has for Australians appears to be not exportable. A British edition of *They're a Weird Mob*, in 1958, sold modestly and did not excite the critics, and an American edition, in 1962, had an equally uneventful reception; Martin Levin, in *The New York Times*, described Culotta and his friends as a 'pretty dreary bunch, talented mainly at drinking beer with their shoes off'.)

O'Grady and his wife were rather anxiously counting their small change when the New Zealand Government at last consented to let them go to Samoa. They arrived there early in 1956, with the half-finished typescript of *They're a Weird Mob* in their luggage. O'Grady's daily job was to train native students as pharmacists; in his spare time he finished his novel, and studied the Samoan people, their language, customs, traditions, history. 'I loved it, but it was hard work,' he says. 'Practically nothing authentic had ever been written about Samoa. I had to get my information from the Samoans themselves, after winning their confidence.' By the time *They're a Weird Mob* was published by Ure Smith of Sydney—Angus and Robertson of Sydney had earlier rejected it!—John O'Grady was more interested in his Samoan researches than in Nino Culotta. He was grateful to Nino for having given him a measure of financial independence, but the novel he wrote in Samoa, *No Kava for Johnny*, was closer to his heart than *They're a Weird Mob*. *No Kava for Johnny* has a solid foundation of fact. One of O'Grady's Samoan students, who was the model for the central character, told him the story, and O'Grady himself appears in the novel, disguised as a big red-headed pharmacist.

O'Grady admits he wrote *Cop This Lot* more or less reluctantly. While he was in Samoa his publisher, Sam Ure Smith, kept urging him to produce a sequel to *They're a Weird Mob*, and the task hung heavily over him for two years or so until it was done. 'I thought,' he says, 'of bringing Nino to Samoa. I thought of taking him to the bush. Then Sam suggested Italy.' O'Grady, with his wife and his son, Denis, went to Europe in 1959. They visited thirteen countries, but Italy was their chief target, and there O'Grady gathered much of the basic material for *Cop This Lot*. He got back to Australia late in 1959, bringing with him three hundred typewritten pages which, twice rewritten, heavily condensed and generally remodelled, became *Cop This Lot* six months later. Then, with *Cop This Lot* selling briskly in the bookshops, he was able to devote himself to the task of rescuing John O'Grady from the clutches of Nino Culotta. Or so he believed, confidently but, as events were to prove, incorrectly.

Precisely where John O'Grady will take Nino Culotta—or, perhaps more accurately, where Nino Culotta will take John O'Grady—in the unspecified future is impossible to forecast. It appears certain, however, that, wherever they go, it will be together, for they are now inseparably linked. As might be expected of Nino Culotta's creator, O'Grady does not talk about 'the message' of his work. He has no high-flown notions about himself or what comes from his typewriter, and perhaps the secret of his talent for writing best-selling novels, which has inspired much discussion, is to be found simply in his conviction that most people read for no other reason than to be entertained. His first aim when he sits down to write has always been to entertain. And so far his aim has been unerring.

FICTION

(Published by Ure Smith, Sydney)

They're A Weird Mob 1957
Cop This Lot 1960
No Kava for Johnny 1961
Gone Fishin' 1962

No Kava for Johnny was published under O'Grady's own name, the other three novels under the pseudonym Nino Culotta.

Gavin Casey

A GOLDFIELDS CHILDHOOD

SOME years ago Gavin Casey wrote a magazine article which began with these words: 'Few people write books, which means that most people are lucky. It is the loneliest occupation there is, and all hard work.' People who don't write books might doubt Casey's assertion, but he refuses to retract one syllable of it. 'Anybody who thinks writing a book isn't a lonely job,' he says, 'has never tried to write one.' Casey should know. Although his output of published books—five novels and two volumes of short stories—is small for a man whose career as a serious writer began in the middle of the 1930s, it is quite large enough to qualify him as an authority on the subject. The loneliness of the writer's life is almost certainly the chief reason why Casey, one of the most talented Australian writers of his generation, has produced few books. He is gregarious by nature, and is able to write books, as he puts it, 'only by sacrificing a whole lot of the time I need for other, pleasanter things'.

Bad health in recent years has taken heavy toll of Gavin Casey's physical vitality, and he looks ten years or so older than he is. He walks with the aid of a stick, and his stiff hair and moustache, once dark, are nearly all grey. His mental vitality is still formidable, however. The cavernous grey eyes, restless, sensitive, imaginative, leap and sparkle as he talks, and, although he can be indignant, even quietly angry on some subjects, laughter is never far from his mouth. Casey has earned little money by serious writing, although pretty well since his first tale was published he has been counted among Australia's four or five best short-story writers; the pick of his stories, such as *It's Harder for Girls* and *Short Shift Saturday*, can stand up in any company; but in Australia his kind of stories bring only small cheques.

At the time of writing, he lives in Manning, one of Perth's newer suburbs, and has been back in his native Western Australia for some years, having spent most of the previous fourteen years living in other parts of Australia and overseas. After going back to live in Perth Casey had sixteen months in hospital, and came out with his lung capacity seriously impaired, but he recovered his health to a point where he could get about, and satisfy, in moderation, his liking for the company of other men, and, again in moderation, his taste for beer. Although not strong enough to work as a daily newspaper-man, he was able to run a weekly page of book reviews and book news for his old newspaper, the Perth *Daily News*. He worked also at creative writing, and in 1961 finished two novels, *Amid the Plenty*, which was published in 1962, and *The Man Whose Name Was Mud*, unpublished at the time of writing, which he describes as 'the story of an unambitious, almost lazy man who succeeds in spite of himself in the post-war period of prosperity'.

Casey has also put a lot of time and work into a story for a film about the aborigines which Cecil Holmes, the Sydney director, plans to make. Casey had never before tackled a full-length film story, but the task absorbed him, not only because he sees films as another medium for the writer, but also because he holds strong views about the rights of Australia's coloured people. 'I believe,' he says, 'that all coloured people throughout Australia should have full citizenship tomorrow—or yesterday, if we can arrange it. I think that has got to be the beginning. Many of the present generation would spend a good time in gaol. So what? The problem would be over in one generation. The way we are going today it will never be over. The do-gooders seem to have no ideas of value. A woman said to me, "We built them a beautiful ablution-block but they don't seem a bit grateful." I said, "Why should they go round wreathed in smiles, like a bunch of vaudeville negroes, because they've got running water to wash in, when you've got a porcelain bath all to yourself?" She couldn't see it.'

His emotional involvement in the question goes back to his childhood at Kalgoorlie, when he saw what he calls 'the poor, dejected, run-down abos and mixed-bloods' on the goldfields, and concluded that no people should exist in such hopelessness and degradation. His novel, *Snowball*, published in 1958, has an aborigine for its central character, and constitutes a demand for justice for the aborigines, and he has written a play, *The Hero Comes Home*, based on some of the incidents in *Snowball*. The film which Cecil Holmes intends making from Casey's story could easily be the most devastating comment yet attempted, in terms calculated to reach a world audience, on the plight of the aborigines; the tentative title is *The Flung Spear*. The Australian economic recession of 1960-61 forced Holmes to defer production of the film until better times should make money easier to get. He did not, however, think of abandoning it.

Casey was born in Kalgoorlie in 1907 and grew up there. In an article on his schooldays (Sydney *Bulletin*, January 18, 1961) he has written: 'The town was big, vigorous and full of life, yet it was not a city that engulfed and limited one. It overflowed into the bush, and this was the real bush, not just a pattern of farms and roads. It was flat country, covered with low, grey scrub, perhaps dull to adult eyes, but fascinating to us. It was full of romantically interesting things, shallow lakes that were often dry but sometimes filled with water and ducks, rabbits to hunt, dams in which to swim, abandoned leases and workings on which to play dangerous but most satisfying games. We used to pedal many miles, hunting and "camping", getting punctures from the "doublegees", cooking bits of meat and heating up the pies our mothers had made in the settlers' huts, seven miles along the trainline to Menzies. You could not get lost in that flat country, because except on the cloudiest of days (and there were seldom days which were cloudy at all) the great cloud of smoke and dust that hung over the big mines of the Golden Mile could be seen for miles. Just head for that, and you were right.'

His father died when he was ten and his mother when he was sixteen, and, after a State school and School of Mines education, he went to work as a cadet for the Kalgoorlie municipal electric light station. Looking back on himself at seventeen or eighteen, he knows he was a brash youth. His career in electricity ended one day when he cheeked his boss, who suspended him. Casey said, 'I'll go for good,' and he did. 'I'm not proud of that episode,' he says. 'The boss was right, I was wrong.' He was not contrite then, however, and he caught a train to Perth and found a job selling motor cars and motor bikes. That was in the late 1920s, and motor salesmen were doing nicely. Casey earned good money until the depression gained a firm hold about 1931. Then, jobless, he went back to Kalgoorlie, and took any work he could find. For a good while he worked in the mines—as a labourer, a blacksmith's striker, an electrician's offsider. 'At that time I really began to see human beings as they are,' he says. 'The depression gave me a new set of values. As a kid, I'd read *The Magnet*, *The Gem*, and *Deeds That Won the Empire*, and never questioned their philosophy. In the depression I discovered how off-beam they were. I've never written anything substantial about the depression, and in spite of what some people say I don't think my books are gloomy. But I'm a product of the depression, and if what I learned then were not reflected in my writing it would be astonishing.' Casting round for ways of making extra money, he got himself into motor cycle dirt-track racing, which was not then the big-money international sport it has since become. He persuaded the committee controlling the trotting ground to let the Goldfields

Motorcycle Club organize a series of dirt-track carnivals, and rode in these on his unpaid-for motor bike. 'I was so broke,' he says, 'that I was more reckless than usual, and I won a fair amount of money.'

He married in 1933, and about the same time a Perth Sunday newspaper, *The Mirror*, appointed him its Kalgoorlie representative. He had to sell advertising space, as well as write a weekly page of goldfields news. He liked the work. He particularly liked reporting the Kalgoorlie riots in 1934. These were the culmination of racial clashes between Australians and foreigners, and Casey says those days were 'pretty wild'. Then the racial enmities simmered down, and the riots stopped. The outdoor entertainment season was ending about the same time, so Casey, seeing little ahead of him in Kalgoorlie, decided to try his luck again in Perth. Business was still flat, but improving, and he went back to work as a motor salesman. More important, he began at that time to write the stories which were to make him an Australia-wide reputation within a few years. His first story ever to be printed appeared in *The Australian Journal* in 1936. It was a piece of slapstick comedy, set on the goldfields, and its title was *Collecting the Evidence*. He wrote more stories and began selling them to *The Bulletin*; in successive years he won *The Bulletin* humorous short story prize with a tale called *Rich Stew*, and *The Bulletin* prize for a short story of any kind with *Mail Run East*.

Casey had nothing against motor car selling, but when he saw a chance to enter journalism he took it. For a time he edited a group of Perth magazines, then went to *The Daily News* as a general reporter and features writer. He was called up in 1942, and did a sequence of army jobs in which, he felt, he wasn't contributing much to the enemy's defeat. So he had no regrets when, in 1943, he became a civilian again. After a spell as State publicity censor, he was sent to the Pacific as a Department of Information writer. 'I got closer to the war then,' he says, 'than I ever had as a soldier.' He kept on writing fiction throughout the war whenever he had spare time, and in 1942 published his first book of short stories, *It's Harder for Girls*, which won the S. H. Prior Memorial Prize, and in 1943 a second, *Birds of a Feather*. His first novel, *Downhill is Easier*, came out in 1946. Like most of Casey's work, these three books were largely based on his observations in the Kalgoorlie region.

After the war he had two and a half years running the Australian News and Information Bureau in New York, then six months in London. He did little creative writing while overseas, but added something to his experience of life. One of his jobs was to get articles about Australia printed in overseas newspapers and magazines, and he once offered an Australian writer's article on two-up to the U.S.

magazine *True*. The editor of *True* said he liked the article but not the pictures. 'Leave it to me,' Casey said. He recruited twenty or thirty Australians from the Anzac Club, New York, and led them to Central Park, in the heart of New York City. There he marshalled them round a spinner with two Australian pennies poised on a kip made from a wooden ruler, and got as good a series of two-up pictures as were ever taken. 'It looked,' he says, 'like the biggest two-up school outside Broken Hill.' The article, duly illustrated, was published in *True*, and seen by hundreds of thousands of Americans.

Casey enjoyed his years abroad, even—perhaps particularly—the crises, such as one which occurred when a recording of a talk between Frank Forde, then Minister for the Army, and Arthur Calwell, then Minister for Information, did not arrive in time to be broadcast, as arranged, over one of the big U.S. radio networks on Australia Day, 1946. The broadcast took place, however; for the occasion, Casey was Calwell and another member of his staff, Lloyd Clarke, was Forde, and millions of American listeners were none the wiser. Calwell laughed louder than anyone did when Casey later confessed the deception to him.

Back in Australia, Casey had two years in Canberra, then six years in Sydney, working at a variety of journalistic jobs, and he went back to Perth probably because, like many Western Australians, he relishes the tempo of life there. He has two sons by his second wife, who is an American; one was born in London in 1947, and the second in Canberra in 1950. He also has another son, Fred, the only child of an earlier marriage which ended in divorce. Fred, who was born in Perth in 1938, is married and himself a father, so Gavin Casey is, somewhat surprisingly, a grandfather.

He does not appear to be troubled by this reminder that time is mounting against him. For some years ill-health cut his literary production to practically nothing, but his later output of creative work indicates that he is by no means 'written out'. This is reassuring, for it cannot be pretended that, as year followed year and he produced nothing but an occasional short story, and certainly nothing resembling the novel of lasting worth so long expected of him, even his staunchest admirers did not begin to doubt. To put it bluntly, they wondered if he had found the loneliness of the novelist's calling too much for him, and could not bring himself to stay long enough with any book to pump it full of the creative magic that is in him; they also wondered if, for all the distinction of his best work, he had ever truly discovered himself as a writer for the printed page and would perhaps, on the evidence of reports about the brilliance of his script for Cecil Holmes, be remembered (if he was remembered at all) chiefly as a writer, not of books, but for the modern medium of films. Australia has had competent film writers, on a commercial level, but never a man whose stories have been both technically and artistically in world class, and it seemed possible that Casey could prove to be that man. This still seems possible, and it is likely to be proved or disproved only when *The Flung Spear* has been made. But it is the rebirth of Gavin Casey the novelist, with *Amid the Plenty*, that really matters. A film has to be the product of many hands, a kind of multiple collaboration, and Casey could stamp any film only with so much of his own mind and his own personality. To fulfil himself as a writer he must go it alone, and that is what he is doing now.

FICTION

It's Harder for Girls. Short stories (Sydney, Angus & Robertson) 1942
Birds of a Feather. Short stories (Perth, R. S. Sampson) 1943
Downhill is Easier (Sydney, Angus & Robertson) 1946
The Wits are Out (Sydney, Angus & Robertson) 1947
City of Men (London, Peter Davies) 1950
Snowball (Sydney, Angus & Robertson) 1958
Amid the Plenty (Sydney, Australasian Book Society) 1962

Colin Simpson

TRUTH IN A HANDSOME FRAME

ANYBODY who supposes the successful author automatically leads an easy life should meet Colin Simpson. He is successful—only one other resident Australian non-fiction writer could be regarded as being more successful—but he still works sixty or seventy hours a week. Simpson, who writes 'searchingly', he says, rather than very quickly or readily, has found the only way he can give all his time to writing books and also earn a good living for himself, his wife and their two daughters is to work hours which would appal any staunch trade unionist. 'I start about nine-thirty or ten in the morning,' he says, 'and usually go on until after eleven at night. I might take fifteen minutes for lunch, stop at five-thirty—for a couple of drinks and dinner, and get back to the typewriter about seven-thirty. If I flag around nine o'clock I stop for a few more drinks, then push on.' This is Simpson's normal routine, five or six days a week when he is writing a book; when he is in the field gathering material the hours he spends looking, talking, listening, making notes, and taking photographs are usually longer.

He could, as he has done in the past, work fewer hours and earn a good living in journalism or advertising, but he prefers to live by writing books. His wife Claire, an artist, whose drawings decorate all her husband's books, also accepts the need for his working long hours; she knows he would not be really happy in any other kind of job. He is not one of those exuberantly energetic men who make everyone else feel slack and weary, but dynamic in a reserved and unostentatious way. Although he is six feet tall and weighs only about ten stone, he is not droopily lanky but actively lean, as you would expect a man to be who has done much travelling in rough and primitive places. He has however never called himself, or thought of himself as, an explorer, even though he has penetrated parts of New Guinea few other white men have visited. 'I just like travelling,' he says. 'And I don't mind if you call me a tourist. How long I'll be able to go on travelling I don't know. The big question is how long I can keep my enthusiasm and my capacity for wonder. They seem to be working well enough at present.'

He wears his straight dark hair longish above the ears and smoothed back from his forehead, and his moustache does not hide the humorous twist of his mouth. His light brown eyes are quizzical, and he has the nose of the man who likes to know what is going on in any place in which he happens to find himself. He is tougher than casual acquaintanceship with his friendly personality might suggest. He showed this in December, 1960, when control of Angus and Robertson, the Sydney house which publishes his books, appeared likely to pass into the hands of people who, Simpson believed, knew nothing about books except as merchandise. He flung himself into that battle and among other things organized a public declaration by fifty-two Australian authors in opposition to the threatened change. He is generally held to have played a decisive part, possibly the decisive part, in rescuing Angus and Robertson from that crisis.

Simpson does his writing at home, working from copious notes and references, including sheaves of photographs which he takes himself; he considers his camera to be no less important than his pen and notebook as a means of preserving the impressions he puts into his books. He lives at East Gordon, one of Sydney's substantial, and conservative residential suburbs, in a pleasant house, which is small but adequate for him and his wife, and their younger daughter, Vivien, born in 1944. Their other daughter, Julie, four years older than Vivien, lives away from home now.

Since publishing his first single-handed book, *Adam in Ochre*, in 1951, Simpson has now and then taken salaried work to help pay his way. He is as highly skilled an advertising man as a journalist, and in recent years he has had two periods—of a year and of ten months—with a Sydney advertising agency. But such jobs have been only temporary strayings from the road he follows; he knows he cannot write good books while giving his mind to some other occupation for forty to fifty hours a week.

As an author, Simpson observes one major rule: he never for a moment forgets the audience he is writing for. This does not mean he panders to so-called popular taste by seeing only the gay and beautiful and refusing to see the sad and ugly, but that he takes great pains to make his books easy to read and to ensure they will appeal to the eye. In short, he does not see why truth cannot be depicted in a handsome frame. One of his beliefs is that most Australians buy books to give away, rather than to keep, and that is why he insists on making his books physically attractive. He surrendered forty per cent of the royalties from the first edition of *Adam in Ochre* 'to pay for the format', as he puts it. For his New Guinea books, *Adam with Arrows* and *Adam in Plumes*, Sir Edward Hallstrom, the Sydney philanthropist, who is passionately interested in New Guinea, paid the cost of the colourplates. Simpson's theories about the kind of books people like must be well-based. At the time of writing, his books have sold about two hundred thousand copies in Australia, New Zealand, the United Kingdom and South Africa. Several of them have had separate American editions, and he has had Danish, Swedish, Norwegian, French and Yugoslav translations.

Colin Simpson started his serious literary life by writing verse. Some of his poems appeared, with poems by Kenneth Slessor and Harley Matthews, in a handsome volume, *Trio*, published in Sydney in 1931; but it is now many years since he wrote verse. 'I stopped,' he says, 'perhaps because there is a process one might call hardening of the emotional arteries, brought on by one's having to earn a living in ways that don't allow enough time for reflection. Possibly my emotional arteries will soften again some day, and I'll come back to verse.'

He was born in Sydney in 1908, but much of his young life was lived at Hill End, an old gold-mining town with a picturesque history, fifty miles from Bathurst, N.S.W. He went to Hill End school until he was twelve. From there, he went on to a Sydney high school and left with a testimonial from his headmaster which said, 'This boy should make a good journalist.' But he was unable to find a newspaper job, and went to work in advertising. When he was twenty the Sydney *Daily Guardian* offered him a journalist's job, and he took it. He stayed in journalism for eighteen years, doing everything from crime reporting to art criticism and aviation. It was his work as an aviation correspondent which led him to write his first book. That was a biography of Sir Charles Kingsford Smith, *Caesar of the Skies* and Simpson did it in collaboration with Flying Officer Beau Sheil.

In 1944 the Sydney *Sun* sent him to America where he studied magazine techniques, and interviewed such celebrities as Henry Wallace, Billy Rose, John L. Lewis, Frank Sinatra, and Claire Booth Luce. He had not been back in Sydney long before he found himself wanting to get out of journalism and into the stranger world beyond the cities. He had done a little travelling off the beaten track; an early newspaper assignment had let him wander round the islands of Torres Strait for two months in a lugger, and the colour of the islands had captivated him. So had the people—for example, a white schoolteacher he stayed with for a fortnight on one island who saw himself as the defender of Protestantism against the Popish Menace. 'We Protestants must stick together!' he told Simpson. 'They're coming, you know. I tell you, they're coming! They're coming with bayonets!' This religious fanatic was many years later to become the central figure of an unforgettable chapter, No White Lilies on Vaituli, in Simpson's book *Islands of Men.*

Time did not dull Simpson's yearning for a life less synthetic than that offered by daily journalism, and in 1947 he resigned his newspaper job and became a wandering documentary writer for the Australian Broadcasting Commission. To gather material for the ABC session, *Australian Walkabout*, and other documentaries, he went all over Australia, out to the islands of the Pacific, and to Borneo. In 1948 he joined an Arnhem Land scientific expedition. The Arnhem Land visit yielded superb radio material, including unique recordings of primitive aboriginal music, and Colin Simpson was marked out as a radio man of uncommon enterprise, tenacity of purpose, and imagination. He seemed likely to stay in radio for the rest of his life, and he might well have done so if, in 1950, the ABC had not apologetically told him it could not renew his contract; the Federal Treasury, it was explained to him, had instituted an economy drive. He decided then to write a book about his ABC travels. He tentatively called it *Australian Walkabout*, but when he sat down to write it he somehow couldn't get away from the Arnhem Land natives. There was so much to say about them! So he scrapped the idea of a literary travelogue, and gave his whole book to the natives. Thus *Adam in Ochre* was written. Simpson does not pretend that any of the 'Adam' books—*Adam with Arrows* and *Adam in Plumes* were to come later—is an authoritative contribution to anthropology. 'I simply wanted to interpret primitive peoples to the layman,' he says.

After finishing *Islands of Men*, which came out in 1955, he felt he had written all he wished to write about Australia and Melanesia, for the time being at any rate. The question was where he should look for his next book. One night in a Sydney club he heard a man say, 'I fought against the Nips in two campaigns, and I hated their guts, but I've just come back from a visit to Japan. And I like them!' Simpson thought, 'Well, they strangled prisoners and shot the sick! But I wonder what they're like in their own country?' He determined to go and see for himself. He went, and from two trips to Japan came *The Country Upstairs. Wake Up in Europe*, published in 1959, was the fruit of a lifelong hankering to see Europe and its people; he went to Europe in 1958, gathered material for his book in five months, and wrote it in ten. 'Art collectors are every bit as interesting as headhunters,' he says.

He gave much of his working time in 1961 to the writing of *Show Me a Mountain*, a commissioned history of Ampol Petroleum Limited. Like any author, Simpson prefers to write on subjects of his own choice, but he found the Ampol people easy enough to work with. 'I was pretty much,' he says, 'the arbiter of what went into *Show Me a Mountain* and what didn't.' One aspect of that task gave him special satisfaction; he not only wrote the book, but also directed its production—everything from the jacket design and the type of binding to the technical layout of the pictures and the style of typography. His absorption in the Ampol history delayed him with a book about Hong Kong, Macao and the Philippines, but he caught up the threads, once *Show Me a Mountain* was in the presses, and this other book, *Asia's Bright Balconies*, came out in the middle of 1962, establishing him as the most ubiquitous Australian travel writer of the day.

Simpson says there are plenty of places left for him to write about. 'There's a pattern to what I'm doing,' he explains, 'I'm interested in civilization, and peace is civilization's only climate; you can't have civilization and war at one and the same time. By going among primitive people I learnt what civilization wasn't. I learnt that people were civilized to the extent that they didn't make war, didn't plug one another with arrows, didn't tolerate male dominance in their society, and so on. I've tried to get something of that over in my books.'

Back in 1952 he published a novel, *Come Away, Pearler*. He wrote it with Hollywood in mind, after working as technical and script adviser on the film *Kangaroo*, but *Come Away, Pearler* has not yet become a film, although it has twice been optioned. He has no plans at present for writing another novel, but does not consider himself committed for life to the writing of non-fiction books. He has ample material for several novels if he should wish to use it. It would be a gamble for an established non-fiction writer to venture into fiction, but Simpson has never been one to shrink from taking a chance. 'I've tossed away safe jobs with wonderful prospects,' he says. 'So I must be, at heart, a gambler. I don't play poker or bet on horses, and I'm trying to wean myself off flutters on the Stock Exchange. These are minor forms of gambling compared with authorship. Every time I sit down to write a book I bet a year of my life that I can produce a profitable one. So far all my books have paid off, although the last chapters of some of them have been written in red ink.' You feel Colin Simpson will go on making his bets on his books—and winning them—for as long as he keeps the itch to travel and the strength to work a typewriter.

FICTION

Come Away, Pearler (Sydney, Angus & Robertson) 1952

VERSE

Trio, with Kenneth Slessor and Harley Matthews (Sydney, Sunnybrook Press) 1931

GENERAL

Caesar of the Skies (biography of Sir Charles Kingsford Smith) with Beau Sheil (London, Cassell) 1937

(Published by Angus & Robertson, Sydney)

Adam in Ochre 1951
Adam with Arrows 1953
Adam in Plumes 1954
Islands of Men 1955
The Country Upstairs 1956
Wake Up in Europe 1959
Show Me a Mountain 1961
Asia's Bright Balconies 1962

Colin Simpson is also the author of *Six From Borneo,* a radio script published as a booklet by the Australian Broadcasting Commission in 1956; and of the narrative to *Australian Image,* a book of reproductions of Australian landscape paintings (Sydney, Legend Press) 1956.

Alan Moorehead

"SOMETHING WAS MISSING"

IN 1959 Alan Moorehead dispelled all doubt that he intends making his home in Europe for the rest of his life. He did this by moving his family into a house on the Italian coast half a mile or so from the Mediterranean. Since the war ended Moorehead has lived mostly in Italy, but always until then in rented houses. The new house, which was built for him and under his supervision, is tangible evidence that the roots he has put down in Europe are permanent. Some of his fellow-Australians shake sorrowful heads over Moorehead's preference for living and working abroad; they feel he is guilty of aesthetic disloyalty by not using his uncommon talents to write about his own country. Such criticisms do not worry him because they mostly come from Australians who are openly or secretly hostile to him for one reason or another. His friends, on the other hand, believe him when he says he has lost none of his youthful affection for Australia, in discovering the wonders of a larger, and an older, world; they also agree with him that there is no good reason why he should not live in Europe and find subjects for his books wherever seems good to him, instead of merely in Australia.

Rum Jungle is the only one of his books with an Australian subject. His fourteenth book, *The White Nile*, which was published in England in 1960, is a history of the White Nile; he spent some years working on it, and it was a critical and a popular success in both the British and American editions. Like two of Moorehead's earlier books, *No Room in the Ark* and *The Russian Revolution*, it was a Book of the Month in America. It is doubtful that Moorehead could have found Australian subjects to equal any of these three in depth of appeal; and, as a professional writer, he constantly watches for subjects which will command a world audience, as well as interest him and challenge his craftsmanship. The Nile was ideal from his viewpoint. After writing *The White Nile* he started work on a book about the Blue Nile, and this was published in 1962.

Moorehead first left Australia in 1936. He came home on a visit in 1945, when he spent six months here writing a biography of Field-Marshal Lord Montgomery, and on another visit in 1952. 'I don't think I shall ever live in Australia again,' he says, 'but I am certainly going to return on a trip, because one must go back to one's roots from time to time, and perhaps a book will come of it.' Moorehead's wife Lucy is English, and his three children, John, Caroline, and Richard, are more English than Australian in outlook. Family considerations were not, however, Moorehead's chief reason for deciding to live in Europe. It was simply that he wanted to live there, because his own instincts and sympathies are European. He likes certain things about Australia, notably the bush, in which he found 'a quality of excitement and revealed truth . . . which we never experienced in the cities', but Europe offers more to please his tastes.

Moorehead's house stands on Monte Argentario, which is a promontory sticking out into the Mediterranean about opposite the island of Elba. Rome is two hours' drive away; this suits Moorehead, who doesn't like Rome and seldom goes there. He has built a shack about a hundred yards from the house, and there he starts writing about seven every morning and goes on for four hours. He does this seven days a week when he is not travelling. 'Building this house,' he says, 'swallowed all my waking hours for six months. I've got ten acres of barren hillside, and I had to build a road to get here, as well as bringing water from higher up the mountain, digging out springs, making terraces for vines, olives and whatnot. I am now an expert on sewerage, bricklaying, hydraulics, floor space (in cubic metres), horticulture, and Italian lawyers.'

Moorehead has gone a long way since he left Scotch College, Melbourne, in 1926, and graduated from the University of Melbourne with a B.A. degree in 1930. He quite likely foresaw even then how far he was destined to travel. He has always shown good judgment in assessing his own capabilities, without either under-valuing or over-valuing himself. He knew long before leaving school where he wished to go and pretty well how he should go there, and he has never swerved far from the planned route. 'Since as long as I can remember—the age of fifteen anyway—I have never wanted to do anything but write,' he says, 'and quite early I planned first to get a job on a newspaper, then a job as a foreign correspondent, and then subside gently into writing books.'

The end of the war was the most critical point in his career. He finished the war with a reputation as the greatest British, and one of the world's greatest, war correspondents, and also with the beginning of a reputation as a writer of books. He had a handsome contract with the London *Daily Express*, whose senior war reporter he had been for most of the war, and he could have gone on as a highly-paid foreign correspondent for the rest of his life. He was thirty-five then, however, and wanted to live by writing books, so he got out of his *Daily Express* contract and went to Italy to live and write. Italy has been his true home ever since, although he sometimes goes away for fairly long periods; when he was writing *Gallipoli* he lived for nine months on a Greek island, so that he might work without interruption.

The years have placed a few marks on Moorehead, but his general appearance has hardly changed since he was a reporter on the Melbourne *Herald* in the first half of the 1930s. He still has most of his dark hair. His shortish compact body is no thicker, and his brisk step is still as jaunty. Time has not noticeably touched the strong dark brows above the bright and watchful eyes, the blunt determined nose, or the generous mouth. Moorehead's mouth is the physical expression of one of his salient characteristics. He is extraordinarily generous, at times quixotically so. Soon after the war a Fleet Street journalist, who had helped Moorehead to find his first London job, came to him asking for a loan of five hundred pounds to buy his way out of an acute personal crisis. Moorehead made the loan at once, without security, although at that time he was battling to establish himself as a writer and needed all his money. As far as any of his friends know, Moorehead never mentioned the transaction to anybody. It would have remained a secret if the beneficiary had not himself told several people about it.

Moorehead was born in Melbourne in 1910, the son of a journalist named Richard Moorehead. His childhood, adolescence and young manhood were outwardly unremarkable, but he says in *Rum Jungle* that, as far back as he could remember, he was 'dogged by a nagging feeling that something was missing'. Moorehead went from school to university, then had five years as a reporter on the Melbourne *Herald*, covering anything from railway rounds and civic receptions to bushfires and grasshopper plagues. For years he planned to travel abroad, and one rainy day in 1936 he left Port Melbourne in the one-class liner *Ormonde*, bound for London. Some weeks later the ship steamed into Toulon harbour. In *Rum Jungle* Moorehead wrote:

> I date my life from this moment. Everything in my memory either falls into that period before I reached Toulon or belongs to the years since then. . . .
>
> I left my friends and walked on alone trying with my schoolboy French to decipher the advertisements and slogans on the walls. Finally I came to an open square, a long oblong space flanked on each side by tall buildings and with an avenue of plane trees in full leaf running down the centre. This was

the crisis for me. As I stood there on the sidewalk I knew that I would never go home again—not at any rate for many years. . . . This was it. This was what I had come for. Here in this market and among these people was the missing thing.

After working for an Australian news bureau in London for a few months he joined *The Daily Express*, as Gibraltar correspondent. Gibraltar was a fairly important post then, because the Spanish Civil War was still being fought. Moorehead did well there, and after a while *The Express* transferred him to its Paris office, then to Rome, about the time war broke out. Foreseeing Italy's entry into the war, he left Rome for the Middle East early in 1940. He was still a minor figure among Fleet Street foreign correspondents, but the Middle East was an inactive war theatre just then, so *The Daily Express* let him carry on there.

France fell in June, 1940, and the bearing of this event on Moorehead's personal career, as well as on the course of the war, was considerable. For one thing, the Middle East acquired new importance, as the only theatre where Britain faced the Axis Powers on land; for another, the Mediterranean was closed to British ships, which meant *The Express* could not have got a senior man to Cairo to take charge in less than three months. So Moorehead went on working as chief correspondent of *The Daily Express* in the Middle East, and after the first Western Desert campaign in the winter of 1940-41 there was never any thought of superseding him. His work then marked him out as brilliant, and everything he did later in the war added something to his reputation. His reporting of the invasion of northern Europe, from D-Day to the surrender on Luneberg Heath, was superlative.

The war launched Moorehead as an author; his three books about the war in Africa, *Mediterranean Front*, *A Year of Battle*, and *The End in Africa*, won high critical praise and reasonable popular success. His first two post-war books, *Eclipse* in 1945, and *Montgomery* in 1946, also derived from his war experiences, but then he deliberately turned his back on World War II subjects. He has since written only one war book, *Gallipoli*, and this describes events which took place in World War I, at a time when he was five years old. '*Gallipoli* is the book that most satisfies me,' he has said, 'and certainly it has had more support from the critics than any other. It is full of holes and things that didn't work out as I planned, but in it I got nearer to saying what I wanted to say than ever before or since.' *Gallipoli* won two of England's major literary prizes, the 1956 *Sunday Times* Book Prize and the Duff Cooper Memorial Award.

Moorehead's talents seem to run to biography, history and travel, rather than fiction, although at one time he had ideas of turning himself into a novelist. He half-finished a novel in Paris before the war, and since the war he has published two novels, *The Rage of the Vulture*, which became a Hollywood film under the title of *Thunder in the East*, and *A Summer Night*. He wrote a third novel between these two. This one was already printed and well on its way to become a book when Moorehead decided to withdraw it. 'I read the proofs,' he says, 'and just couldn't bear it.' He has also written several plays, but has never, he says, 'had the nerve to show them to anyone'. It seems improbable that Moorehead will ever again write fiction—unless perhaps, as he paints, purely for recreation. His published novels are smooth enough, but they somehow lack the vitality which distinguishes his other books. His ideas for books come to him 'out of thin air', perhaps while he is shaving or on top of a bus. Publishers and agents suggest to him anything up to twenty subjects a year, but only once—in the case of *The Russian Revolution* —has he adopted one of these.

No other Australian-born writer has built a bigger international reputation, and he is probably among the twenty most successful English-language writers of the day. He writes regularly for *The New Yorker* magazine, and most of his books are serialized in England and the U.S.A., and translated into six or seven foreign languages. But he is not wealthy, nor ever likely to be. 'Since leaving newspapers,' he says, 'I have never stayed at a first-class hotel or travelled (with very few exceptions) first-class or lived in the rosy glow of journalistic ready cash, and I can report in all honesty it hasn't mattered a damn. The great thing about having no job is that you are never in a hurry, you don't have to send or receive telegrams or telephone calls, and no one can tell you to do anything. On the other hand, a certain amount of worry banks up when you spend a year or even two working on a book and no money coming in.'

Moorehead mistrusts discussions about literary values, methods of work and the like, and won't take part in them. He admits, however, that he has a series of what he calls makeshift rules. These are:

Never write for the market, only yourself.

Never write anything unless you are not only sincere but agog to express yourself.

Rewrite everything until the words are absolutely clear and simple with as few adjectives as possible.

Avoid personal publicity as much as you can, above all television.

Never be satisfied with anything.

Makeshift or not, these rules seem to have served Alan Moorehead well enough through his writing life up to now. They will probably go on serving him well enough for the rest of his writing life.

FICTION

(Published by Hamish Hamilton, London)

The Rage of the Vulture 1948
A Summer Night 1954

GENERAL

(Published by Hamish Hamilton, London)

Mediterranean Front 1941
A Year of Battle 1943
The End in Africa 1943
Eclipse 1945
Montgomery 1946
The Villa Diana 1951
The Traitors 1952
Rum Jungle 1953
Gallipoli 1956
The Russian Revolution 1957
No Room in the Ark 1959
The White Nile 1960
The Blue Nile 1962

Olaf Ruhen

TRAVELLER IN THE BYWAYS

SHOULD Olaf Ruhen ever lose his faculty for devising and writing highly profitable fiction he won't starve. When he was a young man, before he had written a single line for print, and long before he first dreamed of making his living as an author, he lived well for six years as a deep-sea fisherman. Although he is in the fifties—an advanced age for a deep-sea fisherman, if not for a novelist—he is confident he could again live by fishing, for he has forgotten none of the tricks of the game. And, although he has no driving ambition to become an ordinary deep-sea fisherman once more, he is still fascinated by an old dream, which he cherished for many years, of fishing the Antarctic. 'The Antarctic,' he says, 'is the greatest unfished fishing-ground in the world. Where a seal can catch a fish a man could catch a hundred; where penguins can live a whole town could live.'

Before I met Olaf Ruhen one of his friends told me, 'Ruhen doesn't look like a writer. On appearance, you'd expect to find him serving before the mast in a sailing-ship.' Most writers, anyway, don't look like writers (whatever writers look like), but Ruhen looks less like the popular idea of a writer than most writers do; practically everything about him suggests the man of physical action, rather than the man of mental affairs. He is about six feet tall, loosely built, with a lean muscular frame and strong fair hair turning grey. His skin, like the skin of many outdoor men, has a kind of luminous pale brown hue. He is a prolific talker, mostly on serious subjects; and while he talks you feel he is trying his ideas on himself, addressing himself no less than anyone else who is present. His eyes are intent; as they puzzle over some new idea which has risen in conversation, they reveal the thinking side of his character. In fact, Olaf Ruhen is a nicely balanced blend of the doer and the thinker. No other kind of man could have written such novels as *Naked Under Capricorn* and *White Man's Shoes*, or any of his short stories. These are the work of a man who has discovered a philosophy of life; they are also the work of a man who has gone to many off-the-track places, in the Australian outback and the Pacific, and talked on intimate terms with the kind of people found in such places.

Ruhen spends at least half his time travelling, and he says his heaviest expense as a writer is travel. Much of his travelling is done in fairly primitive style, because the places he wants to see can rarely be reached by regular airline, air-conditioned train or de luxe motor coach. He has, however, never been tempted to stay at home and get his background material by reading in libraries, as some writers do. For one thing, he likes travel. For another, he knows the danger of supposing something to be true merely because it has been published. He makes a pastime of tracing to their sources popular anecdotes of Australian history which generations of historians and journalists have perpetuated in print, and he has found many stories of this kind to be largely apocryphal. As an example of the way history is twisted, he cites a familiar tale which has often been published in Australian books, magazines and newspapers. It concerns three hundred and twenty-six Chinamen reported to have been fattened and eaten by natives of Rossel Island, in the Louisiade Archipelago, off the south-east tip of New Guinea, and Ruhen says of it: 'It just isn't true. The French ship *St Paul* was wrecked there all right in 1858, and three hundred and twenty-seven Chinamen and some of the crew landed until help could be brought. But they were under indenture to Hong Kong and Singapore principals, and the wreck offered them too good an opportunity to escape their commitments. They disappeared, and left one of their number to tell a tale that would prevent a search for them. *The Sydney Morning Herald* interviewed the supposed lone survivor when he got to Sydney. Every subsequent account was based on his unsubstantiated story alone. And it was instrumental in delaying the development of New Guinea—the British Government quoted it as an excuse not to move into New Guinea when pressed to do so by the New South Wales Government in, I think, 1863. The natives were too savage, they said; and this reputation has undeservedly stuck to the Rossel Islanders ever since.'

Whatever may be objected against Ruhen's novels and short stories —and some Australian critics habitually treat them with the disdain they reserve for any Australian book which achieves overseas recognition—nobody can say they are based on secondhand research. Ruhen feels the writer, whatever else he does, must be honest with himself. The editors of *The Saturday Evening Post* considered his first novel, *Naked Under Capricorn*, as a serial before it was published as a book in the U.S.A. in 1958; they liked it, but wished Ruhen to change parts of it. Believing these changes would have robbed the story of a measure of truth, he refused to make them, and, although the editors accepted his decision with understanding, they rejected the story. In money terms this was expensive for Ruhen, because *The Saturday Evening Post* would have paid him a dollar fee of between nine thousand pounds and thirteen thousand pounds for American serial rights of the novel.

When he and his wife are not travelling they live in a pleasant house in the Sydney harbourside suburb of Mosman. His taste is either for big cities, or regions like North Australia, in which you can travel sometimes for two or three days without seeing another human being, not for in-between places like Dunedin, New Zealand, where he was born in 1911, and lived his early life. Dunedin's population is just over a hundred thousand, and many people consider it one of the world's most agreeable small cities. Ruhen concurs in this, but believes he would have stifled intellectually if he had stayed there. It was there that he started as a writer, but only after he had tried other jobs, including deep-sea fishing.

The sea was part of Ruhen's heritage. His mother, though born in New Zealand, came of a Shetland Island family, and his father, a German from Schleswig-Holstein, was a Frisian Islander. Young Olaf Ruhen had a normal education in Government schools, and when he left Otago Boys' High School he spent a few years working on farms. Then he found a job with the fishing fleet working from Port Chalmers and the Bluff. After picking up experience, he bought a boat of his own. In his six years as a fisherman, he owned three different boats, including his favourite, the thirty-two foot schooner *Alice*, which he worked single-handed for two years. 'It was a hard life,' he says, 'but I enjoyed it. We were getting seven and six a hundred pounds for sole; today they get several shillings a pound. But I did all right. I remember I once took seven tons of sole in a day.' Ruhen's fishing career ended when he wrecked the *Alice*. That was some years before World War II, and the New Zealand Government was at that time nationalizing the fishing industry. So Ruhen decided to go back to dry land.

He worked for a while in a Dunedin timberyard; then he started a spray-painting business in Christchurch, and was doing well when a Dunedin newspaper, which had published some articles by him not long before, offered him a job. The salary was only four pounds a week, and he was making far more at spray-painting, but he decided to take the job because he liked the idea of writing for a living, although his ambition to make a career of writing was still nebulous. The thing he most wanted to do at that time was to fish the Antarctic, but he believed his only hope of doing so was to get to Australia, and here raise the necessary capital and buy a suitable boat. He found a journalist's life agreeable enough, and also began experimenting with fiction. He wrote a short story and sent it to the Sydney *Bulletin*, which published it. So he wrote more stories, and most of these also *The Bulletin* bought and published. Ruhen began to realize he had a talent for fiction. He was still writing—and still thinking of the Antarctic's fishing possibilities—in 1939. Then war broke out and he had to put his personal plans aside.

There was a little bother about his joining the N.Z. fighting services, because his father had been born in Germany. Ruhen was not the only young New Zealander who had this trouble; many others whose connection by blood with one or another enemy nation was as remote as his, in some instances even more remote, were viewed as possible Axis sympathizers. At last N.Z. decided to permit these men to risk their lives fighting for the country they were suspected of wishing to betray, and in December, 1941, Ruhen joined the Royal New Zealand Air Force. As a bomber pilot, he flew sixteen missions from the United Kingdom. In a raid on Berchtesgaden, on April 25, 1945, his Lancaster was the only one of three hundred and eighty-five heavies whose bombs were officially credited with having hit the Berghof, Hitler's chalet.

Back in New Zealand after the war, Ruhen returned to newspaper work, but stayed only long enough to find his civilian feet. In January, 1947, he went to Sydney. He found work with *The Telegraph* first, and later with *The Sun* and *Sydney Morning Herald*. He was also writing short stories again, and these, appearing in *The Bulletin*, began to attract favourable notice. He reached a decisive point in his life in 1949, when his newspaper sent him to New Guinea to write articles about sheep-raising experiments in the Central Highlands, sponsored by the Sydney millionaire Sir Edward Hallstrom. New Guinea captured his imagination, and he wrote a short story with a New Guinea background. He sent the story to America, and *The Saturday Evening Post* bought it for eight hundred and fifty dollars—more money than he would have earned by selling thirty stories in Australia. *The Saturday Evening Post* published that story, *Uprising on the Watumba*, in 1954. Encouraged, Ruhen wrote more stories which *The Saturday Evening Post* bought, increasing payments until these reached two thousand two hundred and fifty dollars a story. Although he was tempted, Ruhen hesitated to throw away the substance of a daily newspaper job for the uncertainties of a freelance writer's life, but circumstances more or less forced his hand; he quarrelled with his then newspaper, *The Sydney Morning*

Herald, and quit. He had sixty pounds at the time. On Christmas Eve, 1956, he had only six pounds left. That was his nadir, but then his fiction began selling, and he has not looked back since.

Today he writes with his eyes fixed, not on Australia, but on the world. He aims to sell his novels and short stories first to publishers and magazines in the U.S.A.; his best magazine market in America has been *The Saturday Evening Post*, which to the end of 1961 had published twenty-three of his short stories. He tries then to place his work in Britain and the Continent of Europe. 'If I write for the limited public that reads the average Australian literary magazine,' he says, 'I'm not meeting the number of people I want to meet. That's why I concentrate on overseas markets. For instance, thirty-one million people read each issue of *The Saturday Evening Post*. I work too hard at my fiction to let it die after being read by a handful of people when I can reach millions. And fiction can be important; a writer can say things in fiction that he could say in no other way. It's the only form of writing in which you can tell the truth.'

The anonymous writer of an article in the Sydney *Bulletin* on March 15, 1961, remarked that Ruhen 'is sometimes held up as an example of a man who makes a business rather than an art out of writing'. Ruhen denies that he does so, because he does not admit that efficiency and artistic integrity are incompatible. In a signed article (Sydney *Observer*, January 7, 1961) he wrote: 'Writers who enjoy success do so because they have forsworn the sweet dreams of childhood, realizing that they operate in an adult world. It used to be thought that an author needed nothing more than pen and paper for his craft, and most of us started in this way; but the author is a fool or lucky beyond belief if he continues to limit his plant to these items. At a conservative estimate he should make an investment of at least four thousand pounds to provide the essentials for writing—at any rate, for the kind of writing by which I live. My own plant is inadequate; it lacks a tape-recorder, a movie-camera and projector, and currently about four hundred and fifty pounds worth of reference books. I do have an investment of two typewriters, steel filing cabinets, a library worth at least five hundred pounds, camera gear worth two hundred and fifty pounds, a station-waggon, extensive camping gear, a variety of useful types of clothes, and so on. It was necessary to provide a large study in my house, and a telephone. A television set and several radios have paid for themselves. I use two desks, and lately acquired extra bookcases at a cost of seventy-two pounds. I've been waiting months for the builder to provide me with more.'

In the five or six months of each year that he is not travelling Ruhen works at his typewriter for four hours a day, from nine in the morning to one o'clock, five days a week. But the time he spends in the physical act of writing represents perhaps only a fifth of the total time he gives to it; travel, talk and mental preparation account for the rest. Although his stories are, on the surface, gripping action tales, they have a deeper purpose than mere popular fiction has; for Ruhen is a missionary in the cause of better racial understanding. He has made a close study of the problems caused by the impact of white civilization on primitive peoples, including such primitive peoples as the Australian aborigines and the natives of the Pacific. Much of his travelling has been done in New Guinea, a land which fascinated him when he first went there and still fascinates him. On one trip he sailed seven hundred miles up the Sepik River and met men of three tribes who had never before seen a white man and did not even know white men existed. His acquaintances include practising headhunters—whom he has found 'ethically ahead of most white men'.

A writer of Ruhen's gifts, moving round as he does, and having his unwearying curiosity about the world beyond the cities and the people who inhabit it, is never likely to run short of material for stories. So he will probably never satisfy that old ambition of his to fish the Antarctic. At least he will never do so merely because he has no more stories to tell and has to find some other way of earning a living.

FICTION

Land of Dahori. Short stories (New York, Lippincott) 1957
Naked Under Capricorn (New York, Lippincott) 1958
White Man's Shoes (London, Macdonald) 1960

GENERAL

New Zealand: Land for the Artist, with R. C. Goudie (Sydney, Legend Press) 1953
Tangaroa's Godchild (London, Macdonald) 1962

Judah Waten

AUSTRALIAN FROM ODESSA

THE three most talkative men of their time in Australia, barring politicians, are probably writers. The three—not necessarily in order of loquacity—are Alan Marshall, Bill Harney, and Judah Waten. Which of these three would talk the other two down in fair oral fight is uncertain, but there is some support for the belief that Waten's relentless staying-power would carry the day. A more resolute talker than Waten would be hard to find, whether as a public speaker or in private conversation. A story about his talking capacity relates that, when he was wheeled into the operating theatre of a Melbourne hospital to undergo a major operation in 1953, he struck up a conversation with the anaesthetist on the work of the French master, Honoré de Balzac, one of his literary gods. The two argued back and forth, neither yielding an inch, and the debate swayed on as the anaesthetist—possibly hurrying matters a little, in self-defence—went into action, but even as Waten lost consciousness he was still defiantly babbling Balzac's name. It is not claimed that he won that debate, but only that, so far as any anaesthetized man can, he got the last word. He usually does get the last word.

For reasons which will be examined presently, Waten is perhaps the most politically controversial among Australian writers of his own day. He is also the first immigrant from Eastern Europe to have made a reputation as an Australian writer. Dr Joachim Schulz, a German scholar, says in a German-language history of Australian literature,* published in West Germany in 1960 (surely the first history of Australian literature to be written in the German language), that Waten 'opened up a new path with his novels about emigrants'. Even Waten's most steely antagonists could hardly deny this. In this sense at any rate, he is an Australian literary pioneer.

He is a large bearlike man, nearly six feet tall and weighing over fifteen stone. His health has been poor for some years, and he carries more flesh than he should, but his physical and mental vigour are

* *Geschichte der Australischen Literatur* (Max Heuber Verlag, München, 1960).

formidable. His curly hair is black and grows strongly, and his heavy-featured face is double-chinned. The brown eyes are deep-set below arched brows, which have the expressive mobility of an old-fashioned tragedian's, and his big teeth are more often than not showing in an almost boyish grin. I called on Waten at his home, a brick villa in the Melbourne suburb of Box Hill, surrounded by a flourishing garden which is obviously the work of an enthusiastic, if not a highly academic, gardener. He likes gardening, and can make things grow, but he gardens by instinct, not to any meticulous plan. He was dressed in slacks and an open-necked shirt, and we talked in his study, where he has a desk and typewriter, and many shelves packed with orderly rows of books and literary magazines. In this study he wrote his strongly autobiographical collection of short stories, *Alien Son*, and many other short stories, and his three novels, *The Unbending*, *Shares in Murder*, and *Time of Conflict*. There also, when this profile was written, he was working on a new novel about Jewish and foreign immigrants to Australia in the period after World War II.

He spends twenty to twenty-five hours a week at serious writing, and regrets he cannot spend fifty to sixty hours a week at it. The Watens have a daughter Alice, born in 1947, and while Mrs Waten works as a high school teacher, Judah Waten contributes to the family income as a part-time publicity man. He does not however believe his writing output would be large, by the standards of most professional authors, even if he could devote all his time to novels and short stories. In nearly ten years he published only four books and nine or ten short stories, but he is content to write slowly, and knows he will never be able to write in any other way. He writes each novel or short story by hand four or five times, then types it three or four times, pruning and polishing as he goes, and trying all the time to express himself in simpler, clearer words. 'I don't believe in inspiration,' he says. 'You just have to get down to it and keep slogging away. That's what I do, but I've never yet been entirely satisfied with anything I've written.'

When Waten talks of writing, whether his own writing or a friend's, or that of one of his idols, such as Tolstoy, Flaubert, Thackeray, and Sholokhov, and, for what he calls 'nature writing', D. H. Lawrence, his personality changes. The rumbustious, opinionated, often aggressive Waten disappears, and in his place is a quiet man, with a deep knowledge of the classics, as well as of modern writing, who speaks of the things in literature that he loves with something close to reverence. Waten by no means admires only those writers whose works promote socialist philosophy; he can, and does, admire fine craftsmanship purely for itself, just as he can, and does, deplore sloppy craftsmanship by Communist writers of irreproachable party standing.

Writers—like managing directors, floorwalkers, clerks, bricklayers, and everyone else—usually have personal political convictions. The difference between Judah Waten and most Australian writers is to be found in his vehemence about his political convictions. He has been a Communist for many years. This is his own business, in a country where the Communist Party is legal, but his eloquence on the glories of Communism has caused some Australians to shy away from accepting him as a writer; they will not separate Judah Waten the Communist from Judah Waten the writer, and they dismiss him as a writer wearing a political straitjacket. Waten has, however, already made a useful contribution to Australian literature, and will probably make a larger one before he is done. Any reader of *Alien Son* remembers those stories, not for any propaganda content, but for their delicacy of phrase, their pathos, their subtle comedy, and their human warmth. His Marxist beliefs naturally influence his writings, just as any writer's political beliefs, whether Right-wing or Left-wing, influence his writings. His adherence to the cause of world socialism and his dislike of capitalism are apparent in his fiction, but his best work stands on its own legs.

He was born in 1911, at Odessa, Russia, and was only a few weeks old when his father and mother, both Jewish, moved to Palestine, seeking escape from the raging anti-Semitism of Czarist Russia, with its pogroms and other persecutions. About two years later they came to Australia, arriving here in 1914, a few months before World War I began. Australia is therefore the country of Judah Waten's earliest memories; his two sisters, the only other Waten children, were both born here. 'Culturally,' he says, 'I lived in two worlds. There was the Australian world—schools, books, games and so on—and the Jewish immigrant world, with its own Yiddish newspapers from abroad, Yiddish books, and, occasionally, Yiddish plays. As long as I can remember I knew the names of several Yiddish and Hebrew writers, especially Sholem Aleichem and Bialik, and the Russian writers, Tolstoy and Chekhov, my mother's favourites.'

For most of the first war the Watens lived in Midland Junction, a railway town about twelve miles from Perth. Waten senior was the local bottle-oh, and his son, as a small boy, sometimes went out on the cart with him, often acting as interpreter for his father, who was halting and uncertain in the English language. One day they called at a big house, set in a bush-garden, at Greenmount, near Midland Junction, and young Waten listened while his father, in broken English, talked with the lady of the house, a small, delicate-featured, fine-boned woman, with luminous brown eyes. Her name was Katharine Susannah Prichard, and although he does not remember now what the talk was about he still remembers his excitement when his father told him, as they jogged homeward in the bottlecart, that she was a successful novelist. The boy had already formed an ambition to become a writer, and the sight of an author in the flesh stimulated that desire. He had discovered the Carnegie Free Library, in Midland Junction, some years earlier, and spent most of his leisure there, dreaming of the day when he also would have a book on the shelves. 'It was,' he says, 'to be a book about people and great events—a novel, in a word.'

He first wrote short stories when he was thirteen, and at the time he thought they were original stories; now he knows they were merely imitative echoes of whatever writer he happened to admire most at the moment. He had most of his schooling at the Christian Brothers' College, Perth, and, rather surprisingly for one who within a few years was to embrace the Marxist ideology, got on well with the Brothers and his schoolfellows, and speaks warmly of his schooldays. When he was fourteen the family moved to Melbourne, and he finished his education at University High School. Then he worked, by turn, as a junior State school teacher, clerk, shop assistant, and—this being the start of the depression—in the unemployed movement.

He wrote his first novel at nineteen. It was set in Melbourne and was built around a group of unemployed men, but Waten says it was a poor novel, because the characters 'were not flesh-and-blood people'. It was not published, but that early failure did not discourage him; it only made him examine himself and determine that he would have to keep on trying for a long time—studying people, gaining experience of life, working at the craft of writing—if he wanted literary success. For the next fifteen years, while earning a living as, among other things, a taxation clerk, railways clerk, and postal employee, he observed people and events, and sweated over his experiments in fiction. Some of his work was published in *avant-garde* magazines in France and England, when he was abroad for two years in the early 1930s, living for a time in London, for a time in Paris. One story appeared in an issue of a magazine which carried contributions by Ezra Pound, John Dos Passos, and Paul Bowles. 'However,' Waten reports, 'the combined glow of these contributors could not light up my story.'

While in England Waten served a sentence in prison. As an active radical, he was to the fore in welcoming contingents of hunger marchers who at that time converged on London from all parts of England and Scotland. In November, 1932, at a rally in London, he urged the police not to draw their batons against the unemployed. He was arrested, charged with inciting the police to refuse to carry out a lawful command, tried at Bow Street, and sentenced to three months' imprisonment. He served his sentence in Wormwood Scrubs, and was granted the full remission for cleanliness, obedience and industry. Of prison he says: 'It was a profound experience which revealed the futility of prison. For criminals, prison is only a stopping-over place unless they are redeemed, which is only possible if they are taught trades that fit them for life in the outside world. For people like me, it is only a place of enforced confinement, for it cannot change our views. To a Communist to be sent to gaol for his ideas is like a badge of honour.'

His first significant success as a writer was the appearance of a short story, *To a Country Town*, in the 1946 *Coast to Coast* collection of Australian short stories. This was the first of his series of stories about Jewish immigrant life in Australia which became, in 1952, his first book, *Alien Son*. Two years later his first novel, *The Unbending*, which has for background the World War I anti-conscription campaigning in Australia, was published. Three years after that came his second novel, *Shares in Murder*—technically, his most skilful book. After another four years he published *Time of Conflict*, which, while broadly concerned with the economic depression of the 1930s, is, in the author's own words, 'first and foremost, as any novel must be, about people'. Waten's work has been published also in the U.S.A. and the U.K., and, in translation, in the U.S.S.R., Germany, China, and Czechoslovakia.

He has positive views on what a novel should be if it is to rank as a work of art. These cannot be expressed in a few lines, but possibly the most important of them reflects Tolstoy's dictum: 'Simplicity is a necessary condition of the beautiful.' Waten holds that the writer must always strive to develop his ideas to 'a maximum of clarity and accuracy'. Obscurity in prose, he says, is perhaps even more unforgivable than in poetry. Unlike some politically dedicated writers, he does not pretend he would be horrified if his books were to achieve large sales and bring him affluence, but he will not woo popular success on any terms but his own. 'The writer wants fame and money,' he says, 'but he should not write for them, they should not influence his work. Many good writers get both fame and money, but the predominant motive in literature must be your perfection, not somebody else's.' A more concise statement of an uncommonly loquacious man's literary creed could hardly be imagined.

FICTION

Alien Son. Short stories (Sydney, Angus & Robertson) 1952
The Unbending (Melbourne, Australasian Book Society) 1954
Shares in Murder (Melbourne, Australasian Book Society) 1957
Time of Conflict (Sydney, Australasian Book Society) 1961

Kylie Tennant

THE JOBLESS GENERATION

ANYBODY knowing nothing about Kylie Tennant could deduce approximately when she was born by reading any two or three of her novels. They are the novels of a writer who, in her own words, 'is not so much interested in emotions as in how people make a living, because I belong to the generation who couldn't get jobs'. She was born in 1912, and was therefore rising eighteen when the economic depression closed over Australia, and in the late twenties before it lifted. In those impressionable years she saw far more than most Australians did of the depression's impact on men and women, and she saw this, not from a plush-covered seat in the stalls, but as an actor in that bitter, yet sometimes richly comic, human drama.

Her novels—not only the early *Tiburon* and *Foveaux*, but also later books, like *Lost Haven* and *The Honey Flow*—are unmistakably the work of a writer who learned much of what she knows of life in the depression years. This does not mean they are destructive, savage or anti-social, but only that their author is a realist, who lost her rose-tinted glasses a long time ago and has never wanted to find them again. Kylie Tennant is not, however, a cynic; perhaps the salient impressions you carry away from a meeting with her are of her almost boundless enthusiasm, her elasticity of mind, and her surging joy of life. Whether she is driving the family truck, cooking a meal in the kitchen of her home at Hunter's Hill, Sydney, or yarning with a visitor in front of the living-room fire, her energy never flags. 'I've always been interested in political and sociological things,' she says, 'but I've put most of my ideas in the form of novels, because back in the depression you couldn't get the truth published unless you pretended it was a lie. My writing principles are simple. Try to make it interesting, and, if you can, make it funny. While they laugh, they'll think. And every writer wants to make people think.'

Her spiritual code, which is implicit in her novels, is not one that can be handily labelled like a package of chain-store merchandise.

She calls herself 'a Christian of sorts', but her Christianity is no less real on that account. Her father was a Presbyterian and her mother a Christian Scientist, and she was married, and later confirmed, in the Church of England, which, she says, 'I have attended ever since in the amiable frame of mind of the scientist who landed in America and to the query, "Which church?", replied, "Oh, any church. I don't mind where I pray or who with."'

Kylie Tennant wears her curly grey hair cut short. Her grey eyes are set wide apart, under strong brows, in an oval face. Her mouth expresses both resolution and a sense of humour, and as a writer she has had need of these qualities. It is astonishing that she should have managed to get any serious writing done in recent years. Her husband, Lewis C. Rodd, a school teacher, who has now retired, was ill for some years, and she has two school-age children, a daughter and a son. Yet in an uncommonly difficult period, in 1959 and 1960, she published a biography, *Speak You So Gently*, of the Cape York Peninsula missionary, Alfred Clint, and a fictional children's book, *All the Proud Tribesmen*, and began work on a novel, *Tantavallon*, set in the Sydney suburbs. About the same time she also wrote and published two textbooks in social studies, one for eight-year-olds, the other for nine-year-olds; these were designed especially, but not exclusively, for N.S.W. State schools. 'Anybody who wants to learn to write,' she says, 'should try writing for eight-year-olds and nine-year-olds. It's sometimes terrifyingly difficult to find the right word. I never before dreamt how hard writing could be.'

Kylie Tennant was born at Manly. She and her sister, two years younger than Kylie, were the only children of middle-class parents. She was christened Kathleen, but in childhood she somehow acquired the name Kylie, an aboriginal word meaning 'boomerang'; many of her friends do not know she was ever called anything else. Her most enduring memory of childhood is of her aloneness. She could read when she was four, and at seven she was reading Rider Haggard and Dickens. She loved reading, but her addiction to books marked her out at school—Brighton College, Manly—as a freak. 'The other girls weren't interested in these things,' she recalls. 'They looked on me as a complete outsider. I would have given anything to be popular. All I did was to come top in English!' She realized by the time she was nine or ten that she had no talent for being a member of a group, no knack of making the way easy for herself by conforming. Books were her companions; in a few years she read her way right through the local lending library. She also discovered the pleasures of solitary wandering. The Tennants lived fairly close to French's Forest, and she often went there alone, taking sandwiches with her, and stayed all day, exploring, talking to no one.

As a child, she wrote a few stories and some fragments of what she calls 'frightful poetry', but when she left school at sixteen she went, modestly enough, into radio broadcasting, as assistant to 'an old boy with a walrus moustache and a gold watch chain who ran the children's hour'. Her enthusiasm for this job steadily ebbed; there were several reasons for this, including her dislike of having to spend all day behind walls. So she decided to throw the job, leave home, and go to Melbourne. Although few dates mean anything to her, she remembers she took that decision on March 11, 1930, because her eighteenth birthday fell next day.

Since the economic depression had already reached Australia, the step was daring; her parents, her sister, and sober-minded people in general felt she was crazy. She arrived in Melbourne on the eve of winter, with only enough money to keep her for a few days. She knew nobody in Melbourne, except a friend of her family, who ran tobacco and sweets kiosks on Kew and Barker railway stations. She called on him, and he offered her a job behind the counter of the Barker kiosk. The pay was thirty-five shillings a week. Some days she had to start work at six-thirty in the morning, some days at nine, and her usual working day was ten hours. Board at Kew took twenty-seven and sixpence a week of her pay, and her employer kept five shillings, towards the cost of her fare back to Sydney. The other two and sixpence was her own. She was reasonably well content, however. The boarding-house meals were not bad, as boarding-house meals go; and when hunger pangs grew sharp she eased them by eating into the stock of the kiosk. 'I've never been able to eat chocolate since,' she says.

Having no money to spare for entertainment, she decided to use her time exploring Melbourne. She scraped together a few shillings, bought a pair of sandshoes, and became a strictly non-competitive runner. Most of her nights were spent running. When she was feeling particularly energetic she would lope from her Kew boarding-house to Fitzroy and back, just for an evening's entertainment. She roamed all over Studley Park after dark. It never occurred to her that she might be attacked by a back-street or park prowler. Anyway, she could have given most prowlers two yards in ten and outrun them.

In Melbourne she learned much about people, because most of the people she met were utterly different from the conventional suburbanites she had known. Now and then some visitor from Sydney would call on her at the Barker kiosk. Her former head-mistress from Brighton College, Manly, went away grieved and perplexed at having found her one-time star English pupil working, not only unashamedly, but even gaily, at so lowly a job. Her employer's kiosk at Kew railway station was a kind of unofficial rendezvous for young men with nowhere much to go in the evenings. They were mostly manual workers—when in those years of depression they could find work, in the city, the country, or other States—and they would lounge about the kiosk, yarning of where they had been and what they had done. Kylie Tennant, lurking unobtrusively there when she had nothing better to do, listened to their talk and stored it away in her memory.

After nine months or so she decided to head back for Sydney, and she felt it would be interesting, as well as economical, to go on foot. She wanted company, however, so she went to the Lost Dogs' Home, at North Melbourne, and bought a shaggy dog for seven and sixpence. The man she was working for thought her mad to contemplate walking to Sydney, and begged her to use the money he had saved from her wages, at five shillings a week, to buy a rail or ship ticket. In the end she agreed to do so, largely because she woke one morning to find her shaggy dog had escaped from the yard of her Kew boarding-house and disappeared. So she arrived back in Sydney by ship; it is one of the few times in her life that Kylie Tennant has, from choice, travelled anywhere in a respectable middle-class manner, instead of in the manner of the vagabond who is broke.

Having some idea of becoming a psychiatrist, she enrolled at the University of Sydney, and there met a young school teacher named Lewis Rodd, never dreaming how much influence he was to exert on her life. After a year or so she quit the university and went chicken-farming at East Hills, a Sydney outer suburb, with a friend named Naomi Lewis. They lived in a converted tramcar on their poultry block, and the venture failed. 'Naomi and I,' Miss Tennant recalls, 'ate all the chickens.' About the time the last chicken was eaten she had a letter from Lewis Rodd, in Coonabarabran, northern New South Wales, where he was teaching. He had heard she and another friend were contemplating a bird-watching expedition to northern New South Wales, and he suggested they should look in at Coonabarabran. She took the road soon afterwards, travelling alone because her bird-watching friend was unable to make the trip. Thousands of men were on the roads in Australia then, living as best they could, taking any casual work that offered. Many men had their wives or girls with them, but Kylie Tennant found no other woman travelling the roads alone. She dressed in slacks and a sweater, she jumped trains and hitched lifts as the men did, she talked their language, but she never suffered even minor embarrassment on account of her sex.

'Because I was dressed like them and acted like them,' she says, 'the men accepted me as one of themselves, without question.'

Lewis Rodd was still at Coonabarabran when she arrived there. It was a joyous reunion for them, and a few days later they surprised themselves: they got married. Kylie Tennant settled down then to become a schoolmaster's wife, but it did not work out quite like that, because a year or so later she launched herself on a literary career by writing her first novel, *Tiburon*. *Tiburon*, set in a New South Wales country town in the depression, won the Sydney *Bulletin's* S. H. Prior Memorial Prize for 1935. It also achieved critical acclaim, even though Kylie Tennant says, 'It was a poor book. When I think of it today it makes me groan. But then all my books make me groan!' Her second novel, *Foveaux*, a story of the Sydney slums, appeared four years later, and since then she has always been working at a novel, or anyway at a book of some kind. She says all her books have been written in collaboration with her husband. 'We talk them over,' she says, 'I write them. He edits them. I rewrite them. The only thing is that his name doesn't appear as co-author.' She does not mind how many times she has to rewrite a sentence, a paragraph or a chapter to make it express her meaning; she rewrote a chapter of one novel seventeen times before it satisfied her.

None of her novels has had a fictitious background; always, before writing a novel, she has gone out and lived among the people she intended writing about, whether they were hawkers, bee-keepers, fishermen, or slum-dwelling drifters. To get material for *The Battlers*, published in 1941, she travelled the roads in a horse and cart. 'The social strata of the roads are strictly defined,' she explains, 'and at that time those travelling on foot were at the bottom, those on bicycles one step up, and those in horse-drawn turnouts at the top. I knew if I travelled in a turnout the right people would come and talk to me.' When gathering first-hand experience for another novel, eventually published as *The Joyful Condemned*, she dyed her hair, put on appropriate clothing, pretended to be drunk and was arrested and sent to Long Bay gaol. 'That cost me thirty-five pounds in lawyers' fees,' she says. 'However as a newspaper paid me for two articles I covered my expenses. What I didn't cover was the bitter knowledge I came by in that gaol, or waiting in the reception house courtyard between a maniac and a woman being removed to a home for the dying. Now, as a member of a group, I go once a month to the local mental hospital to visit chronic cases who have no other visitors. The book I originally wrote, *Tell Morning This*, was much grimmer and longer than *The Joyful Condemned*. But after the war, with a paper shortage, my publishers felt they could not use their paper ration on a book that might fall foul of the censors. *The Joyful Condemned* is therefore my original novel cut by a third. It was either cut out what shocked them or leave the book in a drawer for years.'

Late in 1961 Kylie Tennant got down again to her interrupted novel, *Tantavallon*, after having suspended work on it for many months for a complex of reasons. She describes *Tantavallon* as partly a study of adolescent girl (which is a challenging theme for any middle-aged writer), but says it is 'much more about what is happening to a Sydney suburb in the change from old houses to great home-unit buildings'. Judging by this description, *Tantavallon* seems likely to demonstrate that, whatever her interest in sociological and political states, she loves people above all, and finds them inexhaustibly interesting; especially, to quote one of her novels, 'the dirty, tragic, cheery people, their bravery and their horrible patience. . . .' Those are the kind of people Kylie Tennant knows best, the kind of people she likes best. That she will ever, as a writer, stray far from these people seems highly improbable.

FICTION

Tiburon (Sydney, Endeavour Press) 1935
Foveaux (London, Gollancz) 1939
The Battlers (London, Gollancz) 1941
Ride On, Stranger (London, Gollancz) 1943
Time Enough Later (London, Macmillan) 1945
Lost Haven (London, Macmillan) 1946
The Joyful Condemned (London, Macmillan) 1953
The Honey Flow (London, Macmillan) 1956

For Children

All the Proud Tribesmen (London, Macmillan) 1959

GENERAL

Australia: Her Story. Notes on a Nation (London, Macmillan) 1953
Speak You So Gently (London, Gollancz) 1959

DRAMA

Tether A Dragon (Sydney, Associated General Publications) 1952

For Children

John o' the Forest and Other Plays (London, Macmillan) 1950
The Bells of the City and Other Plays (London, Macmillan) 1955
The Bushranger's Christmas Eve and Other Plays (London, Macmillan) 1959

Patrick White

LIFE AT CASTLE HILL

LATE in the 1950s the enterprising editor of an American sports magazine offered Patrick White, the Australian novelist, a special assignment. He invited White, for a fee of fifteen hundred dollars and all expenses, to fly to Perth from Sydney, where he lives, and interview the great mile runner, Herb Elliott. The editor explained in a letter that he had chosen White because he wished Elliott to be interviewed for his magazine by 'the writer who means most to Australians'. White replied declining the assignment and suggesting that, if the editor wished to print an interview with Elliott by 'the writer who means most to Australians', he should engage a certain woman author whose radio serials are familiar to listeners from Cape York to Cape Leeuwin. It was realism, not mock modesty, that impelled White to deny he is 'the writer who means most to Australians'; he has greatly enlarged and strengthened his reputation since *The Tree of Man* was published in 1955, but he has no illusions about his standing with Australians in general. He knows many Australians have never read anything he has written, and perhaps half of those who have read him consider him to be a queer kind of literary fish whose novels are peopled by freakish characters acting in an eccentric way. If White is troubled by the reluctance of all but a more or less select few of his fellow-countrymen to admire his work, he conceals it well. Nor is he disturbed—outwardly at least—by the venom which his novels cause many Australian literary critics to secrete. Some of his friends say, however, that his external calm under the gibes of critics is no more than the disguise a deeply sensitive man uses to hide his true feelings, and this could well be true.

His novel, *Voss*, published in 1957, was attacked by Australian critics from coast to coast; probably not more than five or six found anything in it to praise, even grudgingly. After that belabouring, many a man would never have written another line, but the attacks on *Voss* did not cause White to falter. In 1961 he published *Riders in the Chariot*, which many overseas critics acclaimed as the best novel he had written; it was widely approved even by most Australian critics, many of whom had earlier tried to damn White as a pretentious obscurantist or worse. Reviewing *Riders in the Chariot* in the Sydney *Bulletin's* Red Page, the Australian poet and critic Chris Wallace-Crabbe wrote: 'We must never forget that White is a novelist with magnificent gifts. If these gifts are ever fully harnessed, he will be far more than Australia's finest novelist; he will be one of the world's very great writers. With this possibility in mind, we should keep on gently carping. And reading his books.'

Patrick White is a tall lean pale-faced man, with a sardonic mouth. His stare, when he sits across a room, talking to a caller, is almost uncomfortably penetrating. He was educated largely in England, and lived most of his young manhood there, but he now seems to be permanently settled in Australia. This is a matter of deliberate choice. In an article written for the Adelaide literary quarterly *Australian Letters* (Vol. I, No. 3, 1958) White told how, after the war, he faced the prospect 'of ceasing to be an artist and turning into that most sterile of beings, a London intellectual or of returning home, to the stimulus of time remembered'. He came home first to grow flowers and vegetables, and breed Schnauzer dogs and Saanen goats, and only later to resume writing. He stayed because, he says, 'I am interested in seeing Australia become civilized, and I want to contribute something to that process.'

A bachelor, he makes his home with a friend named Manoly Lascaris, a Greek, in what was once a farm, at Castle Hill, about twenty miles from Sydney. One of his worries is that the spread of suburban villas, now pressing hard on the boundaries of his six acres, will force him to move within the next few years. White is the kind of writer who needs a refuge. His type of novel, in which the narrative method is indirect, inferential, oblique, could not be written in any but a quiet atmosphere, where a man can be alone with his thoughts, if necessary for many hours on end. 'Possibly,' he has written, 'all art flowers more readily in silence.' He has elaborated this by saying that, in writing a novel, he does not start with a story; he sees his books as 'a series of encounters between characters'. His Castle Hill place, 'Dogwoods', is at any rate perfectly suited to his need; the old pink stucco house, low and roomy, stands among trees and flower gardens which form a kind of bulwark against the outside world.

White does his writing at a littered desk. A portable typewriter usually stands on the desk, but he writes the early drafts of all his work by hand, typing only the copy which he sends to his publishers. This is not affectation; he is not the first man to find he cannot think when faced with a typewriter. Even if he has an important letter to write, he always drafts it by hand. He finds writing no less hard now than he did when he started writing some thirty years ago. His daily routine at 'Dogwoods' is almost invariable. He gets up at seven o'clock each morning and breakfasts. Then he writes for two hours; or sometimes just tries to write. 'I hate writing,' he says. 'I can't explain why I do write, except by saying that I seem to suffer from a kind of disease which can be eased only by writing.' He works in the garden until lunch, and, after a siesta, puts in another two hours or so at his desk in the late afternoon. After a relaxed dinner, he sleeps from nine o'clock to midnight, then gets up and writes until about four in the morning. Until a few years ago White worked what he called 'office hours', doing all his writing between nine in the morning and five or six in the evening, but he says of his current routine: 'It seems better suited to my middle age. I prefer short periods of sleep. I am able to get more work done in the intervals of waking. The midnight to four a.m. period is valuable; the telephone never rings then. The only trouble arises when one's social life upsets the plan.'

The Whites were among Australia's early colonists, Patrick White's great-grandfather having settled in N.S.W. in the 1820s; but White himself was born in London in 1912, during a visit to England by his mother. He was brought up in Sydney, and had his early schooling there and at Moss Vale, and at thirteen he was sent off to Cheltenham College, England. He came home five years later, and had two years or so as a jackeroo on a station. It was then that he first tried to write a novel. He spent night after night in his room, mentally sweating to put down on paper what he wished to say. By his own account, he failed dismally. The station hands whom he worked among, although good-naturedly tolerant of this odd youth's fondness for writing, dismissed him as a harmless crackpot. White did not mind. All he asked was to be left undisturbed. He probably knew even then that he was destined never to go along with the herd, and he has accepted this fate with enthusiasm ever since.

When he was twenty he went back to England. He studied Modern Languages at Cambridge, still writing whenever he had spare time, and after graduating in 1935 settled into rooms in London and went to work in earnest. He wrote plays and verse chiefly. He also wrote novels, but his ambition then was to become a writer for the theatre first, a poet next, and a novelist a long way afterwards. The plays he wrote went the rounds without waking any manager's interest, but he scored some success in the theatre by writing occasional revue sketches and lyrics which were performed and even paid for.

He had been in London three or four years when one night he had a curious experience: he dreamed an entire poem. Waking, he jotted the poem down, and next day sent it off to the English writer Geoffrey Grigson, who at that time was editing a magazine called *New Verse*. Grigson published the poem, and this set White thinking. He had some months earlier finished a novel, the fourth he had written; this had been seen by most of the London publishers and, like its three forerunners, unanimously rejected. Now White asked his agent to send the novel to Grigson, who was a reader for the publishing house of Harrap. He hoped Grigson, who had liked his poem, would also like his novel. Grigson did. He recommended its publication, and so White's first published novel, *Happy Valley*, appeared in 1939. It had a good critical success, but its sales were modest, both in England and the U.S.A., where it came out somewhat later. He finished another novel, *The Living and the Dead*, in the first months of the war. When it appeared in 1941, many critics gave it high praise. 'To read it,' wrote the late Edwin Muir, in the London *Listener*, 'is an experience resembling one's first experience of the work of Joyce and Lawrence. . . . Compared with what he does in this book with the raw material of experience, most novels seem to do nothing at all.'

White served in the war, as a RAF intelligence officer in the Middle East, with a year in Greece after that country's liberation; he remembers that year, 'after all those years of death', as one of the significant parts of his life. Demobbed in 1946, he wrote *The Aunt's Story*, which came out in 1948; many of his admirers consider it to be his best novel. It is White's own favourite, 'because I wrote it immediately after the war, when I had been cut off from any intellectual life for years, and also because I feel that, in it, I said most nearly what I wanted to say.' Each of his three later novels, *The Tree of Man*, *Voss*, and *Riders in the Chariot*, has vehement detractors, as well as ardent admirers, but they have added to his stature as a novelist.

Overseas and Australian critics have compared him, at one time or another, with an extraordinary range of eminent writers; the list includes Joyce, D. H. Lawrence, Gertrude Stein, Faulkner, Katherine Mansfield, Hemingway, Virginia Woolf, Sinclair Lewis, Herman Melville, Remarque, Malraux, Tolstoy, Henry James, and Knut Hamsun. He was even labelled 'the Antipodean Thomas Hardy' after publishing *The Tree of Man*. The closest students of his work consider none of these comparisons valid; they believe his novels, and even the mechanics of his literary style (if the word 'mechanics' may properly be applied to his literary style), come wholly from within White himself.

Late in 1961 Australians were first afforded a glimpse of White the playwright, who had been obscured for so long by White the novelist.

A play, *The Ham Funeral*, which White wrote just after the war, was produced in Adelaide by the Adelaide University Guild. This play, inspired by the Australian artist William Dobell's sardonic painting, *The Dead Landlord*, and the story behind it, had earlier been considered by theatre managers in Sydney, London and New York, but had not achieved production. In 1960 it came to the notice of the drama advisory committee of the Adelaide Festival of Arts. This committee recommended that the play should be produced at the 1962 Festival, but the board of governors of the Festival decided against it. It was then that the Adelaide University Theatre Guild arranged to produce the play. This impelled White to sit down and write another play, *The Season at Sarsaparilla*, which he sent to his agent in London. He says, however, that, as a writer, he is not deeply interested in the theatre, principally because 'there are too many difficulties, and warring personalities destructive of one's own'.

He appears to have no intention of abandoning the novel for drama, but only a rash man would dare to make positive forecasts about his literary future; even positive assertions about his literary past are dangerous. In this category is the assertion, which has been widely made, that *Voss* is merely an imaginative fictionization of the story of the explorer, Ludwig Leichhardt. The truth is that White conceived the basic idea of Voss when, serving in the Western Desert, he began thinking of a novel built around a central character who was, like Hitler, a megalomaniac. He felt it would be interesting to involve this character in an unconsummated Tristan and Isolde love affair with a woman he was physically separated from; this subsidiary theme was suggested to White by his work of censoring letters written by airmen to the wives and girls in England whom they were cut off from by the war. 'For some of that time in the desert,' he says, 'I had a posting in which I was free to wander, and I covered a lot of ground. It was then that I began to realize the possibilities of the desert, and that the Voss character really had a chance to develop.' White does not pretend Voss and Leichhardt did not have much in common, but he was unaware of these similarities until, long after the main lines of the novel were established in his mind, he began studying the lives of early Australian explorers, Leichhardt among others, in preparation for writing it. In short, Leichhardt did not beget Voss; it merely happened that certain aspects of Leichhardt's life and character matched those of Johann Ulrich Voss, as White saw Voss when the novel was still only a hazy outline in his mind.

Behind the mask of his rather chill reserve, White possibly worries about the manifest failure of many people to understand his novels;

but, if he does so, his concern remains hidden. Even the most immoderate assaults by the critics—especially several Australian critics who derided him with a kind of malicious glee—did not break his spirit, but in the end appeared only to strengthen him. The dominant impression you carry away from three or four hours' talk with White is that he wishes to get on with his work in his own way, and that nothing but death is likely to stop him.

FICTION

Happy Valley (London, Harrap) 1939
The Living and the Dead (London, Routledge) 1941
The Aunt's Story (London, Routledge) 1948
The Tree of Man (London, Eyre & Spottiswoode) 1955
Voss (London, Eyre & Spottiswoode) 1957
Riders in the Chariot (London, Eyre & Spottiswoode) 1961

VERSE

The Ploughman and Other Poems. Illustrated by L. R. Davies (Sydney, Beacon Press) 1935

Mary Durack

PIONEERS BEHIND HER

SOME years ago Mary Durack took a hard look at herself and felt none too pleased with what she saw. She wondered if she was one of those writers who make a dashing start on a literary career, then lose their way. She had published seven books, all but one either collections of light sketches or children's tales illustrated by her sister Elizabeth. Further back, at the ripe age of ten, she had seen a collection of her verses printed and published. But at forty she had not finished writing even one of the big ambitious books she wanted to write, and it was beginning to look as if she never would finish one of them. 'I had heaps of stuff on paper, chapters of novels and notes on characters,' she says, 'but not one completed book, or anything that looked like becoming a completed book. A good deal of my precious writing time was also going into "fugitive" stuff—the occasional short story, verse, radio feature. My question was not perhaps so much where I was going, as where so much time and effort had gone and whether the dream of doing something worth while "when there was time" was anything more than an excuse for lack of discipline and real ability.'

That was how she felt about it at any rate, even though, to onlookers, there seemed to be ample justification for her inability to find time to write books. She had married Horrie Miller, a pioneer airline operator, in 1938, and her domestic obligations were heavy. At the time she set about examining herself to determine where she had failed to make her mark as a writer she had four daughters and a son, aged from fourteen down to four, and since then she has added a son to her family; she also had to run the Millers' large home at Nedlands, a Perth suburb. The most energetic woman might have considered this to be a full hand, but the best excuses she was able to find did not satisfy her. And that was where the Durack blood took over. When her forebears wished to pioneer a new piece of country in the North they did not sit round thinking about it until the obstacles looked insuperable; they went out and did it. In the same way, Mary Durack sat down and wrote her book. She had enough material, either on paper or in her mind, for three or four novels, and she decided to put it all into one book. It was a prodigious task of compression, but within eighteen months her novel, *Keep Him, My Country*, was finished. She posted it to London, and a publisher accepted it at once. When it was published in 1955 it carried the English Book Society's recommendation; it was also the book-of-the-month choice of the literary magazine *Books and Bookmen*. To Mary Durack, *Keep Him, My Country* was less important for any popular acclaim it won than because it allayed her doubts about herself; and the publication late in 1959 of *Kings in Grass Castles* demolished any lingering fears.

But she recognizes now that she cannot do work that is really worth while in a hurry; this is evidently a matter of temperament which nothing will alter. She says she seems to get things to a certain stage—short stories, plays, novels, even poems—and then finds herself called away by some urgent and immediate commitment. She puts aside the part-finished task, hoping to return to it later when the way ahead is clear. 'This is not a neurosis or an excuse,' she says. 'At least I hope it's not. It is, I suspect, just life the way it has worked out for me.'

Although Mary Durack does not admit this herself, she is obviously not ruthless enough in rejecting the demands that other people, often people she has never seen, make on her time. Like every writer who makes any kind of name, she finds her mail heavy with letters from admirers of her work and aspiring authors seeking her advice. She confesses she can no more leave a letter unanswered than she can leave the telephone ringing or shut the door in someone's face. She also finds it impossible to dismiss with a bare acknowledgment a letter on any subject that interests her; a reply which starts out to be a short note more often than not expands into three or four typewritten pages and encourages a prolonged exchange of correspondence. So a substantial part of her time and energy goes into the writing of letters and adds not a single word to the volume of her literary output.

She is a handsome woman, with brown curly hair and wide-spaced blue eyes, and for some reason she appears a good deal taller than she is—five feet one inch without shoes. She has a strong jaw, which, like her thrusting stride, suggests she has inherited all the purpose of her pioneering grandfather, Patsy Durack, the dominating central figure of *Kings in Grass Castles*.

Critics of Australian literature have long been perplexed by the best Australian writers' preoccupation with the bush, and many people have asked Mary Durack why she does not forget the bush and write about the city. 'The bush background has always,' she explains, 'been so alive to me. I shouldn't care to say I'll always want to write about the bush, but there are subjects there which light me up more than any other subjects do. It isn't that I dislike the city or find it uninteresting; it's just that my love of the bush is almost psychopathic.'

Broome is the setting of a novel she has been working on for some years. Other writers have written novels of Broome, but these have chiefly concerned pearls and pearling. To Mary Durack, the fascination of Broome lies chiefly in the people who live there. In her novel, pearls and pearling are merely incidental to her dramatization of the sociological situation of the men, women and children of mixed blood whom she calls 'the unused by-product of the pearling industry'. She says of them: 'I know these people as I know my own brothers and sisters. My principal character is a man of mixed aboriginal, Malay and English blood, brought up in the polyglot atmosphere of Broome. I know many men like him. These northern mixed-bloods, a good-looking, fun-loving people, represent a problem mainly because the economy of the country cannot properly use or absorb them. But they are not, like the mixed-bloods of the south, outcast, hopeless and mostly miserable. These are the people of the country—about ten to every one white. They are better adapted than the white man to the climate and conditions, better than the full-blood to the cultural clash.'

She suspended work on the pearling novel in 1961 to visit Kimberley, at the request of the Roman Catholic Bishop of Kimberley, and write a series of newspaper articles on the past and present of the native missions. She travelled with a photographer, and her articles, put together, would have made a sizeable book. In moving round she came upon a wealth of fascinating material about early missionary efforts around the Dampier Land Peninsula, the coming of a group of Trappist monks from France in 1890, their high hopes, remarkable achievements, and—in the end—their admittance of defeat. The mission, she discovered, passed into the hands of the German Pallottines in 1901, and the task began again with the people who seemed at first so amenable, and so adaptable, but proved always to be bewilderingly elusive. 'I roamed most of the peninsula,' she says, 'and talked with practically every native and coloured person around, and gathered as much as possible of this strange story. Inevitably the background is the pearling industry and the polyglot people it brought to this part of Australia with the resulting racial mixtures that have always so interested me. I felt I must write a documentary book giving a picture of the work that has gone into these missions, in how much they have failed and in how much succeeded, and if possible giving some understanding of the peculiar problems they have had, and still have, to contend with.'

Mary Durack was born in Adelaide in 1913 and has lived roughly half her life in cities, but the outback has always filled her mind. Her earliest memories are of the bush and cattle; her very first memory is of clutching her father's hand, and pretending she wasn't terrified, as he counted the cattle running down a race into a cattle-boat at Wyndham. With her eldest brother, she had her early childhood in the Kimberley area of Western Australia, living on either Ivanhoe station or Argyle station, the great Durack properties. When she and her brother were nearing school age, her parents moved the family home to Perth. The Durack children—three brothers and another sister were born after Mary and her first brother—were educated in the city. Those being days of slow travel, the Durack children did not go back to the North until school was finished; but they were never far from the outback. Their father divided his time between Perth and Kimberley, and always on trips home he brought with him fragments of the North—crocodile skins, native weapons, cockatoos, galahs, outlandish stones; sometimes he came down accompanied by an aborigine who wished to see the city.

Mary Durack's writing gift showed itself almost as soon as she learned to put words on to paper. She started by writing verse. Her parents proudly collected these melodious jingles, and paid to have them published in a book called *Little Poems of Sunshine*. 'It was about the worst thing that ever happened to me,' Mary Durack says. 'It set me apart, as a kind of freak. I longed to be good at basketball, but instead I was a child-poet.' Some people wouldn't even believe that ten-year-old Mary had written *Little Poems of Sunshine* unaided; one day a teacher at her Perth convent school, with a few sceptical words, sent her out of the classroom and told her not to come back until she had written a poem. She sat under a tree in the playground all day and wrote nothing. 'That,' she says, 'put a mark on me for ever.'

All the time she was living in the city, she was hungering for the North, and as soon as she left school, at sixteen, she persuaded her parents to let her go back to Kimberley. To her, that was a homecoming. She was always writing then, although she never thought her stories or verses might be worth publishing. Then she wrote some articles about station life in the North, and sent these to *The West Australian*, which printed them. The sight of her own words in print gave her heart. Her sister, Elizabeth, two and a half years younger than Mary, also went North on leaving school. Elizabeth, who has since made a reputation as a fine artist, was at that time a talented, if inexperienced, black-and-white artist, and she illustrated some of Mary's articles. These were published, and the sisters, finding they collaborated well, joined in producing a series of outback sketches, with words by Mary and pictures by Elizabeth. The Sydney *Bulletin* published these, and later issued them as a book entitled *All-About*. The book went through several editions, so the sisters did a second, *Chunuma*. This also sold well, and was quickly followed by a third book.

Neither had the smallest inclination to leave the outback and lead a literary life in the city. For three years they took over Ivanhoe station, sharing the cooking and the cook's award wage of three pounds ten shillings a week. They often saw no white faces but each other's for weeks, sometimes for months. There was no flywire, no refrigeration, no electric light or power, but they loved the life. 'This Ivanhoe time was significant, as far as our understanding of the blacks was concerned,' Mary Durack says. 'They regarded us as their responsibility and looked after us all the time, always most tactfully and never being obtrusive about it.' One day she took the old station jalopy out to deliver stores to a stock camp. The engine suddenly choked and died, and she was debating whether to go on or back—about fifteen miles either way—when two armed warriors sprinted toward her out of the long grass. They were naked except for loincloths, and smeared with the remains of white corroboree paint and emu feathers, but, peering hard, she recognized them as two of the station boys who had been on walkabout.

'What's the matter, Mary?' one said. 'Had a bit of a stick up, eh?' He whisked up the bonnet, fiddled with the engine, removed a part, sucked it, and put it back. 'Bit of dirt in the carburettor,' he said. 'That's always happenin' to this old bus. Give her a kick over—she ought to be right now.'

She was.

In 1936 the Durack girls decided they ought to see the world. They had five hundred pounds each, which they had saved from the earnings of their books and their wages as joint cooks at Ivanhoe. They stayed overseas until their money ran out, towards the end of 1937; they spent most of their time in London, but also explored the British Isles and the Continent of Europe, and even managed a glimpse of North Africa. In London Mary worked on a novel which she had started to write before going overseas. It came to nothing in the end, but the work was not wasted; nearly twenty years later she used it as the basis of *Keep Him, My Country*.

When they returned to Australia, the sisters separated, Elizabeth going to a job in Darwin, Mary to work with West Australian Newspapers. She conducted a correspondence feature, The Friendly Corner, and a children's section in *The Western Mail* for a year or so, until her marriage in December, 1938. Most of her married life has been lived in Perth, but whenever she can she escapes to the second home she and her husband have at Broome. 'Something happens to me as soon as I get off the plane on Broome airfield,' she explains. 'A heavy weight drops from my shoulders. I always wonder if it will happen this time. And it always does.' Much of her writing since 1950 has been done at Broome. She says she writes better and more prolifically there.

As a writer, Mary Durack has all the intensity of the perfectionist. She touch-types all her own work, and *Kings in Grass Castles* was written four times before she was reasonably content with it. The book is a big one, three hundred and ninety-nine large printed pages, so the physical work alone of writing and rewriting it was heavy. This saga of the pioneering Duracks, a moving and powerful frontier tale, and no less gripping because it is fact, not fiction, is a testament of Mary Durack's love of the wide and lonely Australian lands which her family played a salient part in opening up. 'I've nothing against cities,' she says, 'but I'd still rather live in the North. Barring accidents, I'll die there.' It is impossible to doubt that she will do so, in her own good time; for Mary Durack, whatever target she has in view, is a woman of gigantic determination.

FICTION

Keep Him, My Country (London, Constable) 1955

For Children

* *Piccaninnies* (Melbourne, Offset) 1940
* *The Way of the Whirlwind* (Sydney, Consolidated Press) 1944
* *The Magic Trumpet* (Melbourne, Cassell) 1946

VERSE

Little Poems of Sunshine, by An Australian Child (Perth, Sampson) 1923

GENERAL

* *All-About*: The Story of a Black Community on Argyle Station, Kimberley (Sydney, Bulletin Co.) 1935
* *Chunuma* (Sydney, Bulletin Co.) 1936
* *Son of Djaro* (Sydney, Bulletin Co.) 1937

Child Artists of the Australian Bush, with Florence Rutter (London, Harrap) 1952

Kings in Grass Castles (London, Constable) 1959

* Illustrated by Elizabeth Durack.

David Martin

ALWAYS A WINDMILL

'I HAVE hardly ever felt myself an outsider wherever I have been,' says David Martin, in his slightly accented English. 'I am homesick for more than one country, and I seem to belong as much in one place as in any other.' This faculty of Martin's bothers some of his friends, who wonder if he will ever settle anywhere. Whether or not he has put down permanent roots in Australia remains to be seen, but it seems probable that he has done so. He came to Australia in 1949, not intending to stay long, but now says he is a fixture. This does not mean he never intends to travel again. In 1958-59 he spent some months in the Far East, chiefly in Thailand and North Vietnam, and two years previously went round the world, and if he thought he was anchored forever in Australia or any other country he would suffer something of the feeling of a man serving a life-sentence in a penitentiary. But, although he hopes and expects to travel overseas in the future, he believes he will always return, because he now considers Australia his home. A. A. Phillips, writing in the Australian literary quarterly *Meanjin* (No. 1, 1961), said: 'David Martin is the most improbable Australian writer who ever existed—if indeed he should now be classified as an Australian writer.' Improbable or not, Martin is numbered among Australian writers by any but those Australians in whom parochiality is an incurable disease. To exclude him would be to say that a man cannot be an Australian unless he was born under the Southern Cross with the strains of *Waltzing Matilda* ringing in his ears; in short, that Australianism is a matter of technicalities of birth, not of the individual's mental outlook and sympathies.

Martin was a writer with a limited, but solid, reputation in England before he saw Australia or ever thought of living here, but, after discovering certain qualities which he likes in Australia and Australians (as well as some qualities which he disliked on first acquaintance and dislikes still), he undertook what he calls 'a gradual penetration of the Australian scene'. This took more than ten years; it was a kind of probation which Martin imposed both on himself and his adopted country. That he has completed it became evident in 1962 when he published his first novel with an Australian background, *The Young Wife*. About the same time he said: 'I want to write a series of Australian novels now. I don't know how many—perhaps three. There are a number of things in Australia I want to discuss, not as a visitor standing off and watching, but as an Australian. I suppose it's part of the process of becoming an Australian.' Not only the locale of these novels, but also most of the characters in them, will be Australian; this will distinguish them from *The Young Wife* in which all the major characters are Greeks and Cypriots living in Melbourne.

Martin had difficulty for a long time, he says, in writing, against the Australian background, prose that satisfied him; but little by little, as he experimented, his feeling of 'not enough drama here' diminished, and at last fell away altogether like an outer skin. The novel he was working on at the time of this writing is set in an Australian country town. In common with many writers, he dislikes talking about work in progress, and would say of this novel's theme only that it investigates some established Australian beliefs, particularly masculinity. It is unlikely that his findings on these beliefs will flatter the Australian ego and please the mass of Australians. 'I am,' he says, 'intensely and passionately devoted to reality. I hope however I shall be able to write at least one novel in the few years immediately ahead which will be a best-seller and also of top quality. These things are not mutually exclusive. Reality is what I want—not just realism.'

Martin and his wife, with their son, live in a small unpretentious house, which they are buying, in a quiet side street of the Melbourne suburb of Coburg. Mrs Martin, an English woman, whose maiden name was Elizabeth Richenda, is a great-granddaughter of Elizabeth Fry, the Quaker and nineteenth century prison reformer; she contributes to the family income by working as a teacher at a Melbourne girls' school. David Martin's only steady job is as Australian correspondent of the Indian newspaper, the Madras *Hindu*, but his earnings from this work are comparatively modest. He gives as much time as possible to writing, even if it means turning lucrative jobs away, and works for immediate pay—chiefly as a social psychologist, doing motivational research, for, among others, such bodies as the Broadcasting Control Board—only for a few months of each year. He does not seek long-term financial security, nor is he putting by anything for his old age. 'You can be content with very little,' he says, 'if you are doing what you want to do.'

Martin is a tall man, with good shoulders and powerful arms. His face is narrow, and the gentle curves of his mouth are emphasised when he smiles. His head is bald on top and fringed with hair fair, and he wears a moustache and a short clipped beard. His blue eyes are near-sighted, and when he sits talking he habitually looks sideways, often with his horn-rimmed glasses resting on his forehead, past his companion; this is a result of a small eye defect. He never loses the thread of what he is saying, but part of his mind sometimes seems to be occupied with other matters than the conversation he is conducting.

He was born Ludwig Detsinyi, in Budapest, Hungary, in 1915. He changed his name by deed-poll soon after arriving in Australia, having been known as David Martin in Australia, and also for some years in Britain, where he was naturalized. His father was a Hungarian, and his mother a German from the Rhineland, and he and his twin brother, Rudolph, now a business man in London, were brought up like the children of any affluent European Jewish family of that period. He lost his mother in infancy, but his father married again. He has always felt closest to his brother.

He admits to a certain ambivalence about Germany, where his parents settled when he was quite young, but on the whole his detestation of that country is stronger than his love of it. When he thinks of his boyhood, it is often of the schools where he and his brother were educated; they were sometimes the only Jewish boys at these schools, and were, he says, bullied appallingly. He remembers with gratitude the masters of that period who hammered into him a knowledge of the English language, on which he was ultimately to depend for a living—one of the five languages he speaks fluently—but recalls with pleasure only a few other things about his schooldays; or about Germany itself: 'I still have a great yearning for Germany at times, especially for its pine forests and the Baltic coast,' he says, 'but always mixed up in my memories is the bullying and sadism, and the overstrong element of the tragic in the German character. Although no two worlds could be more different than the German and the Australian, sometimes in the depth of the bush one catches a whisper that could be of the German forests. It is perhaps the one point of kinship.' He left Germany when he was seventeen, and has never been back. He was a member of a Left-wing Berlin youth group at the time, and had parental troubles following the discovery of a batch of anti-Nazi leaflets which he had hidden in his gramophone. That was in 1934. His parents endured the Hitler tyranny until 1938 when they fled to England. Some other members of the family were less fortunate; sixteen of them, including his mother's father, became victims of the Nazis.

After leaving Germany he lived in Holland and in a collective settlement in Palestine. He also served with the International Brigade in Spain, as a first-aid man; at times he was attached to the Abraham Lincoln Battalion, an American volunteer unit, and there he first developed a fluency in spoken English. Martin does not like to talk much about the Spanish Civil War: 'All wars are terrible,' he says; 'civil wars most of all, and though we fought for a good cause, that does not make death and suffering more lovely.' Implied in this is a certain unorthodoxy within the framework of his own materialism; an unorthodoxy which, in the past, occasionally caused some of his comrades to look at him askance. He was a member of the Communist Party and he left it in somewhat complicated circumstances some time after the Hungarian revolt of 1956. To himself he remains 'a radical humanist—just as I've always been. No man can destroy his past, nor should he want to, I think.'

After Spain, he went to England and was firmly settled there—firmly settled, that is, for him—by the time World War II broke out. He worked there as a newspaperman and for the British Broadcasting Corporation. He had always written in German, his mother-tongue, but soon after reaching London he wrote a poem in English, and all his writing since then, whether in verse or prose, has been in English. A German publisher some years ago put out a German-language edition of one of Martin's books. Martin insisted that someone else should translate it; he felt his own German was no longer equal to the task.

He first saw Australia in 1949, after spending a year in India, as correspondent of the London *Daily Express*. He came here not long after his play, *The Shepherd and the Hunter*, was produced in Sydney, and after looking about him decided to stay for a while. He kept the pot boiling for the best part of a year as editor of a Jewish weekly newspaper in Sydney; then he and his wife and their son, who was six at that time, went off and lived in a place called Putty, on the edge of the Hunter Valley, in northern New South Wales. Putty lies on the old coach road from Sydney to Singleton, and is merely a few houses strung along a creek. His wife took charge of the little bush school, which had only six or seven pupils at that time, while he put into verse a nineteenth century Swiss tale about a cat named Spiegel, a Municipal Sorcerer named Florian, a witch named Martha, and sundry other characters having little in common with twentieth century Australia and nothing at all in common with the old bush settlement of Putty. Perhaps, for David Martin, that was the essential point; Spiegel's was an ideal tale for him to write while he was still in the early stages of assimilating, and being assimilated by, Australia.

He did not try very hard to get *Spiegel the Cat* published when it was finished, and it eventually appeared as a book in 1961, printed and published in Australia, with illustrations by a Sydney artist, Roderick Shaw. Martin liked Putty, and still thinks back to his time there with pleasure, but a year of it was enough for him; then the Martins packed up and came to Victoria, where friends helped them to settle in.

His working methods, he says, have changed in recent years. At one time he worked at high speed when writing prose. Writing by hand, with his ears stoppered with rubber plugs to deaden distracting noise, he finished in a month a book of autobiographical short stories, *The Shoes Men Walk In*, published in 1946; he wrote the short novel *Tiger Bay*, published in the same year, in three weeks. Now he works on a typewriter, and much more deliberately. Before starting to write a novel, he spends long weeks in making a closely detailed synopsis of the characters and action; when writing, he works about six hours a day—three in the morning, three in the afternoon—turning out his narrative at the rate of fifteen hundred or two thousands words a day. He revises carefully, and does not expect to finish a novel in much, if anything, less than a year.

In deciding to write a series of novels about Australia and Australians, Martin has had to postpone an old ambition to build a novel on a subject which has fascinated him for a long time: the Anabaptist uprising in Munster in 1534. The Anabaptists set up a state of their own and held it for something over a year until superior force overthrew them, and, to Martin, the episode is 'an apocalyptic kind of story, having certain parallels with our own time'. He has merely deferred, not abandoned, that project; he will go back to it some day, but to do the theme justice he must visit Germany, and he will not be ready to do that for some years yet.

What David Martin will ultimately achieve as a writer is only to be guessed, but his target is unmistakable. He once wrote a poem about Don Quixote which ends with the line, 'By such madness has the world been saved', and he will never reveal more of himself than he did in those eight words. 'I love Quixote,' he says, 'because he was the most profoundly human of all men. He would break a lance for anything. So long as the world produces men like that, and writers who will write about them, so long will there be some hope for mankind.' Martin himself has all his life yielded to the temptation to tilt with his pen at windmills wherever he has found them—at those windmills which rear against the twentieth century sky as challengingly as Don Quixote's against the sky of medieval

Spain—and he could not stop now. He has, he admits, come upon quite a few inviting windmills in Australia, and it would be against his nature to leave these undisturbed.

FICTION

The Shoes Men Walk In. Short stories (London, The Pilot Press) 1946
Tiger Bay (London, Martin & Reid) 1946
The Stones of Bombay (London, Wingate) 1950
The Young Wife (London, Macmillan) 1962

VERSE

Battlefields and Girls (Glasgow, MacLellan) 1942
From Life (Sydney, Current Books) 1953
Poems of David Martin, 1938–1958 (Sydney, Edwards & Shaw) 1958
Spiegel the Cat (Melbourne, Cheshire) 1961

DRAMA

The Shepherd and the Hunter (London, Wingate) 1946

Morris West

WINDOW ON PITTWATER

MORRIS WEST was in high spirits on the evening, late in 1960, that I called at his Avalon Beach home, overlooking Pittwater, twenty-odd miles from Sydney. There were two reasons for his cheerfulness. First, the Royal Society of Literature had that day announced in London that he had been awarded the W. H. Heinemann Foundation for Literature for his novel, *The Devil's Advocate*. Second, a few hours earlier he had destroyed about two hundred typewritten pages, representing two-thirds or so of a novel he had been working on for seven or eight months. West's delight in the award of the Heinemann Foundation, which is designed to 'encourage the production of literary works of real worth', requires no explanation; it is an honour any novelist would be elated to win. But why he should have taken pleasure from seeing months of hard writing disappear into the incinerator is not apparent, unless you are familiar with the way the minds of novelists work. By 'novelists' I mean writers of fiction who, however much they prize the material rewards yielded by a commercially successful book, aim to produce something more lasting than a row of potboilers. This description fits Morris West.

Although some Australian literary critics and literary cliques smile patronizingly when his name is mentioned, they can't quite contrive to dismiss him as a mere commercialist. West says he is a professional writer, and his first concern is that his books should enable him to keep his family—he has two young sons, and a young daughter—in decent comfort. If, after the butcher, baker, grocer, doctor, rate-collector, and all the rest have been paid, one or more of his novels should prove to have enduring value, he will be well pleased, but his primary aim is to be a good craftsman, to write novels that men and women in his own time will enjoy reading. He is inclined to believe that, if he does so much, he will have done more than most of those who look down their noses at him. He had decided that the two hundred or so pages of the new novel which he scrapped on the day of my call were not quite right, according to his standards of craftsmanship. Having decided this, he knew the novel itself—a study of the problems besetting a twentieth century scientist in our technocratic society—would never satisfy him unless he began anew. So when he had destroyed what he had written he was a happy man. He started out again on that novel, but perhaps he was subconsciously out of sympathy with the theme, the characters or some other aspect of it. At any rate he never did finish it. After working on the second version for some months he once again lost patience with the novel and scrapped it when he had most of his story—between eighty thousand and ninety thousand words—on paper. In its place he wrote an entirely different novel, *Daughter of Silence*, a tale built upon the trial of a girl charged with shooting a man in an Italian village. (Asked why he likes using Italy as the locale of his major books, West briefly considered the question, then said, 'Why do some men like kissing red-headed girls?')

When *Daughter of Silence* was published late in 1961 it immediately went to the top of American, British and Australian lists of best-selling novels. About the same time West's dramatization of the novel opened on Broadway and was well received by many of the New York critics. Howard Taubman, drama critic of *The New York Times*, expressed the hope that its author would in future devote himself exclusively to writing for the theatre. West was gratified by this suggestion, but not tempted to act upon it; his chief literary interest is, and seems likely to remain, the novel. The short life of his play on Broadway probably strengthened him in this preference. *Daughter of Silence* closed after running only a few weeks.

Morris West, tall, hazel-eyed, with big shoulders and the body of a slightly overweight Australian Rules ruckman, is a friendly man, easy of manner, and a stimulating talker. He was hardly known as a writer, except to a small circle of admirers, until 1957, the year in which he turned forty-one; then his book, *Children of the Sun*, describing his experiences among the slum urchins of Naples, carried him to international fame in a few months. This is the only non-fiction book he has written, possibly the only non-fiction book he will ever write, although he has a private ambition to write a biography of the poet, Robert Browning, and might eventually succumb to it.

While *Children of the Sun* was his first big literary achievement, it was his novel *The Devil's Advocate* which established him, with both critics and public, as a talented fiction writer. He was a late starter, as professional writers go. 'I always wanted to write,' he explains, 'but I got sidetracked.' He was born in 1916, in the Melbourne suburb of St Kilda and educated at St Kilda Christian Brothers' College, and, having a fancy for teaching, he became a Christian Brother. He stayed with the order until 1940, teaching in Sydney, Young and Goulburn; but, when the time to take final vows approached, he decided he lacked the vocation, and resigned. The war had begun then and, after a few months as a State school teacher in Victoria, West enlisted, and was sent to Darwin as a cipher officer. While there he wrote his first book, *Moon in my Pocket*, which he published under the pseudonym of Julian Morris. It was a fictionized account of his life as a Christian Brother, and it had at least one positive result. This was that, for reasons which don't matter here, it led to his being released from the Army to become private secretary to the late W. M. Hughes, Australia's one-time Prime Minister and then a private M.P. West had heard somewhere that none of Hughes's private secretaries stayed in the post for more than a few months, and that many lasted only a few days, but he took up the appointment with a willing heart. He was summoned one day by his employer, who said: 'You and I have got to part. I regret it, you know, but for a moderately intelligent young man you've done some —— silly things!'

And so Morris West arrived back in Melbourne, his native city, wondering how he, a man of thirty, with a limited experience of how to make a living, would find an acceptable job. He worked for a year as publicity manager of a Melbourne radio station, then went into business as an independent producer and writer of recorded radio programmes. The trouble with this venture was that it was too successful; for, although West was continually plagued by his desire to write novels, he could not bring himself to abandon the thriving business he had built. Early in the 1950s he sold a controlling interest in the company and moved to Sydney to establish a N.S.W. branch, hoping that at last he would find a little time to write novels. He didn't. The N.S.W. branch, successful from the start, was soon absorbing all his time. There seemed to be no escape; he was caught in a kind of gold-plated trap. The programmes the company produced sold readily in South Africa, Canada and New Zealand, as well as Australia; when West was in the U.S.A. nearly ten years later he found that one or two of them, like echoes from another life, were still going out from small-town radio stations.

In 1955 a more or less unexpected demand for income-tax dues arrived on his desk. As the only means of earning money to pay it, he somehow found time to write a novel, *Gallows on the Sand*. This story of a search for lost treasure, set on the Queensland coast, was reasonably popular with Australian readers, and West decided to write another novel in like vein. This, *Kundu*, a New Guinea romance, won little critical or public acclaim in Australia or the U.K., but an American paperback publisher liked it, and bought the U.S. rights for three thousand dollars. That was the first turning-point. At last Morris and Joy West had enough money to live for a few months while he tested his ability to survive as a professional writer. They discussed the hazards. Then, stifling his fears, he quit his Sydney job, and they took ship to Italy, and found lodgings in Sorrento.

West intended writing a novel in Sorrento, but somehow the novel refused to leap the gap between his brain and the paper in the type-writer. Their money dwindled, and the future lost its glow. One day Joy West was browsing through a book. She came on a chapter describing the work of Don Mario Borrelli, the Priest of the Naples Urchins. She found it absorbing, and the story gripped Morris West also. He went into Naples and found Borrelli. They talked; then West went out to discover the slums of Naples for himself. And so *Children of the Sun* came to be written.

The Wests reached London about the middle of 1956, but, although the book was almost at once accepted by a publisher, they and their infant son had to live somehow until it came out in 1957. They scraped along with the publisher's advance on *Children of the Sun*, and with money earned by an adventure novel, *The Big Story*, which West wrote in London, but it was a hard battle. Looking for an inexpensive place to live for a few months, they tried Austria, and settled into a pension in the village of Bad Gastein, south of Salzburg. They say they will never forget New Year's Eve, 1956. Although money was on its way to them from England, it had not arrived and, flat broke, they spent the evening playing canasta. They would not even have been able to toast the new year if the keeper of the pension had not arrived at midnight, bearing a thimble-sized glass of schnapps for each of them. But at last the tide was running their way. At Bad Gastein West wrote an adventure story, *McCreary Moves In*, and sent it out under the pseudonym of Michael East. It was snapped up, for both European and U.S. publication (as also was a later Michael East tale, *The Naked Country*, which he wrote to relax his mind after a bout of serious work). He also used his time at Bad Gastein to do research for *The Second Victory*, but before that novel came out in 1958 *Children of the Sun* was published. Its impact was immediate and heavy. Within weeks West was widely known in the U.K., not only to novel readers, but also to televiewers through his TV appearances.

Back in Australia, he gave two years to the writing of *The Devil's Advocate*—'a two-year gamble in time and money', he has called it. The success of the gamble exceeded probably even his best hopes;

MORRIS WEST

PAUL BRICKHILL

HAL PORTER

NANCY CATO

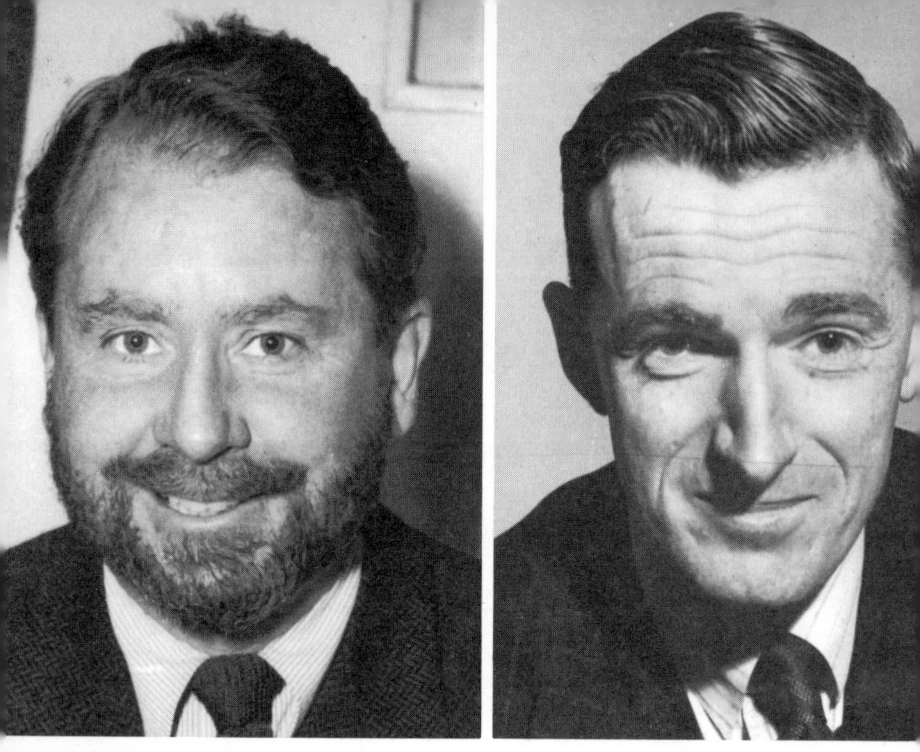

JON CLEARY

FRANK HARDY

D'ARCY NILAND AND RUTH PARK

when *The Devil's Advocate* was published in New York and London late in 1959 it was sniffed at by some connoisseurs, but acclaimed by many others (it won the James Tait Black Memorial Prize, as well as the Heinemann Foundation), and was also bought with enthusiasm by the public. Even in West's native Australia some critics of standing were impressed, if rather against their will. One of the most interesting comments by a responsible critic came from a fellow Roman Catholic, the poet Vincent Buckley, who wrote (*Meanjin*, No. 2, 1961): 'In *The Devil's Advocate* Morris West has broken through the pattern of the circulating library romance to a minor triumph of a humanist Christianity, which is marred chiefly by his unenterprising conception of a narrative language. . . .' In 1961 a stage version of *The Devil's Advocate* opened on Broadway, but closed after four months. The play was written (as well as directed and produced) by Dore Schary, a successful Hollywood producer. Some critics felt that Schary's transcription missed the essence of the novel. One of them said privately: 'Schary dodged the central issue of the book and lapsed into the facilities of sentiment. People who were enamoured of the book felt cheated.' This probably explains why West himself dramatized *Daughter of Silence*. Although he had never before had a play staged it was not his first experiment as a playwright. He sold an earlier play in England, then bought it back because, he says, he could get no satisfaction from the producer.

West's confidence in himself has grown under the influence of success, but he says he is always haunted by the fear, between one book and the next, that he won't be able to write another book that anybody but he will wish to read. This is a fear that assails many creative writers, and it must have surged high in him when he wrestled with the novel of the twentieth century scientist which came to nothing in the end. He will probably never conquer that fear, and, if he ever does so, he will almost certainly be a lesser writer than he is, for the kind of novel he has made his reputation with, however smoothly it runs in print, is the product, not of gentle meditation, but of mental conflict. West would be the last man to wish that changed.

FICTION

As Morris West

Gallows on the Sand (Sydney, Angus & Robertson) 1955
Kundu (Sydney, Angus & Robertson) 1956
The Big Story (London, Heinemann) 1957
The Second Victory (London, Heinemann) 1958
The Devil's Advocate (London, Heinemann) 1959
Daughter of Silence (London, Heinemann) 1961

As Julian Morris

Moon in my Pocket (Sydney, Australasian Publishing Co.) 1945

As Michael East

McCreary Moves In (London, Heinemann) 1958
The Naked Country (London, Heinemann) 1960

GENERAL

As Morris West

Children of the Sun (London, Heinemann) 1957

Paul Brickhill

AN END TO LOOKING BACKWARD

MANY a man spends a few months searching his soul—if he has a soul to search—when the thirties fall behind him and the fifties loom ahead. Paul Brickhill did this, but, for him, the process lasted seven or eight years. This was in character, for Brickhill has a passion for thoroughness in whatever he does. He has never been able to work in any other way, whether the immediate task is to write a book, fly an aeroplane, or do anything else. Even before the war when he was a Sydney evening newspaper reporter he always hankered to dig deeper into the guts of a story than the demands of the deadline would permit. 'I went out once on a safe-blowing at Botany,' he recalls. 'It was a routine affair, with no special point to it. So I wandered round the corner and found some people living over a shop who had been wakened by the explosion and seen the whole thing. They were frightened to talk, but I kept at them and persuaded them to tell me all about it. Feeling I had done something worth while, I telephoned the story to the office, but instead of a compliment I got my pants kicked off for having missed the first edition with the colourless report that the safe had been blown, which didn't matter a damn anyway. That was really the first division between newspapers and me. I like to take my time with a story, to uncover the drama in it and bring the drama out. Working for a newspaper, there was hardly ever time to do that.'

That anecdote is important for the light it throws on the character of Paul Brickhill, a shortish, dark-haired, dynamic man who talks as emphatically and lucidly as he writes. It does something to explain why, after publishing four best-selling books between 1951 and 1954, he more or less dropped from public view for some years. An occasional interview with or article about him appeared in print, but nothing came from Brickhill himself to show that he had not permanently forsaken his writing career. He could go on living comfortably if he were never to work again; the earnings of his early books ensure that, in all foreseeable circumstances, he and his wife and their two children will never want. But Brickhill's failure to publish a new book as year after year passed did not mean he was idling; on the contrary, for most of those years he was working perhaps harder than he had ever worked before, in the effort to find himself. It is true that, for two years or so after *Reach for the Sky* was published in 1954, he turned his back on professional writing. He did so because, first, he did not wish to add to his earnings, largely for the benefit of the tax-gatherer; and, second, because he was well occupied at that time with business problems arising out of the immense success of *Reach for the Sky*. Brickhill however has the temperament which makes men write, whether their work is recognized or unrecognized, rewarded or unrewarded; it is a compulsion roughly approximating that of the alcoholic. So a time came when he knew he must write another book to satisfy his inner craving. The only problem was what he should write.

He started two or three books, and put each aside after doing a few months' work on it. He wrote in England, in Australia, and in New Zealand, but was content with nothing he produced; what he wrote read smoothly enough, but left him unsatisfied. He decided to write a book about the Australian immigration programme. He studied the subject from every aspect, and concluded that here was excellent material for a book of wide human appeal. He sat down to his typewriter with enthusiasm to begin work on that theme, but somehow it eluded him. He tried it as fiction, and he tried it as a factual narrative, but it would not come. It would not come at any rate for Paul Brickhill. He began to grow worried. He had several periods of illness, and as he lay in hospital, in enforced idleness, he sometimes wondered if he would ever again find himself as a writer. He knew he could have picked up his career where he had left it, by doing what he had proved himself able to do superlatively well—that was, write war books; his books had all recounted his own or other men's experiences in World War II, and limitless material of a like kind was to be found if he cared to look for it. But Brickhill had taken a decision and was determined to abide by it. 'I had decided,' he says, 'that I would never write another war book. I felt that writing about the war was looking back over my shoulder at a sterile thing. Now I wanted to write about constructive things.'

It was a long road, but at last he reached the end of it. He found a theme for a novel, set in the Paris of today, running insistently through his mind; he could not rid himself of it, and at last the outline of a story took firm shape. The central figure was a young man, an Australian, involved in a murder campaign conducted by Algerian terrorists. Brickhill says the novel, which he called *The Deadline*, is 'a suspense story, basically, but by implication it raises the question of the tendency of men of ideals on both sides to fall, under pressure, into the attitude that "the end justifies the means"'. He turned to fiction at least partly because 'non-fiction fact tends too often to be anti-climatic rather than dramatic'. He has found that in writing non-fiction he becomes involved with too many people having different versions of the same incident, and he prefers to be independent of the moral obligation which he feels to do justice, or to try to do justice at any rate, to all his informants. This does not mean he will never again write non-fiction books; he hopes in future to write both fiction and non-fiction which will satisfy him, as well as his readers.

Precisely how successful Brickhill will be in attempting to break out of the prison in which success threatened to confine him has yet to be seen, but he is beyond doubt an extraordinarily determined man once he sets his mind on any objective. He was born in Melbourne in 1916, while his father was working on a Melbourne newspaper, but by the time the boy was taking notice of the world about him the family was living in Sydney. He was educated principally at North Sydney High School, and soon after leaving school he took a copy-boy's job on the Sydney *Sun*, not because journalism had laid a spell on him, but because a boy, living round the corner from the Brickhills and already a copy-boy on *The Sun*, persuaded him to do so. This boy, three months or so older than Brickhill, did not stay long with *The Sun*, but presently, finding he wished to be an actor, went off to storm the theatre. To the astonishment of his boyhood contemporaries, he achieved post-war fame as an actor rivalling Brickhill's as a writer. His name is Peter Finch. Brickhill stayed with *The Sun*. After a year or so, he became a cadet reporter, and did all the wearisome chores—shipping, markets, and the like—which cadet reporters do. He graduated to the status of a full-fledged reporter; and, for the last year or so before World War II broke out, spent most of his time writing feature articles. When war came he was invited to join the newly-created Department of Information, but *The Sun* would not release him. He went on writing feature articles and vaguely wondering if he should do something about the war. France fell, and the British Expeditionary Force withdrew from Dunkirk, and Brickhill, suddenly realizing the war was a serious business, enlisted in the Air Force. He trained in Canada, went on to the United Kingdom, and was posted to North Africa as a flight lieutenant. On March 17, 1943, he was flying about ten thousand feet above the Mareth Line, in Tunisia, when a Messerschmitt 109 dived out of a cloud and shot his Spitfire down. He freed himself and parachuted out, when his aircraft had only a thousand feet left to fall. He was captured, and presently found himself in Germany, a prisoner in Stalag Luft III, between Berlin and Breslau.

Prisoners of war in German camps knew long before the end came that Hitler's Reich was doomed, and RAF officers in Stalag Luft III were mildly intoxicated by the prospect of liberation when word of the Red Army's approach reached them in January, 1945; they believed they would be free within a few days. Then one night, with the Russians only twenty miles away, their hopes were dashed. They were marched out into the snow, and began the journey to another camp at Bremen, three hundred miles to the west. They travelled for two days locked into cattle-trucks, with only room to sit down, and went the rest of the way on foot by forced marches along frozen roads. Shelter when they halted was poor, food short. About seventy of them died before reaching their destination. Through it all Paul Brickhill clung to a grubby bundle of manuscript, rolled in a blanket. Weak from nearly two years' imprisonment, he collapsed twice, but each time struggled up and on. At several stages of the journey he lightened his burden by jettisoning such precious items as cigarettes, razor blades, even food, but always something checked him when he was tempted to throw away his manuscript; to have abandoned it then would have been almost like abandoning a child he had fathered. He nearly lost it at the very end of the journey. As he was entering the Bremen camp, a German guard pointed to his rolled blanket and demanded, 'What have you got in there?' 'I've got a tommygun in there,' Brickhill cheekily replied, hiding behind a grin his fear that the treasured manuscript was to be wrenched from him. The guard laughed and waved him on. And when he was freed some three months later the manuscript, if slightly grubbier, was still intact.

That manuscript had an important part in Brickhill's personal story, because it provided much of the material for his first book, *Escape To Danger*, which was published in 1946. Some of his fellow-prisoners in Stalag Luft III had survived in circumstances which made his own exploits seem about as exciting as a vicarage croquet match, and he had begun collecting their stories. He had also been an active member of the 'X Organization', an escape organization in the camp, whose members dug three tunnels, hundreds of feet long and thirty feet below ground, under the noses of the constantly patrolling guards. Seventy-six officers escaped by this means—Brickhill, who suffers with claustrophobia, was barred from the tunnels—but only three of them reached England, and fifty were murdered by the Gestapo. *Escape to Danger* told something of the story of the 'X Organization' and of the men whose tales of personal war experience Brickhill had collected and kept with him even when he had barely enough strength to carry the manuscript. This was his first book, but he says, 'I was never happy about it. It bore all the marks of haste.' Since he wrote sixty thousand words of it, and edited and assembled the rest, in seventeen of the twenty-eight days' P.O.W. leave granted him on his return to London, this defect is understandable.

Brickhill's chance of making a living solely as an author appeared slender then, and for a year or so he worked as an Australian newspaper correspondent in London and on the continent of Europe, then for two years in New York. In 1948 he arrived back in Sydney, with one book to his credit, and no firm plans for writing any more books. It was eight years since he had gone abroad to train as a war pilot, and, feeling he was back pretty well where he had left off, he went to work on the sub-editor's desk of *The Sun*. He did not like the work much. He could not persuade himself that he wished to spend the rest of his life as a newspaperman, and, when a London publisher wrote urging him to do a book telling the whole story of the 'X Organization' and the tunnel escape, he hardly hesitated. In April, 1949, he left Sydney for London. While he was researching that second book, *The Great Escape*, someone suggested he should write a book about 617 Squadron—the 'dam-busters'. He was lucky, of course, to have such a subject dumped into his lap. Or was it luck? In fact, two different writers had earlier tried to write the 'dam-busters' ' story and failed. Yet Brickhill's book became a world best-seller, a radio feature, and a film. Three or four years later Douglas Bader, the legless RAF ace, wrote to Brickhill, who was then living in the South of France—he had married an Australian girl in 1950—and suggested he write the book which became *Reach for the Sky*. Another writer had worked on the Bader story, then abandoned it, because the Rank organization thought little of its film possibilities. In Brickhills' hands it was an immense success; the film version stands high on the list of memorable British films.

Brickhill says he enjoyed writing his war books, although to make a dramatic narrative out of fact sometimes presents huge problems; this bothered him because he is, in his own words, essentially a dramatic narrative writer. He is no longer interested in writing merely for money or success, but he feels, on the other hand, that no book which is not some sort of success is worth writing. 'One of the main articles of my creed,' he explains, 'is that the basic purpose of writing a book is not to show how clever I am. A lot of writers churn out portentous prose that is simply dull, although it may be a critical success. I don't want to write a critical success that people can't be bothered reading. If I have something to say I want it to be in such a form that people will want to read it. I suppose I could sum it up by saying that I aim to avoid being dull or pompous and try to be readable and interesting.' Any of the books that made Brickhill's name is a tangible illustration of what he means by those words.

FICTION

The Deadline (London, Collins) 1962

GENERAL

Escape to Danger, with Conrad Norton (London, Faber & Faber) 1946
The Great Escape (London, Faber & Faber) 1951
The Dam Busters (London, Evans Brothers) 1951
Escape—or Die (London, Evans Brothers) 1952
Reach for the Sky (London, Collins) 1954

Hal Porter

COUNTRY BOY AT LARGE

ANY Australian author who believes he could write masterpieces if only he could escape from mundane Australia to urbane Europe should consult Hal Porter. Porter went to Europe in January, 1960, intending to write a novel of early Tasmania, built round Thomas Griffiths Wainewright, artist and critic—and, some gossip says, professional poisoner also—who was transported to Van Diemen's Land for forgery in 1837. He took with him most of the material for the novel, either in notebooks or in his head, and, after completing his research in the British Museum, sat down to start writing in his room in a quiet Bloomsbury hotel. The words refused to come, so he tried an inn on the Riviera. The words still eluded him, so he found a pension in Venice, hoping that there the mystic juices of authorship would flow; they wouldn't. Porter was growing worried. The Commonwealth Literary Fund had granted him a thousand pounds to write the novel, and he had begged a year's leave of absence from his job as Shepparton's city librarian. Yet, with more than half the year gone, he had written nothing. Deciding on strong measures, he bought an air ticket to Australia. He arrived home well after the middle of the year and went to stay at Hedley, in South Gippsland, with his sister, Ida Rendell, and her husband, a farmer. There he plunged in to the writing of his novel. From the first it went like a racing bird, and was finished in three months. Five or six weeks later a London publisher accepted it, and before the end of 1961 the novel—*The Tilted Cross*—was in the English and Australian bookshops.

Porter, a strongly-built man, has watchful blue eyes, and fair hair which is starting to recede. He wears a clipped moustache above a smallish mouth, from which talk flows more or less incessantly in a cheerful, lively, impious stream. He has one quaint oral mannerism—quaint, that is, for an Australian; he customarily addresses other men, whether or not he knows them well, not as 'sport!', 'mate!', or 'pal!', but as 'dear boy!' It is a measure of the strength of his personality that nobody seems to mind.

Porter does not pretend his experience with *The Tilted Cross* proves that Australia's climate is peculiarly kind to novelists, but only that, once an author is ready to write, he can write no less well in Hedley —or Tennant Creek, Proserpine, Collingwood, or Woolloomooloo —than in Mayfair, Montmartre, Antibes or Positano. As a personal choice, however, he would undoubtedly rather write, or follow any other occupation, in the country than the city, although he has lived many of his years in one city or another. 'I like the country for many reasons,' he says. 'There's more time in the country to know people, to think, and to work. I couldn't bear catching the 8.55 to work every day, and rushing into Young and Jackson's on the way home for two beers, then rushing out again.' Porter's ordinary conversation suggests that drinking is his favourite diversion; most of his tales of his own escapades, including a wonderful anecdote about a night in Sydney when he spent four hours in Darlinghurst lock-up, have an alcoholic tang. He is not a boozer, however. In 1949 he took the, for him, novel job of managing the George Hotel, in the Melbourne seaside suburb of St Kilda, and for the six months he was in the post did not have one drink. He drinks nothing while he is in a period of serious writing; when he was flying back to Australia to write *The Tilted Cross*, he had a last ceremonial drink at Singapore, then went teetotal until the novel was finished. 'I find my brain works better,' he says, 'if I go on the waggon while I'm doing a protracted writing job.'

His chief relaxation while writing *The Tilted Cross* was the fashioning, in papier mâché, of an extravagantly baroque representation of the Buddhist goddess of mercy, whom the Japanese call Kwannon and the Chinese call Quanyin. This showy affair which, with the intricate frondlike tracery surrounding it, was about three feet six inches high and nearly as wide, was painted terracotta, with gold highlights. He built it on a foundation of chicken-wire, twisting the wire into the desired shape with his strong-fingered hands, and pulping old newspapers for papier mâché. For the goddess's face, he used, as a mould, a mask of his own face which the artist, William Dargie, did some years ago. 'I like to do something with my hands when I'm working on a piece of writing,' he says. 'If I went sunbathing or sat in a chair to think, my mind would go blank and I wouldn't get any thinking done. Kwannon was exactly what I needed.'

After finishing *The Tilted Cross*, Porter went back to work early in 1961, as city librarian of Shepparton, in the Goulburn Valley, a hundred and thirteen miles north of Melbourne. Having been appointed in 1958 to create a public library for Shepparton he had arrived to find a shabby library with two hundred pardonably apathetic subscribers; within six months he had established a modern library which two years or so later stocked eighteen thousand books and counted three thousand subscribers, and was still growing. The old wooden building which once housed Shepparton's Mechanics' Institute was converted into an attractive cottage for Porter to live in, with the new library occupying the adjoining block. Since the library was next door, he kept few books on his own shelves, but one well-thumbed book was always there; this was a paper-bound copy of *The New A.B.C. of Australian Vegetable Growing*, by Herbert Rumsey. For Porter is an ardent gardener. He himself planned and laid out the garden, surrounding his cottage, and then tended it with devotion, lavishing no less time and care on an ailing or a sickly plant than, in his writing, he lavishes on some ugly or inaedquate phrase.

He was born at Bairnsdale in 1917, and educated at the local State school and the high school. He has two sisters, both married, and a younger brother, who is also married. Porter himself married in 1938, but the marriage was dissolved in 1943. At sixteen he went to work on the Bairnsdale *Advertiser*, a weekly sheet, and reported cricket matches, church socials, weddings, council meetings, court cases, accidents, and other routine news. He was soon writing his own column, Around the Town, under the pen-name of The Rambler. 'I let myself go on that, dear boy,' he says, with a reminiscent light in his eye. 'I pictured the courthouse as a magic castle, made impassioned pleas for the preservation of the old hop kiln, and implored my readers to see the beauties of the Mitchell River above the weir on a fine spring day.' Despite these ironic words, Porter has a deep affection for Bairnsdale; to him, it is the most desirable town in Australia, as Bairnsdale people are, to him, Australia's most desirable people. He believes he will one day settle permanently in Bairnsdale. 'The only place I have seen where I think I'd rather live for good,' he says, 'is the Japanese island of Shodo Shima. I went there for two nights in 1950 and had to drag myself away after five weeks.'

After a year of country journalism, Porter went to Melbourne, expecting to find work on a Melbourne daily newspaper. He didn't, and after a fortnight he was wandering along Collins Street, puzzled by Melbourne's indifference to him and his talents, when he met his old headmaster from Bairnsdale high school. The ex-headmaster advised the ex-pupil to try school teaching, and a week or so later Porter was appointed to North Williamstown State school. He quickly discovered he was a good teacher; he also discovered, to his astonishment, that he genuinely liked teaching. 'Children,' he says, 'always know whether or not they are being properly taught. You can't fool them.'

Teaching absorbed only part of his energy. He also studied art at National Gallery night classes, and acted with the Gregan McMahon Players. Although he played important parts for McMahon, he knew that what he calls his 'fuzzy voice' would always disqualify him from the top class of actors. He somehow managed to write, as well as teach, act, and paint, and his poems and short stories began appearing in print. In 1937 he left teaching, took a flat in Collins Street, Melbourne, and there plunged into the artistic life. He earned money by designing contemporary shop fittings, by writing radio features, by acting, and by selling short stories and verse, and he was building a name as a writer when, on September 3, 1939, the day World War II was declared, he was run over by a motor car. He did not walk again for nine months.

When he was on his feet, he took a schoolmaster's post in Adelaide, and there his first book was published in 1942. It was modestly entitled *Short Stories*. He stayed in Adelaide until 1946, then went schoolmastering in Hobart, and later in Sydney, in Ballarat, and, for the Australian Army Education Service, in Japan. English was always his chief subject, but he sometimes tried other fields; he still recalls with relish that for a whole term he taught Divinity to the Sixth Form at Knox Grammar School, Sydney.

All the time he was writing. He has never stopped writing for long in the last twenty-five years, although sometimes, for one reason or another, he has published nothing for two or three years. Like every experimental writer, he has written a multitude of words he has never published or wished to publish. Before the war he wrote a novel 'all about North Williamstown—the school, the bank manager, the tennis club clique, the yacht club, the lascars and sailors from ships'. His devout hope, he says, is that the manuscript of that novel won't be unearthed and published after his death—or worse, perhaps, while he is still alive. When he speaks of that work now he always accompanies the words with a stage shudder.

He liked schoolmastering, but in 1954 Bairnsdale wished to establish a modern municipal library, and Porter, a qualified librarian, was given the job of establishing it. Four years later he went to Shepparton with a like task to do. He enjoyed running libraries, but prefers writing novels, short stories, poems and plays, and few of his friends were surprised when he turned his back on salaried security late in 1961, announcing that in future he intended devoting all his energies to authorship. He could hardly have taken the decision without some heavy soul-searching, however. Although his literary earnings had for some years been a useful part of his income, he had never called himself a professional writer, and only a few months before resigning his post at Shepparton he said: 'I've never tried to live by writing. I feel if I did I'd be finished, because I'd start to write what editors and the public want, instead of what I want.' Porter's published work shows that, for better or worse, he always has tried to write what he wants, so presumably he reappraised himself and his abilities and concluded that he would be strong enough to go on writing as he pleased. The decision was fairly sudden, though doubtless hastened by his London publisher's enthusiasm for the possibilities of *The Tilted Cross*, and by invitations to him from magazines in the United States to submit short stories and requests from European publishers for permission to put out translated editions of his short stories and of an earlier novel, *A Handful of Pennies*.

When *The Tilted Cross* appeared many British literary critics endorsed the publisher's good opinion of it, but, with a few exceptions, Australian critics were less enthusiastic. Porter was not unduly troubled on this account, for he long ago discovered that Australian writers must make do with rather less critical acclaim in their own country than they get abroad. He was inspired, however, to write a two-page article on the subject of literary critics in general and Australian literary critics in particular (Sydney *Bulletin*, January 6, 1962). Under the heading "Reputation's Blowflies Or, Read Any Good Books Lately?", he wrote, among other things: 'Criticism, as performed in Australia, is, generally, a slapdash and non-creative act, most often —either obliquely or outright brutally—a destructive one. It engages the attention, therefore, of the non-creative intelligentsia, those spearholders on the literary stage: the author *manqué*, the academic saboteur, the "cultured" journalist, the Little Magazine denizen, the one-slender-vol. poet, supernumeraries with an ideological, religious, moral or personal axe to grind.' While doubting that Porter had been altogether wise, in his own interests, to state the case for the author against the critic, many Australian writers felt he had stated it exceedingly well.

For a man well into middle age who has been writing fiction and verse all his adult life, Porter has not published many books. His output has not been small, but he has been less diligent than some authors in making book-length collections of his work. When able to write without interruption or distraction he is prolific, and one reason he decided to leave his job as Shepparton's librarian, was that his salaried work was 'beginning to cover so large an area that my spare time was being cut into'. Having freed himself of other commitments, he settled down to an ambitious writing programme, with the aim of systematically doing a large body of writing, including novels, verse, two or three volumes of autobiography, and of course short stories—always, and above all, short stories. Short stories, which have won him more notice than any other of his work, are his first literary love. If the complexities of his technique, and what critics have called the 'jewelled phrases' that stud his prose, do not please every reader, they at least make it hard to dismiss him. Porter usually writes a short story in two sittings. In one, he does a complete draft, and, in a second, completely rewrites it, working with the pen, in his deliberate, slightly backhand, script. He is one of Australia's few modern authors—and probably one of the few authors anywhere—who submit hand-written stories to editors, and have them printed. He sometimes types a story, after making the usual two hand-written drafts, so he will have a carbon copy, but he is a purposeful, rather than a skilful, typist, and to type a story takes him three times as long as to write it.

He is also writing for the theatre—for him, a new literary field. His acting experience with Gregan McMahon, in pre-war Melbourne, and a post-war period as a professional producer at the Theatre Royal, Hobart, gave him an insight into the theatre's needs, and he believes he will prove himself able to write as effectively for the theatre as he writes for the printed page. The judges of the Sydney Journalists' Club drama award for 1961 strengthened his confidence when they named his play, *The Tower*, as co-winner. Those who dislike Hal Porter (and he has a cocky air which annoys some people) believe that, in attempting to storm so many literary citadels, he overestimates his abilities, or at least his versatility. This is possibly so, but Porter has heard that accusation before and has always—so far anyway—managed to justify his confidence in himself. On every precedent, he seems likely to go on doing so.

FICTION

Short Stories (Adelaide, Advertiser) 1942
A Handful of Pennies (Sydney, Angus & Robertson) 1958
The Tilted Cross (London, Faber & Faber) 1961
A Bachelor's Children. Short stories (Sydney, Angus & Robertson) 1962

VERSE

The Hexagon (Sydney, Angus & Robertson) 1956

Nancy Cato

GIRL AND A RIVER

NOBODY, except perhaps a Freudian psycho-analyst, could explain why a young woman should fall in love with a river. Nancy Cato can explain in only the vaguest terms why she fell in love with the Murray. 'I think I feel as I do about the Murray,' she says, 'because I was born in South Australia, which is mostly dry. I know that, when I first saw this body of water, coming from two thousand miles away, it was a most stimulating and exciting experience.' Nancy Cato first saw the Murray when she was eighteen, but the wonder it woke in her gives no sign of subsiding. On the contrary, the Murray probably means more to her now than it ever did. The first two novels she published, *All the Rivers Run* and *Time, Flow Softly*, and a later novel, *But Still the Stream*, form a trilogy, embracing the history of the Murray from the 1890's, and with the whole length of the river from the mountains to the sea for background. While the river is a real one, and the details of floods and droughts and the waning of the steamer trade are historically accurate, the river is also—on another level—a symbol of life and time. The action of another novel *Green Grows the Vine*, which was published in London in 1960, also takes place on the banks of the Murray, on an irrigation settlement. It has a modern setting, and—except for the river background—has nothing in common with the trilogy. 'I wrote it,' Miss Cato says, 'as relaxation from the others. But I couldn't get far away from the Murray.'

The Murray has a big place, not only in her prose writings, but also in her verse, some of which has been collected and published in two books, *The Darkened Window* and *The Dancing Bough*. Among her river poems is one entitled 'Paddle Steamer', which captures in a few lines her feeling that the Murray is bigger than the men who exploit it. After picturing the men 'who hasten up and down, and chop and slay', the poem ends:

> Their day will come; and in the endless river
> The waters of Time shall smooth behind their wake
> And not a ripple mark their noisy passing.

Nancy Cato and her husband Eldred Norman, who was for many years one of Australia's foremost motor car racing drivers, live, with their two school-age sons and school-age daughter, in Hope Valley, an Adelaide outer suburb. Their home is an ageing house of sandstone blocks, rambling and friendly, with high-ceilinged rooms and wide vine-screened verandahs. It stands in what was once a vineyard. In Miss Cato's view, the house has only one real disability; that is, it is about forty miles from her beloved Murray, where the river, flowing south, heads through Mannum toward Lake Alexandrina, and the Southern Ocean. To be completely at ease with her surroundings, she would need to live on the very banks of the Murray. Some quality of the river has enthralled her and she is never quite content when she is away from it for long; when starting out on a trip abroad in 1961 she drove to Melbourne by way of Goolwa, at the Murray mouth, and got permission to drive over the barrages, as her final act before taking a ship for Greece.

She counts it among the unlucky breaks of her life that she should have been in England in 1956, when the Murray burst its banks in the greatest flood in its recorded history—even greater and more destructive than the 1890 flood. 'I nearly went mad when I got word in England about the flood,' Miss Cato says. 'I had to wrestle round when I got home and pick up the story of that flood secondhand, which was a poor substitute for having seen it with my own eyes.' Her interest in the 1956 flood was not merely that of a Murray-lover in a Murray disaster; her novelist's appetite for dramatic material was also implicated. *But Still the Stream*, the third volume of her Murray trilogy, opens in 1916 and ends in 1956 with the flood. She was not, however, wholly dependent on hearsay in describing what happens when the Murray floods. By the time she returned most of the flood-water had gone, but the aftermath could be clearly seen in the river towns. Also the river had flooded heavily in 1953, and at that time she was in Adelaide. She packed a suitcase at once and hurried to Echuca; there she talked her way on board the river steamer *Coonawarra*, and spent the next three weeks or so travelling down through flood-waters. 'That was a modest flood, compared with the one in 1956,' she says, 'but it was still something to remember. When you looked out a window of the *Coonawarra* you were apt to find yourself staring at the top of a tree, and pretty well close enough to touch it.'

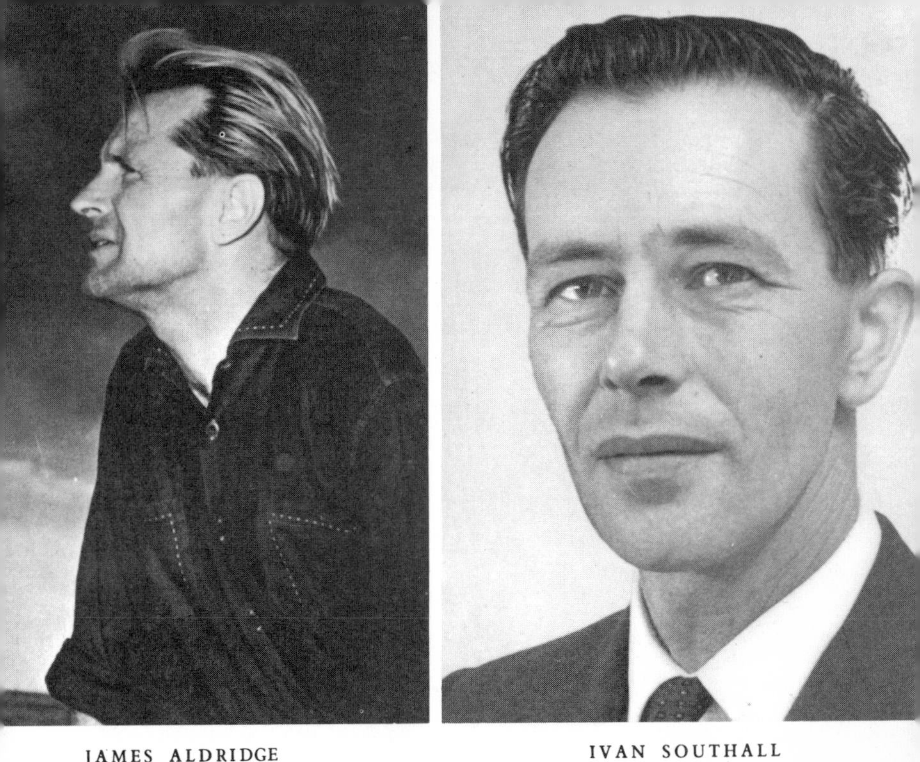

JAMES ALDRIDGE

IVAN SOUTHALL

MAX HARRIS

GEOFFREY DUTTON

G. M. GLASKIN

DAVID FORREST

ELIZABETH HARROWER

RANDOLPH STOW

Nancy Cato, a fifth generation Australian, was born in Adelaid in 1917; her father was a member of an old Tasmanian family. She has travelled fairly widely in the Australian inland, as well as to Europe and the East, but most of her life has been lived, and her work done, in Adelaide. 'I'd rather live in a tent than a house,' she says, 'but only in a warm climate. I once lived in a tent on a coral island in the Barrier Reef, and again for five weeks in Central Australia, and I loved it. For one thing, you don't have to sweep the floor; you just move the tent.'

She wrote a large amount of verse as a child, but most of her early verse, which she began pouring out when she was nine, merely echoed *Palgrave's Golden Treasury* and other poetry anthologies of her youth. She did not at first see anything in her own surroundings worth writing about; it all seemed too mundane to inspire poetic flights. Then, one day near Adelaide, she looked at a paddock of the husky weed soursob, blossoming like tender yellow flame. The sight captured her imagination, and she wrote a set of verses about it. She was sixteen then, and those verses were her first on any Australian subject. She has never since hankered to write on anything but basically Australian subjects, although on her trip abroad in 1961 she conceived an idea for a novel set partly in Europe—'as a change from the outback of Australia and the Murray', she says. Her liking for Australian backgrounds and characters is not an expression of aggressive nationalism; she merely finds that Australian things move her more deeply than any others.

Her verse had gained a little notice when, having left Presbyterian Girls' College, Adelaide, and won the Tennyson Medal by gaining top place in the South Australian Leaving examination in English, she began thinking of a job. About that time *The News*, Adelaide's evening newspaper, announced a contest for girls and boys under eighteen; the task was to write an imaginary interview with Oliver Twist. Nancy Cato came first, and *The News* offered her a cadet reporter's post. She stayed five years with *The News*, doing everything young Australian reporters of that period had to do. For example, she covered what was called 'the North Terrace round', making daily calls at the zoo, the public library, the museum, and other assorted institutions in the North Terrace area. She did this assignment faithfully, and turned in many news items, but even the most enthusiastic young reporter finds, once the early novelty wears off, the writing of paragraphs about the hippopotamus's health or the purchase of another painting for the National Gallery grows wearisome. Her years with *The News* were, however, valuable to Nancy Cato. First, she learned to write when she had to, not just when she felt inclined to; to this day, having been trained on an evening newspaper, whose first edition went to press about two o'clock, she finds she works best in the morning. Second, her experiences—not so much outside *The News* office, as of men and women she worked beside in the office—gave her ample material, if she should ever need it, for several novels.

Some years ago, perhaps seeking a change from writing about the Murray, she wrote a satirical novel entitled *Keep It Brief*, concerning a newspaper called *The Standard*, published in an Australian city. 'The city,' she says, 'was not identified by name, but it could have been Adelaide twenty years ago. For one thing, it was a city where you could starve to death after seven o'clock in the evening, because everything was closed!' No publisher who saw *Keep It Brief* liked it well enough to publish it, but Miss Cato still keeps the manuscript, now somewhat dog-eared, tucked away in a drawer. Several chapters have been published as short stories. Glancing at it once in a while, she finds it readable, but does not know whether she will ever rewrite it and publish it. She will possibly do so when—if ever—she has written the Murray out of her system.

In her five years with *The News*, she wrote and published a few poems and short stories, but nothing substantial, although she planned several novels on paper, down to the chapter headings. At that time, however, she did have the stimulating experience of studying English Literature at the University of Adelaide under Professor J. I. M. Stewart,* who has written novels under his own name but is most widely known for his erudite mystery-detection novels published under the pseudonym of Michael Innes. He was Jury Professor of English Literature at Adelaide from 1935 to 1945.

In 1941 she married and left journalism, and at once started work on a novel. She had spent a grape-picking holiday at Renmark some months before, and the atmosphere of the town, sharpened by her longstanding love of the Murray, had gripped her imagination. She constructed a novel against this background, and it was at least a businesslike attempt, even though it went the rounds of Australia's publishing houses and was rejected. When the disappointment of that early rebuff passed, she found herself thinking more fondly than ever of the Murray, as the setting of a novel. Eldred Norman's mother had been born on the banks of the Murray, above Echuca, and from her own memories and the diaries of her father, who had taken up land there in 1864, was able to reconstruct the days when aboriginal bark canoes were as common as the paddle steamers of a later era. Nancy Cato's imagination was fired by her mother-in-law's stories

* For other references to Professor Stewart see the profile of Max Harris.

and she began exploring the river for herself, and eventually her explorations extended from Echuca to the sea. Travelling wherever possible in one or another of the old paddle steamers, she came to know the large and small river towns, and the people living in them. She was relentless in her pursuit of early documentary records, reflecting aspects of life on the Murray fifty or sixty years before, and tireless in tracking down men and women who remembered the river then. Among her records is a fifteen-page letter, written in faultless copperplate script, from an old man living in retirement in England. At the turn of the century, he was cabin boy of the famous river steamer, *Gem*, and sent Miss Cato his reminiscences because he heard she was hunting for material. Staying at the family weekend shack at Goolwa, with the river at the door and within sound of the sea, she found the idea of a long novel gradually taking shape in her mind. This expanded to a trilogy when she realized she needed a wider canvas to develop her theme. Although the first of the trilogy, *All the Rivers Run*, was not published until 1958 and the third, *But Still the Stream*, until 1962, they were the end-product of many years' work.

In 1956, before the first volume of her river trilogy was accepted, Nancy Cato visited England and stayed three months in London. She wrote hard there, trying to turn into an acceptable book the novel, inspired by her grape-picking experiences at Renmark, which she had written soon after her marriage. It wouldn't go, so one morning she caught a bus to London Bridge, with some hundreds of typewritten pages under her arm. Standing on the bridge, she sent the sheets cascading into the river and watched them float away and drown in the dark brown waters of the Thames. She was relieved once this ceremonial deed was done; it was like laying a ghost that had haunted her for years. She used some of the background of that unpublished novel in *Green Grows the Vine*, but the action and the main characters were completely different.

Perhaps, with her trilogy finished, Nancy Cato will abandon the Murray as a fictional background, for she has many other interests, including the sea ('I've loved the sea ever since I went to Hobart by ship as a child,' she says), painting, swimming and travel. On her 1961 travels abroad she swam off the shores of every country she visited except England, which was too cold, and Russia and Poland; and she carried sketching materials, as well as a typewriter. She once studied oil painting at the South Australian School of Arts and buys modern Australian pictures, and in 1957-58 she was art critic of the Adelaide *News*. But, if she finds she cannot escape the Murray, or does not wish to, plenty of the river remains for her to write about; for, as computed by Ernestine Hill in *Water Into Gold*,* the Murray is three thousand five hundred and thirty-two miles long, 'from the source of the longest tributary to the mouth'. That represents the background of enough novels to keep an imaginative writer like Nancy Cato busy for several lifetimes.

FICTION

All the Rivers Run (London, Heinemann) 1958
Time, Flow Softly (London, Heinemann) 1959
Green Grows the Vine (London, Heinemann) 1960
But Still the Stream (London, Heinemann) 1962

VERSE

The Darkened Window (Sydney, Edwards & Shaw) 1950
The Dancing Bough (Sydney, Angus & Robertson) 1957

* Ninth edition (Melbourne, Robertson & Mullens) 1951.

Jon Cleary

THE STORY COMES FIRST

JON CLEARY made probably the most important decision of his professional writing life when he was thirty-five. That was in 1953, and he was an established popular novelist with an international reputation, but, as he puts it: 'I stood aside and examined myself. I knew I did not have the mental equipment to be the Great Writer I had started out to be, so I totted up my assets. I had a gift for narrative, for conveying atmosphere, and for writing dialogue, and I decided then to employ these gifts to the best of my ability. That's what I've done, and that's what I intend going on doing.' Most writers who ever cherished a dream of writing some work of great and lasting quality could not bring themselves to admit they had relinquished it. Cleary's willingness to do so once he knew his limitations is a measure of his capacity for being honest with himself.

To suppose, however, that Cleary has become a pure money-grubber is wrong. Unlike many authors, he is astute in business; the bargains he drives with publishers once inspired another Australian novelist to say of him, 'In the unending battle between authors and publishers, Cleary is worth a couple of brigades to the authors.' But, although his income in recent years has probably equalled that of any Australian writer, the mere making of money is not his objective. Some years ago he declined a Hollywood TV offer, which would have given him twenty-five thousand pounds a year, because he wasn't keen on the proposed subject and didn't want to be anchored in one place for too long. 'I like,' he says, 'to be able to get up and go when, within reason, I wish.'

The Clearys—including their two schoolgirl daughters, Catherine and Jane, who take changes of country, climate and schools in their stride—are ardent travellers, but they look on Australia as home. They have built a house at Stokes Point, on Pittwater, north of Sydney, and have no wish to settle anywhere but in Australia. 'I'm not an uncritically nationalistic Australian,' Cleary says. 'I think we have lots of faults, more than we care to admit, but I can't imagine myself wanting to be anything but Australian.'

He has helped to familiarize the world with Australia and Australians since he became a writer. Six of his ten novels are set in Australia, two of the others are set in adjacent territories, and all of them have Australians among the major characters. In *The Country of Marriage*, a novel published this year, he breaks new ground—new for him, that is—by setting it in England, but one of the two chief characters is an Australian girl married to an Englishman. And, surprisingly for a Cleary novel, it isn't an adventure story, but, in his own words 'a strictly urban book, without action'. Cleary enjoyed writing it, because it gave him an opportunity to break away from outdoor action themes which he has exploited with high success. He has been working on an outdoor novel, set in Burma, but plans to try another city story, one about politics, which will have Sydney for background.

Cleary is just five feet six inches tall and stockily built, and he walks with a slight sailorly roll, although he has never been to sea except as a passenger. He is blue-eyed and brown-haired, and his pointed brown beard shows grey streaks. The beard is not an affectation. 'I wear it because I dislike shaving,' he explains. 'Also, travelling as we do, I often find myself in places where it's impossible to use an electric shaver. I've had the beard over ten years, and I think I'll stick to it—I'm only tempted to shave it off when I find myself alongside a beatnik, or a French student with his thin jawline growth.' People who think the beard is a mark of eccentricity don't know Cleary. He has no literary or artistic poses, and has never even kept a scrapbook of his reviews or articles published about him; he says this is 'a conceit I don't encourage in myself'. He refuses to join any organizations, whether devoted to good or bad works, and his only club is a cricket club, of which he is a playing, not a social, member.

He was born in 1917, in the Sydney working-class suburb of Erskineville, the eldest of seven children—five boys and two girls—who were brought up as Roman Catholics. Jon Cleary is still a practising Catholic, though sometimes at odds with what he calls 'the Irishism' of the Catholic Church in Australia. His father, who died in 1948, had a variety of jobs, and was a general mechanic at Taronga Park Zoo for the last fifteen years of his life. There was never any spare money in the Cleary household, and when Jon turned fifteen, in the depression year of 1932, he had to leave the Marist Brothers' College, at Randwick, to which he had won a bursary. Like his father, he took any job that paid a reasonable wage. He was an animated cartoonist, passport photographer, silkscreen artist, bush worker, baker's delivery boy, salesman, laundryman, textile machine operator, commercial traveller, signwriter. 'For one whole morning,' he recalls, 'I operated a machine that punched holes in washers. I was sacked by lunchtime because the foreman reckoned I wasn't cut out for the higher branches of engineering.'

When war came he tried to enlist in the RAAF, but was rejected, because of astigmatism in one eye. A few months later he joined the AIF, and went to the Middle East, as a gunner in an artillery survey regiment. He came back to Australia in 1942, and spent the rest of the war in New Britain and New Guinea as a writer in the Military History Section. He says the war finished for him the day he was demobbed. 'I never collected my campaign ribbons, never joined a service organization, never marched in a memorial parade,' he says. 'I didn't dislike the army, but I hate war. I think I'd join up again, if ever another war broke out, but while peace is with us, however brittle, I don't want to remember times when I saw men killed.' His only war book, *The Climate of Courage*, is based on fact. Its emphasis is on the men, not on the atmosphere of war, and Cleary, having got it out of his system, has no desire to write any more about war.

He started writing in the war, and surprised himself by selling a number of short stories to American magazines. When the war ended he had about fifteen hundred pounds in the bank, and decided to go abroad and see if he could make a living by writing fiction. He fixed two years as the trial period; if he didn't succeed in that time, he would come home, find some safe mundane job, and settle into it. Another passenger in the ship he took to England was a Melbourne girl named Joy Lucas, and she and Cleary were married three weeks after reaching England. Joy Cleary published a novel, *Strike Me Lucky*, in 1959, but she has no ambition to become a regular writer and no immediate plans to write another book. Her one venture into authorship was extraordinarily successful, however; an American film company bought her story, and Jon Cleary worked on the script of it. He is not sorry, though, that she prefers a housewife's life to a literary career. 'Selfishly,' he says, 'I think one writer in the family is enough. I don't discuss my work with Joy. When I knock off for the day that's the end of it, and I think it could be pretty stifling for both of us if we were surrounded by the atmosphere of writing.'

Cleary's two years abroad lengthened into seven. He and his wife returned to Australia late in 1953, with their daughters Catherine and Jane, born in 1948 and 1949. In 1956 they went abroad for another two years, and on that trip Cleary took with him the typescript of probably the most ambitious novel he has attempted.

It was concerned with Sydney over the twenty-five years from 1930 to 1955, and politics figured strongly in it. It was a hundred and eighty-five thousand words long and took him fourteen months to write. His publishers rejected this novel. They said overseas readers would not be interested in its political aspect; they also believed readers outside Sydney would not be much interested in it anyway. 'I think they were right,' Cleary says, 'because since then I have seen novels on wider political backgrounds than mine that have flopped resoundingly.' That novel continues to haunt him, however. Its characters never ceased to interest him, and elements of it will help to provide the basis of the political novel he has in mind now.

After his political novel was rejected the Clearys went to Spain. Jon had done no writing for five months, and was chafing to get back to work. He researched his motor racing novel *The Green Helmet*, then wrote it in twenty days—a chapter a day. That is the most profitable three weeks' work he has ever done. *The Green Helmet* was a big seller as a book, was taken by the Reader's Digest Condensed Book Club, was published in ten foreign languages, and was made into a film.

Cleary does not usually write his novels nearly so fast as he wrote *The Green Helmet*. He drafts them in longhand, in a rather neat deliberate script, at a rate of fifteen hundred words a day; he stops as soon as this quota is done, preferring to start each day with something in his mind, rather than write himself out and lie awake at night wondering what he will say tomorrow. Sometimes he finishes his quota by lunchtime; other times, when the going is hard, he stops for an hour or two and goes for a walk or a swim, then comes back to it. He rarely works at night, unless he has had a particularly bad day. From the longhand draft, he types his own fair copy, amending, expanding, cutting, and generally editing the narrative as he goes. 'I think my main object is to entertain,' he says. 'I have a few comments to make, but I am not a messenger. I always look for a subject that will provide a strong story—I think story is still the basis of all good novels—and people who interest me.'

His talent for devising plots, characters and dialogue which are, above all, entertaining is probably the essence of Cleary's natural gift for cinematic writing. Several of his novels, including *The Green Helmet*, *Justin Bayard* (the film title was *Dust in the Sun*), and *The Sundowners* have been filmed, but he had to work hard to make himself a skilled writer of film scripts, which isn't at all the same thing as being a skilled writer of novels. He learned this craft by working with old hands on the script of his own novel, *The Sundowners*, and the script of another writer's story, *The Siege of Pinchgut*. He now divides his time between novel writing and screen scripting, which is excellently paid and helps him to fill in slack time between novels. The novel remains his first love, but he writes a novel in six to nine months and publishes one only every fifteen to eighteen months, and he is a man who likes to be occupied. For years he wrote short stories in his spare time, but some years ago he lost interest in short stories and found he needed another outlet for his unused literary energies.

When anyone asks Cleary what is his best book he is apt to reply, 'My next one'—and mean it. Like most writers, he always feels he can do a shade better next time, and believes that is the only way a writer can go on improving. He likes parts of some of his novels—parts of *You Can't See Round Corners*, of *The Sundowners*, of *The Climate of Courage*, of *North From Thursday*, and of *The Country of Marriage*—but not all of any of them. 'But I've enjoyed writing all my books, and to enjoy what you are doing is, I think, the important thing,' he says. 'Contrary to the opinions of certain critics, I don't whip off potboilers. Some of my books admittedly haven't come off, and could have been much better, but, at the time of writing, I wrote them as well as I could.'

Cleary says he cannot be specific about his ultimate aim as a writer, but if he could some day, when Australia's social structure settles down, write a novel of Australia as good as John P. Marquand's novel of America, *Point of No Return*, he would be content. From choice, he reads biography and history, but Marquand is one of the modern fiction writers he most admires, along with Graham Greene, Peter de Vries, James Thurber and Irwin Shaw—'four Americans to one Englishman, which just about sums up my opinion of British writing today,' he says.

He now sells well in Australia, but his earlier books sold only modestly here; he sells particularly well in Holland, and his sales are going up all the time in Britain and the United States. His most successful book, *The Sundowners*, has sold over a million copies in all editions, including paperbacks and translations, but he has not yet become what the book trade calls an 'impact' author. 'My daughters keep me on my toes, anyway,' he says. 'They won't consider me famous until I am a household word in Iceland. Don't ask me why Iceland. They could have been really difficult and chosen Greenland.' The way things are moving at present, however, his prospect of becoming a household word in Iceland—and in any other place where people read for amusement—seems reasonably bright. He is hopeful about Iceland at least, because he likes to stand well with Catherine and Jane.

FICTION

These Small Glories. Short stories (Sydney, Angus & Robertson) 1946
You Can't See Round Corners (New York, Scribners) 1947
The Long Shadow (London, Werner Laurie) 1949
Just Let Me Be (London, Werner Laurie) 1950
The Sundowners (London, Werner Laurie) 1952
The Climate of Courage (London, Collins) 1954
Justin Bayard (London, Collins) 1955
The Green Helmet (London, Collins) 1957
Back of Sunset (London, Collins) 1959
North From Thursday (London, Collins) 1960
The Country of Marriage (London, Collins) 1962

Frank Hardy

FAREWELL TO BENSON'S VALLEY

A SLIGHT, dark man, wiry and thin-featured, stood in the Melbourne Criminal Court dock on June 18, 1951, wondering if he was about to go to gaol. His name was Frank Hardy, and he was being tried on the unusual charge of criminal libel—specifically, of having criminally libelled Mrs Ellen Wren, in his novel *Power Without Glory*, published in 1950. The jury returned a verdict of not guilty. Hardy was discharged, and a few more pages had been added to the story of one of the most controversial novels ever written by an Australian. Any novel which more than a handful of people remember as much as a year or so after its first publication is a rarity. Yet tens of thousands of Australians still remember *Power Without Glory*. Their reasons for remembering it range all the way from admiration to detestation of it; but, for whatever complex of reasons, *Power Without Glory* stays alive in a large number of minds. No novelist could be displeased with such a tribute to the durability of his work, and Frank Hardy, the country boy who wrote a city novel which swept Australia, does not conceal his satisfaction.

Hardy, who at the time of writing lives at Manly, N.S.W., in a flat overlooking the Pacific, published only four books in the U.K. or Australia in the twelve years immediately following the appearance of *Power Without Glory*. These were a travel book, *Journey Into the Future*, describing a visit to Soviet Russia; *The Man from Clinkapella*, a small volume of short stories; a novel, *The Four-Legged Lottery*; and *The Hard Way*, an autobiography. All these books are competent, and sold reasonably well, but none of them had the quality to make of it another *Power Without Glory*. Nobody knew this better than Hardy did, for he is a shrewd judge of his own work. The simple fact was that, after *Power Without Glory*, he was, as a creative writer, temporarily exhausted, struggling in a slough of mental inertia. This was inevitable. The events associated with that novel's publication, coming on top of years of painstaking and tedious research, imposed a heavy and prolonged physical and nervous strain on him.

Hardy would be willing now to forget *Power Without Glory*. He does not regret having written it, but it belongs to his past, and he prefers to look ahead, not behind. 'I believe *Power Without Glory* interrupted my natural development as a writer,' he says in his light incisive voice, 'and I've only now got back to the line I originally started out to follow. *Power Without Glory* gave me wonderful experience, because, in it, I was confronted with every conceivable literary problem. But, after writing and publishing it, I did not recover my creative force until 1956. In that "dry" period I started several novels, but couldn't get ahead with any of them. For a time I did no writing at all and worked as a seaman on the coast. Now I believe I've found my way back. It was through writing my autobiographical book, *The Hard Way*, that I recaptured the thought processes and work habits which had temporarily deserted me.'

Hardy is now writing more prolifically—and, he believes, writing better—than ever before in his life. Having published *The Hard Way* after a self-imposed delay of six years, he finished, or was in course of finishing, a book of short stories, a comic novel, and a book of what he calls 'pub folk tales'. (There are twenty-one of these 'pub folk tales', and eight of them were published in the U.S.S.R. in 1960 in a paperback entitled *The Pub Yarns of Billy Borker*.) He intends to publish all these three books sooner or later, and also a novel, based on his experiences as a coastal seaman. But none of these is the book he wishes posterity to remember him by; nor, he confesses, is *Power Without Glory*. His overriding ambition is to write a trilogy of novels woven around the life of Henry Lawson, whose work Hardy profoundly admires. This trilogy would dwarf *Power Without Glory* both in philosophical conception and physical size. 'The way I plan it,' Hardy says, 'this trilogy will be the story, not only of a man, but of a people and a tradition, of how a new kind of people—the Australians—came to exist on the earth.' Any writer might quail before such a project; it is a fair indication of the revival of Hardy's confidence in his own powers that he has—or, at least, betrays—no doubt of his ability to do what he plans.

Hardy, the third of eight children, was born in 1917, in Southern Cross, a village near Warrnambool, but Bacchus Marsh is the place that dominates his youthful memories. His parents settled there when he was eight, and although, after leaving school at thirteen, he moved freely about Victoria, as a seasonal worker in orchards, market gardens, milk factories, packing sheds, and the like, Bacchus Marsh continued to be his home ground. He did not see any big city until he was sixteen, when he visited Melbourne for one afternoon to watch a football match. Then, at twenty-one, he went to live in Melbourne, after deciding, quite dispassionately, that he must quit Bacchus Marsh. 'I had the happiest days of my life in Bacchus Marsh,' he says, 'but I knew that if I stayed there I would go to seed.'

His affection for Bacchus Marsh has never diminished. One of the books he has in hand is a collection of short stories about a small town called Benson's Valley, which is modelled on Bacchus Marsh. The stories, linked by their common background, and the recurrence in them of certain characters, form a portrait of a typical small town near an Australian capital city. When Hardy began work on this book he went to Bacchus Marsh to yarn with old friends and acquaintances and collect ideas for story situations and characters. He found many of the locals still remembered him; dozens came to chuckle with him over his widely known short story, *A Load of Wood*, based on an incident which occurred in Bacchus Marsh in the depression years. *A Load of Wood*—which has been published in twenty-seven languages, including two Indian dialects, printed in five anthologies, and filmed—will be one of the stories in *Legends from Benson's Valley* due to come out in 1963.

Hardy had to struggle to make a living in his early Melbourne years. Having a little talent as a black-and-white artist, he now and then sold a cartoon; otherwise he worked at any job that offered and contrived to scratch a livelihood. In 1942 he joined the army as a private and was posted to Mataranka, North Australia, as a storeman. In need of mental occupation, he launched a troops' newspaper, *Troppo Tribune*. He wrote much of the contents himself, turning out paragraphs, word-sketches, and doggerel in large quantities. Most of the writing he did then was amateurish, rough-hewn and hurried, but it must have shown promise, because one of his army friends, a Sydney journalist in peacetime, persuaded him to try his hand at a short story. A few days later Hardy finished the first short story he ever wrote. He called it *A Stranger in the Camp*. It was his version of a bush tale he had heard his father tell many times. Hardy's father worked all his life in country milk-collecting depots, and was, his son claims, a born story-teller who never wrote his stories down, but told them always by word of mouth. 'He used to polish his stories like jewels,' Hardy says. 'I heard every one of them many times, and he would add something at each telling. When I was a kid I used to think he was an old fibber, but when I grew older I realized he was perfecting his stories exactly as a writer does.' *A Stranger in the Camp* won first prize in a Sydney competition. Encouraged, Hardy wrote another story; this was the now famous *A Load of Wood*.

There was no longer any doubt in Hardy's mind what he intended doing with his life; he intended becoming a writer, and when he was invited to join the staff of the army magazine, *Salt*, in Melbourne he took the post for experience. By the time he left the army in February, 1946, he had written a good number of short stories, and wanted to attempt something bigger. He had been reading Theodore Dreiser's novels, and he concluded, while under their influence, that Australia was ripe for a city novel about a tycoon absorbed in the quest for money and power. *Power Without Glory*, published in August, 1950, was the novel he wrote. The late John Wren was widely identified as the central character, John West, whom Hardy introduced with these words: '. . . the first noticeable characteristic was his bandiness, but, at close range, his eyes were the striking feature. They were unfathomable, as if cast in metal; steely grey and rather too close together; deep-set, yet sharp and penetrating.' Hardy's counsel insisted, when addressing the jury which tried the charge of criminal libel against his client, that 'the book character John West' was a composite-fictional character. But most readers of *Power Without Glory* continued to see John West and John Wren as one.

Whatever disputes the literary quality of *Power Without Glory* inspires, there can be no argument about the monumental character of the work which gave the novel birth. When Hardy was writing it, he was already married, with two young children, and he worked sixteen hours a day, sometimes more, to make a living and get ahead with his novel. He earned money when and where he could, chiefly, as he records in *The Hard Way*, as a spare-time reporter and general handyman for an obscure trotting newspaper. It was a fierce struggle, and Hardy will probably never again have to battle in this way while writing a book. Although he has periods when money is tight, his writing earns him enough to let him chart his future with some assurance; world sales of *Power Without Glory*, for instance, exceed five hundred thousand copies.

Whether or not Hardy knows it himself, the novel is obviously the literary form he finds most satisfying. He has written hundreds of short stories (only a fraction of which he has published) and several full-length stage plays; one of his plays, *Black Diamonds*, was staged in Sydney and also in Berlin. But when he discusses his own writing any mention he makes of anything but his novels is in the nature of a digression.

His major interest now is in the Lawson trilogy, and this promises to be his major interest for many years to come. He has drafted the early chapters, and done much research into Henry Lawson's life and times. Among the lesser books he has in hand, he is particularly hopeful of a comic novel, *Up The Garbos!*, describing events which follow the sacking of two garbage collectors in a Sydney suburb for sorting bottles in working hours. Hardy, who has a lively sense of fun, is particularly responsive to slapstick comedy, which is probably the strongest element in *Up The Garbos!*. And he wished to write a comic novel because, as he puts it, 'Australians have the subtlest, most many-faceted sense of humour of any people in the world. They find humour in the most serious situations. Yet most of our literature is deadly grave.' He knows, however, that he is likely to have difficulty in finding a publisher for *Up the Garbos!*. If all else fails, he will probably publish it himself.

One interesting aspect of Frank Hardy's literary work is the wide variety of themes he has tackled, even though, as he confirmed in *The Hard Way*, he is a convinced Communist. In a television interview he commented upon this (as some critics see it) apparent contradiction, in these words: 'My interest in literature arose from my experience in life and from my political experience and beliefs. I can say that the philosophy of Marxism, the theory of conflict within people and between people, of conflicts in society, has made it possible for me to be a writer. . . . I feel completely integrated as an Australian, as a working man, as a writer, and as a Communist. That is not to say I am free of conflict. No one is. Conflict is the very basis of existence. . . . There is a conflict I have to constantly watch and resolve. As a committed writer, I take part in political activity and often meet people at a point of struggle, people changing in the process of conflict. Then I must find time to transmute this experience into literary works. But this is not a conflict between me as a writer and my political views.'

Frank Hardy in his mid-forties is unquestionably the same Frank Hardy who in his early thirties wrote *Power Without Glory;* he is still, as he would say himself, 'politically motivated'. He has grown in maturity as a man, however, and it is inevitable that this growth will influence his work as a writer. The only question is how deep the influence will ultimately prove to be.

Farewell to Benson's Valley

FICTION

Power Without Glory (Melbourne, Realist Printing & Publishing Co.) 1950

The Man from Clinkapella. Short stories (Melbourne, Realist Printing & Publishing Co.) 1950

The Four-Legged Lottery (London, T. Werner Laurie) 1958

GENERAL

Journey into the Future (Melbourne, Australasian Book Society) 1952

The Hard Way (London, T. Werner Laurie) 1961

A Russian-language edition of a selection of short stories, *The Pub Yarns of Billy Borker*, was published in the U.S.S.R. in 1960.

James Aldridge

"IT ALL COMES OUT LIKE BLOOD"

JAMES ALDRIDGE finished writing his eighth novel, *The Last Exile*, in London in November, 1960. He had worked on it for four years, which was twice as long as he worked on any of his earlier novels. The size of *The Last Exile* gave some justification for the time Aldridge took to write it; it is four hundred thousands words long, or rather more than four times as long as the standard novel. Four years to write four hundred thousand words is slow going for Aldridge, however; he earned his living as a newspaperman before he became a novelist, and in those days he was fast at writing anything from a frontline battle report for a daily newspaper to an extended profile of some European political celebrity for an American national magazine. 'It took me two years to write *The Diplomat* and three years to write *Heroes of the Empty View*,' he says. (*The Diplomat* was published in 1949 and *Heroes of the Empty View* in 1954.) 'And four years for *The Last Exile*. I get slower, because I suppose I demand more. I think when you have written a book, finished it, and published it, you begin to see only then how it should have been written. It would be perfect if you could write a book, put it away for a year or two, and then sit down and rewrite it. That should produce masterpieces, but who could do that?' Aldridge usually writes the first part of a book a dozen times before he knows his characters—in his own words, 'to find out what sort of people I've got'. Even then, he is apt to go back when he has the whole book on paper and rewrite the beginning, because only at the end does he know thoroughly the people he is writing about.

He is one of the few Australian-born writers whose names are known in practically every country where novels are printed. Most of his books have been translated into ten or twelve languages; *The Diplomat* has been published in twenty-five languages or more, including Kurdish, and in Soviet Russia, where all Aldridge's books sell well, it has sold in millions. He is the most popular living British writer with Soviet readers, and one of his more agreeable economic problems is to spend the roubles his novels earn; these earnings accumulate for him in Moscow, and cannot be spent outside Russia. He has solved this problem, in part, by staying a few months in the Soviet Union every other year or so. For instance, in 1960 he and his wife and their two school-age boys had three months in the Crimea, where he did some writing and much sun-bathing and skin-diving.

Aldridge, an exceptionally handsome man, could be the prototype for the perfect Nordic of Adolf Hitler's National-Socialist dreams, which is ironic because his hatred of Nazism has never wavered. He has thick straight blond hair, regular features, and far-looking blue eyes. He is just under six feet tall and solidly made, with muscular hands which seem, and are, capable of doing many practical things other than work a typewriter. He published his first novel, *Signed With Their Honor*, in 1942, when he was in his early twenties, and every novel he has since published has added something to his reputation (which is not the same thing as saying that each of them has been a better novel than the ones that went before it).

Some Australian critics try to disqualify Aldridge as an Australian writer, because none of his novels is set in Australia and few of them have Australians as characters. Aldridge does not seem to be worried by such judgments. Since he was seventeen or eighteen he has been more concerned with the world at large than with any particular corner of it, and with human beings at large than with any national group, and so it is the world at large and human beings at large that he writes about. For example, *The Last Exile*, published in 1961, is a novel of Egypt; it focuses on the last days of British influence in Egypt, and has the Suez Canal conflict as its climax, but manages to encompass the whole story of British rule in Egypt. Aldridge has a special title to write about Egypt; his wife, who was Dina Mitchnik before their marriage in 1942, is Egyptian, and each of their two sons has an Arabic, as well as an English, given name. William's Arabic name is Da-ud, meaning David, and Thomas's is Hilal, meaning New Moon. The Aldridges have a more or less permanent base in London, where they live in a flat. They spend about half their time in England and half somewhere else—perhaps in France, Switzerland, Russia or Egypt. They had as long as a year in Egypt some years ago, and more recently a year in France.

Aldridge has never written a financially unsuccessful book, and he and his wife and their two sons could live comfortably on his royalties, but he sometimes takes a journalistic assignment, less to supplement his income than to keep his newspaper touch. Unlike some successful authors, he neither wishes nor tries to forget his journalistic beginnings, nor does he scorn the opportunities for self-expression he still finds by writing for newspapers, as well as for book publishers. 'I like,' he says, 'to keep a foot in both camps.' Every medium of writing interests him, as a channel for communicating his ideas. In 1955, between novels, he surprised his admirers by publishing a practical guide to a sport he has practised in many waters, entitled *Undersea Hunting for Inexperienced Englishmen*, which is illustrated with his own drawings. He has never had time to study the craft of writing for the theatre, but as long ago as 1947 he had a play staged in London. This play, *The 49th State*, was on the theme of American power over Britain, and he believes it would have been more popular in England a little later than when it was staged.

Considering what Aldridge has done since, aged nineteen and unknown, he left Australia for London in 1938, it is ironic that in Australia he should have been unable to find a job as a cadet newspaper reporter. He was born at White Hills, Bendigo in 1918, and christened Harold Edward James, but all his friends know him only as 'Jimmy' and would hardly recognize him under the weight of all his given names. His parents were English, and his father worked as a country newspaperman in Victoria for many years. Young Jim, after attending country State schools and Swan Hill High School, went to Melbourne when he was sixteen, and found a copy-boy's job in the Melbourne *Herald* office. He was fascinated by journalistic techniques, but could persuade nobody to give him a trial as a journalist. Despairing of ever breaking into Australian journalism, he scraped together the tourist-class one-way fare to England and went abroad in 1938. In London he found a modest job, writing picture titles for *The Daily Sketch*, at nine guineas a week. But at least he was doing journalistic work at last.

When war broke out he wanted to be a frontline correspondent, but he knew he might as well cry for the moon unless a miracle were to happen. He made the miracle happen by foreseeing the invasion of Finland by Soviet Russia well before the event. He was not alone in believing Russia would move against Finland and occupy certain territories as a measure of self-protection, but he appears to have been the only young British newspaperman who acted on the belief. He decided to go to Finland and await the Soviet invasion. No London newspaper was much interested in what he did, but the Melbourne *Herald's* London office gave him mild encouragement, and, taking with him what was left of his meagre savings after paying the steamer fare, he caught a ship to Finland. He arrived in Helsinki early in November, 1939. Three weeks later, on November 30, the Red Army attacked Finland, and suddenly Helsinki became one of the world's great news centres. When the fighting ended four months later James Aldridge was recognized in England and the U.S.A., as well as Australia, as one of the formidable correspondents of World War II. He had shown, not only that he had a knack of being on hand when big news broke, but also that he could describe what he saw in vivid, simple prose. Most of his stories from Finland were published in the London *Times* and *The New York Times*, as well as in Australian newspapers. He spent two months in Soviet Russia after the Russo-Finnish war. Then he reported the campaign in Norway, saw the Balkans in the last months before Hitler overran them, and eventually reached the Middle East. From Cairo, he operated for nearly two years as chief correspondent of the American agency, North American Newspaper Alliance, reporting the Western Desert war, Mussolini's campaign against Greece, and the overthrow of Greece by Germany.

In 1941 he went to America, taking with him some short stories about the fighting in Finland. These stories were not published at the time, although some were incorporated in later books, but a New York publisher's editor named Angus Cameron read them and liked them. Cameron, of whom Aldridge says, 'He taught me so much that I can safely say he taught me how to write', persuaded him to write a novel about the Royal Air Force in Greece. The American magazine *Collier's* published the story as a serial, called *Flight to the Sun*, and paid Aldridge twenty-five thousand dollars for it. It was also published in New York and London as a book, under the title *Signed With Their Honor*. Both titles derive from the closing lines of Stephen Spender's poem, 'I Think Continually of Those Who Were Truly Great':

> . . . . those who in their lives fought for life
> Who wore at their hearts the fire's centre.
> Born of the sun they travelled a short while towards the sun,
> And left the vivid air signed with their honor.

On the evidence of *Signed With Their Honor* and his second novel, *The Sea Eagle*, published in 1944, Aldridge might have settled into a well-padded career as a writer of skilfully told middle-brow novels, having entertainment as their chief purpose. This was not his aim, however. He wanted to be more than a mere teller of diverting tales, and each of his later books has cut deeper than either of those first two novels, in its examination of human motives and political and sociological implications.

'My philosophy as a writer,' he says, 'begins with my philosophy to life itself. I am a Marxist, and this is my point of view, and always has been, since I was sixteen anyway. So the philosophy is political, but the philosophy of the craft, too, comes into it. I come from a long line of craftsmen, and I thank my lucky stars that I can lean on this. To have the right philosophy hardly means a thing if you don't have the real respect, the deliberate approach, to the craft itself.' Aldridge's fascination with craftsmanship—perhaps the air pilot's or the seaman's craftsmanship, perhaps the carpenter's or the blacksmith's—is evident in his books. His minute observations of the most humble kinds of craftsmanship are revealed by descriptions such as this, of a boy watching a country milk roundsman, which occurs in one of his Australian short stories, *Victory for a Bush Boy*: 'Edgar watched as Bugs twice plunged the tin dipper with a long handle into the polished metal can and brought forth two clean pints of rich milk. A little dip extra, and he hung the ladle hook on a bar in the milk can, clanked the hinged top down, and was out of the gate into the next house in no time. He was a craftsman. . . .'

Aldridge writes so well about Australia—so vividly, so lovingly—that many of his admirers hope he will sooner or later make Australia the locale of a novel. He says he will write about Australia some day, but exactly how this will come about he doesn't know. He has no plans at present to live in Australia or to come back here and stay long enough to gather material for writing. He came home for twelve months in 1945, and he had arranged to visit Australia, with his wife and sons, in 1960, but fell ill, and cancelled the trip. He will come back, however, when he is ready to, because 'I can't escape Australia and don't want to'.

In a sympathetic estimate of Aldridge, Eric Partridge, the Australian-born author, philologist and literary critic, has written (*Meanjin*: No. 3, 1961): 'James Aldridge is a born writer, no less at home with the vast canvas than with the concentrated particularity. . . . If only he will remember that fiction is fiction, not a vehicle for polemic, and will allow his immense literary potential its full scope, he will soon stand in the forefront of British novelists. This quiet, modest writer, this most likeable of men, has a multitude of friends: and they all hope that he will refuse to become lost in the deserts of sociological theory. We already have a superfluity of theorists, but we can never have enough great writers.' What Aldridge thinks of this finding is not known, but he is not content with all he has done, or even with anything he has done, as a writer. He believes he is groping toward something, not that he has found it. 'I still feel I am just learning to write,' he says. 'There are a dozen books I *need* to write, and my aim is to get them done, and for each one to teach me more and more. It all comes out like blood; I wish it would come easy.' For a novelist of international standing, that is a refreshingly frank confession of imperfection, but Aldridge is a refreshingly frank man. Even his fiercest political antagonists would grant him that, if they would grant him nothing else.

FICTION

Signed With Their Honor (London, Michael Joseph) 1942
The Sea Eagle (London, Michael Joseph) 1944
Of Many Men (London, Michael Joseph) 1945
The Diplomat (London, The Bodley Head) 1949
The Hunter (London, The Bodley Head) 1950
Heroes of the Empty View (London, The Bodley Head) 1954
I Wish He Would Not Die (London, The Bodley Head) 1957
Gold and Sand Short stories (London, The Bodley Head) 1960
The Last Exile (London, Hamish Hamilton) 1961

GENERAL

Undersea Hunting for Inexperienced Englishmen, with line drawings by the author (London, Allen and Unwin) 1955

D'Arcy Niland and Ruth Park

TWO CAREERS UNDER ONE ROOF

A MARRIAGE between talented careerists is widely held to be in mortal peril once the first glow fades. If this is statistically so, Mr and Mrs D'Arcy Niland are exceptions to the dire rule. Each has won uncommon notice as a writer, but their marriage in 1942, which has yielded two sons and three daughters, has been conspicuously normal and happy. Three out of four Australians chosen at random could probably tell you who D'Arcy Niland is, without two seconds' hesitation; the success of his best-selling novel, *The Shiralee*, which became an equally popular film, firmly established his name. Many fewer could identify Mrs D'Arcy Niland, unless you were to mention her professional name—Ruth Park; then the same three out of four Australians would at once answer that she is as successful a writer as her husband. And, in spite of the strain that two careers in one family theoretically place on any marriage, the Nilands' marriage seems certain to survive any foreseeable shocks without the slightest abatement of either career.

Considered individually or together, D'Arcy and Ruth Niland must be as busy as any two professional writers anywhere. They acquired the habit of being busy in the early years of their marriage when, for them, the difference between working and not working was liable to make the difference between eating and not eating. 'When we started out as full-time writers,' D'Arcy Niland says, 'we wrote anything and everything. We had to. We wrote radio copy, paragraphs, jingles, short stories, articles. Ruth even wrote advertising "copy". We did gag scripts for Dick Bentley, and we peddled songs. Words were our business.' At first the Nilands often found it hard to pay rent and buy food; now they have their own house in Balgowlah Heights, Manly, N.S.W., and their own car, and no worries about tradesmen's bills. Everything was bought with the earnings of their typewriters. After you have been with them a few minutes, you understand why their marriage has succeeded. Superficially, they are opposites, but in one thing they are twins: each passionately believes in the writer's craft, and has understood from the start what the other wants from life, and why. D'Arcy Niland is dark, short, compact, a welterweight run slightly to flesh, who presses his opinions with courteous, but inflexible, intensity; Ruth Niland, a slim redhead, with a generous mouth and quizzical eyes, is more casual. Or perhaps it is truer to say that she merely appears so, because, when any of her basic views is challenged, she defends it with a fire of crackling words.

They first met only because D'Arcy Niland, not long before World War II broke out, happened one day to be discussing his writing ambitions with Sister Mary Fidelis, of the Sisters of St Joseph, a Roman Catholic teaching order. Sister Fidelis had taught him at St Joseph's school, Glen Innes, N.S.W., his native town, and knew how he ached to be a writer. 'If you write to this lady in Auckland,' she told him, jotting down a name and address on a piece of paper, 'she'll help you.' He went away and, after heavy labour, produced a letter, rich in orotund phrases and resounding sentences, designed to impress the literary lady in Auckland, whom he pictured as an ageing spinster, with a terrifying contempt for split infinitives and a vocabulary rivalling Noah Webster's. Presently the reply came. It was not at all orotund or resounding, and in the course of it the lady in Auckland, whose name was Ruth Park and who turned out to be seventeen, said: 'You sound as though you wear a frock coat and Piccadilly weepers like two bundles of kapok—and you make me feel like an old lady with her hair in a bun!' He admits he was so annoyed that he did not write back for about three months.

He has never been quite sure why Sister Fidelis, who had heard of Ruth Park from a New Zealand Sister of St Joseph, advised him to send that letter which started so much; at that time Ruth was working on an Auckland newspaper, *The Star*, and had gone no further than he had toward making a name as a writer. Sister Fidelis's motives do not matter. What does matter is that, just after World War II began, Ruth Park took a holiday in Australia, and she and D'Arcy Niland met. The holiday over, she went back to New Zealand, and plugged away again as a reporter, working at her writing on the side; D'Arcy, back in Sydney, returned to his job as a railway porter, working at his writing on the side also. Then in 1942 Ruth Park came back to Sydney. She had been promised a Sydney newspaper job, but did not intend to settle in Australia; Australia was to be merely a temporary stopping-place on her way to the bigger world overseas which she planned to conquer. She did not take the newspaper job; instead she married D'Arcy Niland soon after reaching Sydney, and almost at once they began a wandering life in the New South Wales outback.

D'Arcy, born and bred in the country, knew the bush well; he had spent his early working years in the bush, taking any jobs that offered. For a time he was a circus hand; he also had a spell as a boxer in a travelling tent show. The early travels of the newly-wedded Nilands were more or less involuntary, because D'Arcy, an experienced shearer, was under the control of the wartime manpower authorities, and had to go wherever he was sent. Not that the Nilands minded. This was one way for Ruth to become acquainted with Australia, and she went happily along, moving from shed to shed with her husband, seeing the bush, hearing the talk, registering the characters. After a year or so the Nilands found themselves back in Sydney; and, though D'Arcy presently had to go bush again, Ruth stayed in the city because she was pregnant.

Her home—any kind of place to live was hard to find in Sydney in embattled 1943—was only a room over a barber's shop in Devonshire Street, Surry Hills, but it was a refuge for Ruth while the baby was coming, and somewhere for D'Arcy to be with her, between jobs. In the end the room proved to be much more. Her life there gave Ruth the characters and the locale for her first novel, *The Harp in the South*, which was to win *The Sydney Morning Herald* first prize of two thousand pounds for a novel in 1947. '*The Harp*,' she says, 'wasn't fiction, but a literal report of what I saw. Living there, I learned what loving, and loveable, people there are in the slums. Although they mightn't worry about some of the Commandments, their code is based on charity. I'd rather be broke any time in Surry Hills than Potts Point.' Working for wages in a Surry Hills ham-and-beef shop, she saw strange sights and met strange people—strange to her, at least. One day a young man came in and borrowed a hammer. He returned it some time later, having battered his girl to death with it. Ruth could not understand the murderer's scrupulousness about returning the hammer until her husband, who had lived in some tough parts of Sydney and understood the slum-dweller's philosophy, explained it. 'Of course he returned it,' D'Arcy said. 'If he hadn't, that would have been stealing!'

It was in the room over Devonshire Street that the Nilands, about 1944, began working as full-time writers. They did so in defiance of the advice of many older, and technically wiser, people who said they hadn't Buckley's chance of living in Australia merely by writing. Later in their joint autobiography, *The Drums Go Bang*, they wrote: 'The chief character in our life was the postman, as he is in the lives of most would-be writers. High in our front door was a perpendicular slot through which he pushed the mail to fall on the floor. . . . One morning nine manuscripts came through the slot in the door one after the other. They hit the floor with the thud known as dull, while we watched, too horrified to speak.' But in the end they confounded all those well-meaning friends who had said it couldn't be done. The rate of rejections gradually diminished, the incidence of acceptances—and cheques—increased. Their first big success came when *The Harp in the South* won *The Sydney Morning Herald* prize. Its disclosures disturbed Sydney's conscience, and stimulated slum clearance work, even though Ruth Park, when she wrote the novel, had 'no idea of doing anything sociological'. *The Harp in the South* is primarily a story, not of a place, but of people, and this is the quality which made it a best-seller, not only in Australia, but also in countries such as England, the U.S.A., Germany and Holland, where Surry Hills means nothing. Ruth has gone on writing successful novels ever since then, and one, *The Witch's Thorn*, sold five hundred thousand copies in the U.S.A. alone. And D'Arcy Niland, after publishing about five hundred short stories in Australia and overseas, scored international success with his novel, *The Shiralee*, and smaller, but still respectable, successes with other novels.

The Nilands no longer have to write with an eye on the next meal, and, for each of them, the novel seems likely to remain a first interest. This does not mean they give their working lives wholly to fiction, however. For a long time D'Arcy Niland was fascinated by the story of Les Darcy, probably the most tragic figure in the history of the Australian boxing ring. He yearned to write a biography of Darcy, and over the years gathered material for this book as opportunity to do so offered. On a trip abroad in 1961 he visited the U.S.A., where Les Darcy died at Memphis, Tennessee, in 1917, aged twenty-one. 'In America,' he says, 'I had the good luck to find some apparently untapped material which throws new light on the last few months of Darcy's life.' At the time of this writing, he was working on the Darcy biography but did not know how long he would take to finish it.

Either of the Nilands is always prepared to try something new. Some years ago Ruth wrote a factual book about Australia, *The Golden Boomerang*, at a German publisher's request. As *Der Goldene Bumerang*, this sold well to Germans and other German-speaking Europeans who were thinking of Australia as a land worth settling in, and became a kind of immigrants' textbook. D'Arcy also once wrote a textbook, but of a different kind. Entitled *Make Your Stories Sell*, this was modestly intended as a practical guide for Australian and New Zealand short story writers, but the Australian edition came under the eye of an American publisher; he liked the book and put out a U.S. edition, although its author had never dreamed it would reach print outside Australia and New Zealand. Both Nilands write for TV, separately and together, and in 1961 a television play, *No Decision*, which they wrote in collaboration, won a prize of a thousand pounds in a British competition. They are interested in the theatre also as a medium for their work, and hope, some time, to turn Eve Langley's novel, *The Pea Pickers*, into a musical play.

Professionals, they consider writing to be, not some kind of inspired miracle whose esoterics vulgar earthlings cannot comprehend, but a business which must be worked at systematically. D'Arcy Niland (who once described his technique of collecting material in these down-to-earth words: 'It's all copy. Every time I sit on a bus or ferry I salt away what I see and hear') speaks for both of them when he says, 'I write with the idea of interesting and entertaining people. If they get something out of it, I'm happy.' The number of people throughout the world who read the Nilands' books is compelling testimony that this working philosophy is a profitable one.

By Ruth Park

FICTION

(Published by Angus & Robertson, Sydney)

The Harp in the South 1948
Poor Man's Orange 1949
The Witch's Thorn 1951
A Power of Roses 1953
Pink Flannel 1955
One-a-Pecker, Two-a-Pecker 1957
The Good-Looking Women 1961

For Chidren
The Hole in the Hill (Sydney, Ure Smith) 1961
Uncle Matt's Mountain (London, Macmillan) 1962
The Ship's Cat (London, Macmillan) 1962
The Road to Christmas (London, Macmillan) 1962
The Shaky Island (London, Constable) 1962

GENERAL

The Drums Go Bang, with D'Arcy Niland (Sydney, Angus & Robertson) 1956

A German-language edition of a non-fiction book by Ruth Park, *Der Goldene Bumerang*, was published by Carl Schuneman Verlag, of Bremen, Germany, in 1955.

By D'Arcy Niland

FICTION

The Shiralee (London, Angus & Robertson) 1955
Call Me When the Cross Turns Over (Sydney, Angus & Robertson) 1957
Gold in the Streets (Sydney, Horwitz) 1959
The Big Smoke (Sydney, Angus & Robertson) 1959
The Ballad of the Fat Bushranger. Short stories (Sydney, Horwitz) 1961
Logan's Girl. Short stories (Sydney, Horwitz) 1961
Dadda Jumped Over Two Elephants. Short stories (London, Panther) 1961

GENERAL

Make Your Stories Sell (Sydney, Angus & Robertson) 1955
The Drums Go Bang, with Ruth Park (Sydney, Angus & Robertson) 1956

Ivan Southall

THE RIDDLE AND THE ANSWER

FEW young men can ever have launched themselves as writers with a stranger set of working tools than Ivan Southall used. These were a motor mower, a 1928 Austin 12 motor car, and an obsolescent L. C. Smith typewriter. That was in November, 1947. The motor mower and the 1928 Austin 12, having served their purpose, disappeared from Southall's life many years ago, but the typewriter, looking about as incongruous as a Farnum biplane on a jet airfield, is still with him. It works with unfailing, if noisy, efficiency. In the fourteen years or so since Southall decided to become a professional writer, he has published five non-fiction books for adults and one for children, one children's novel and nine boys' adventure books, as well as six paperback novels and three shortish commissioned documentary books. 'I haven't made a fortune,' he says, 'but I don't really want to. All I want to do is live by writing, and support my family in reasonable comfort, and that is what I am doing.'

Southall is a slender man, six feet one inch tall, who cannot get his weight more than a few ounces above ten stone, no matter how much, or what, he eats. Since he is healthy this does not matter. He is olive-skinned and dark-haired, and the brown eyes under his dark brows have an introspective light. His lean face tapers from a high wide brow to a chin with a firm thrust. The Southalls, who have a son, born in 1947, and three daughters, born in 1950, 1959 and 1961, live in a quiet valley in the Dandenongs, on the Old Emerald Road, Monbulk, some thirty miles from Melbourne. They own just under thirteen acres of land, with its own small creek and fern gully, but lease eight acres to a Dutch migrant bulb-grower; Ivan Southall finds that keeping the rest in order is as much as he can manage in his spare time. The place was a run-down farm when they found it and, having paid five pounds deposit on it, moved there from East Brighton in January, 1950. They lived at first in a rough shack which went with the place. Now they have a modern house, with a self-contained bungalow twenty or thirty yards away, which Southall uses as a workroom; he did all the building himself, with his wife's help, and with the occasional assistance of friends and relations.

He did not publish his first serious adult book, *They Shall Not Pass Unseen*, until he was midway through his thirties. *They Shall Not Pass Unseen* is a popular, but accurate, history of 461 Squadron, RAAF, in which he served as a wartime Sunderland pilot in U.K. Coastal Command. In 1958 came *Bluey Truscott*, a biography of one of Australia's most spectacular World War II pilots, and in 1960 *Softly Tread the Brave*, describing the work of the RN Rendering Mines Safe Squad, notably the feats of two Australians, John Stuart Mould and Hugh Randal Syme. Although *Softly Tread the Brave* was tenth on the Australian best-seller list for 1960, its total sales disappointed its admirers. It seems likely, however, to achieve a permanent place among World War II documentary books. Its quality indicates that, in the writing of imaginative non-fiction, Southall has found his literary métier.

The danger seemed to be that he would remain a writer of war books and nothing else, and Southall had no wish to become a prisoner of one subject. In 1960 he proved to himself that he could write effectively of other things than war by turning out in six weeks a book which he calls 'a novel for children', entitled *Hills End*, published in 1962. This tells the story of seven children, cut off by a hurricane-force storm in a Queensland country town, who have to survive by their own resources. 'I was talking to my younger brother Gordon when he and his family visited us here one day,' Southall says. 'I was looking at his three children and my three, and I said to him, "I wonder what would happen to these kids if they were left to fend for themselves?" He said, "They'd die." I thought about it for a year, then sat down and wrote it.' When *Hills End* was out of the way, he began gathering material for the most ambitious book he had contemplated until then. This was *Woomera*, also published in 1962, which is an intimate description of life and work at the Woomera rocket range. The research and writing cost Southall thirteen months of full-time work and a year of part-time work; he spent many weeks at Woomera itself, and talking with the men who run and staff the Weapons Research Establishment at Salisbury, South Australia. This was hardly out of the way when he plunged into research for a factual story about the Anglican Bush Brothers, who began work in the Australian outback in 1897; he had it ready for the printer under the title *Parson on the Track*, by the middle of 1962.

Southall wanted to be a writer from the age of twelve when he scribbled his first stories in school exercise books. In 1942 he published, at his own expense, a book of short stories, *Out of the Dawn*, but he did not begin writing systematically until he was twenty-six, married, a father, and a decorated war pilot back in civilian life. He was born in the Melbourne suburb of Canterbury in 1921. He won a scholarship from Mont Albert Central to Box Hill Grammar School, but his father—a Presbyterian home missionary turned life assurance salesman—died in Southall's first year there, and the boy had to leave school and go to work. After trying other jobs he became a copy-boy on the Melbourne *Herald*. He was continually writing short stories and articles, and wanted to be a journalist, but, unable to find a place on *The Herald* reporting staff, he went into the process department, as an apprentice. He was still an apprentice when he joined the wartime RAAF, and began training as a pilot in 1942. He arrived in the U.K. in October, 1943, and was posted to 461 Squadron as second pilot of a Sunderland; six months later he became captain of his own flying-boat. Southall flew fifty-seven missions in all, and on August 12, 1944, his Sunderland sank a U-boat in the Bay of Biscay; for this feat he was awarded the D.F.C. and two members of his crew of eleven were mentioned in dispatches. At the end of 1944 he was posted to Kodak House, then RAAF headquarters in London, as a writer in the historical section. For him, the most important result of this posting was that at Kodak House he met Joy Blackburn. She was a Londoner, working as a photographic filing clerk in the public relations department, and Southall and she married in September, 1945. A year later they left for Australia, and in Melbourne Southall went back to process engraving.

When he finished his apprenticeship in November, 1947, he knew he must procrastinate no longer if he intended becoming a writer, but he also knew his earnings as a writer would be insufficient for some time to keep him and his wife and their infant son. So he scouted round East Brighton, where he was living, and found householders who were willing to pay him to cut their grass every two or three weeks; then he bought the motor mower and the 1928 Austin 12—he already had the obsolescent L. C. Smith typewriter—and left his process engraver's job. The motor mower presented no difficulties; he mastered it after a few minutes' practice. The Austin was a different matter. 'I had twelve hundred hours in my pilot's logbook,' he says, 'but I had never driven a car. I had to learn how.'

Thereafter he spent three and a half days a week driving about East Brighton, cutting other people's grass; the rest of his time he tried to write stories on the typewriter. His reputation as a grass-cutter grew; he was soon cutting grass four and a half days a week and spending that much less time at the typewriter. His reputation as a writer, however, stood still. Then his wife rebelled. She said some blunt things about her chagrin at discovering she had married a grass-cutter, not a writer. Southall knew she was right; he was frittering his life away to no purpose, and it could not go on. It was then he remembered two boys' stories he had written long before the war; he had scribbled these out in notebooks and all but forgotten them, but now he wondered if there was something in one or both of them worth resurrecting. He dug out the old notebooks and read the stories. One was called *Full Throttle to Fortune*, and the other *Wings of Vengeance*, and the central characters in both were two young men, Alan Grant and Dick Waters, who had a dog named Tickler as their faithful companion. Southall rewrote *Full Throttle to Fortune* in two weeks. He greatly lengthened it, but used the same two leading characters, only changing the faithful Tickler's name to Rex, possibly because Rex sounded more sophisticated. When his wife read the story she said, 'It's all right. But Dick Waters! What a dreadful name! You'll have to find something else. Why not Simon Blackburn?' Simon Blackburn was an ecclesiastically distinguished member of her family, the late Bishop Blackburn, and she chose his name because it had a good manly ring. Ivan Southall also liked the name, but decided to shorten it to Simon Black. He called the first book—originally *Full Throttle to Fortune*—*Meet Simon Black*; the second, *Wings of Vengeance*, became *Simon Black in Peril*. 'Simon,' says Southall, 'has been a very good friend. He's been my bread and butter for a long time, and kept us in business.' In Australia the Simon Black books have sold a hundred and thirty thousand copies, and one—*Simon Black in Space*—has been adopted as a supplementary reader for New South Wales State schools. Some have been translated into French, Norwegian, Dutch and Swedish, and two adapted for radio, and broadcast over the Australian Broadcasting Commission network.

Southall had a distressing experience some years ago. He started to write *Simon Black Takes Over*, and had a desperate battle to make the story flow. Disconcerted, he wondered if he was outgrowing Simon Black. He was troubled, not merely—or even chiefly—because he feared the loss of his best source of regular income, but because he did not care to contemplate a world in which he would be unable to turn to Simon Black for excitement, companionship, and escape. 'Through Simon Black,' he says, 'I have hair-raising adventures, as all men hanker to do, and I didn't welcome the thought that it was all going to be taken from me.' As things turned out, it wasn't. When he began writing *Simon Black Takes Over* he must have been having one of the dry periods which all authors experience. Since then he has met no obstacles of the kind and has written of Simon Black's adventures with all his old verve and relish.

When he and his wife and their son, then nearly three, went to live at Monbulk in January, 1950, he had two hundred and fifty pounds. This was soon exhausted, so he took a job helping a Monbulk carrier, who two days a week delivered a load of stuff from the Dandenongs to the Victoria Market, in Melbourne, and on the return journey fetched supplies for ten or eleven local shops. For four years, every Tuesday and Thursday, Southall got up at one-thirty in the morning, often after punching the typewriter until ten o'clock the night before, and was away until five in the afternoon. It was hard work, but it paid him an invaluable nine pounds a week. He was glad enough to drop the market excursions when rising earnings from writing permitted him to do so, but, in a later period of money shortage, he worked for some years as a local grocer's Friday delivery-man, at three pounds a week. Such odd jobs seem to be behind him now. Except when he is away gathering material he writes from about ten-thirty in the morning until ten at night, with an evening meal break of two to three hours.

He does not like writing potboiling books, such as the six paperback novels he churned out for a Sydney publisher in 1959 and 1960. These were all stories of the air war, and good action writing, but they gave him little satisfaction. 'I wrote one every three or four months, while doing other work,' he says, 'and I had to sweat over them. I don't intend writing any more; by the time I had written six I'd said all I had to say in that medium.'

Southall, a serious man, has a strong religious strain, which he probably inherited from his home-missionary father, but he says he neglected his spiritual life from the time he went to the war until five or six years after settling at Monbulk. Then a new minister, the Rev. John Blacker, took over the Monbulk Methodist circuit, and looked about for young men to help him in his work. One he chose was Ivan Southall. Within three months Southall was a lay preacher, and nearly every Sunday he conducts a service in a church in some Melbourne suburb or nearer country centre. He seems to have a special gift for retelling Bible stories in terms children understand. He says his sermons and addresses, to both adults and children, are a revolt against normal conventions. He does not moralize, but tries to relate life as it is to the Scriptures as they are, and will attack any convention he considers absurd, no matter who supports it. He is invited back to many churches. Others, which he has offended, or possibly failed to interest, do not ask him to come again. He is always sorry if he learns that views he has expressed have given offence to a congregation, but he will never modify his opinions for fear of upsetting his listeners. He would rather say nothing than do that. 'I believe in what I'm doing,' he says, 'or I wouldn't be doing it. Without faith, I can see no reason for life, nor any answer to the riddle of the world. All this would have no meaning.'

A belief in man's spiritual survival is the underlying theme of all Southall's books, even the most ephemeral of them. It is also the theme of several books for adults and children which he has either partly written or planned. He considers he has not yet made a contribution of value to Australian writing, and in pessimistic moments he doubts that he ever will. If he does so, however, it will probably take the form of a book, or a group of books, on the theme of man's spiritual survival. That is the belief that Ivan Southall lives by, and that he will ever cease to live by it is highly improbable.

FICTION

Out of the Dawn. Short stories (Melbourne, National Press) 1942

For Children

(Published by Angus & Robertson, Sydney)

Meet Simon Black 1950
Simon Black in Peril 1951
Simon Black in Space 1952
Simon Black in Coastal Command 1953
Simon Black and the Spaceman 1955
Simon Black Takes Over 1959
Simon Black at Sea 1961
Hills End 1962

(Published by Angus & Robertson, London)

Simon Black in China 1954
Simon Black in the Antarctic 1956

GENERAL

(Published by Angus & Robertson, Sydney)

They Shall Not Pass Unseen 1956
Bluey Truscott 1958
Softly Tread the Brave 1960
Woomera 1962

(Published by Lansdowne Press, Melbourne)

Parson on the Track 1962

For Children

Journey Into Mystery 1961

Southall is also the author of six paperback novels published by Horwitz, Sydney, in 1959-60, and of three commissioned documentary books; these are: *The Weaver from Meltham* (Melbourne, Whitcombe & Tombs, 1950); *The Story of the Hermitage* (Melbourne, Cheshire, 1956); and *A Tale of Box Hill* (Melbourne, Box Hill City Council, 1957).

Max Harris

MIDDLE-AGE OF A BOY PRODIGY

ANYBODY acclaimed as a boy genius is apt to find the going hard when he leaves boyhood behind. Max Harris knows how hard the going can be. When Harris, now in the early forties, bustles through Adelaide, on his way to or from the bookshop in which he is a partner, there is nothing about him to suggest he was once, to some idolators, a youthful prodigy of literature. 'For years,' he says, 'I've been the oldest *enfant terrible* in the business, but now I'm living it down.' This is true. Harris is not only a successful bookseller, but also one of the most industrious writers in Australia, with a large weekly output of words, in serious prose, verse, and high-grade journalism. In his spare time, such as it is, he takes a leading part in editing the monthly, *Australian Book Review*, and the quarterly, *Australian Letters*, and he also edits *Verse in Australia*, a yearly anthology of Australian poetry; these editorial activities enable him to exert a strong influence on many young Australian writers, and steer them toward an aesthetic philosophy which Harris sums up as 'Australianism without bushwhackery'. For good measure, he is making a mark as a literary, drama, film and art critic on national television. The young Max Harris's admirers erred in proclaiming him a boy genius, but they had something on their side; before turning twenty-three, he published two books of verse, *The Gift of Blood* and *Dramas from the Sky*, and a novel, *The Vegetative Eye*. None of these was a popular success, and *The Vegetative Eye* was mercilessly dismembered by some critics; but, whatever the Max Harris of those days thought of the critics who drew-and-quartered him, the Max Harris of today agrees with much, though not all, of what they said.

Few Australians remember the title of any book Max Harris wrote in his boy-genius period; what many Australians remember still is that he was a central figure in the celebrated literary hoax of 1944, known as the Ern Malley affair. Harris was co-editor of the experimental literary quarterly, *Angry Penguins*—at that time being published in Melbourne—when it devoted a whole issue to the poetry of one

Ern Malley. The claim by *Angry Penguins* that Ern Malley's poetry was a major literary discovery created an excited controversy which ended with the disclosure that the poems had been fabricated by the poets, James McAuley and Harold Stewart, one afternoon when they had nothing better to do. Seeking to debunk the work of 'modernist' poets, McAuley and Stewart assembled what they claimed to be a series of meaningless verbal fragments in verse-form, and invented Ern Malley to go with them, then foisted them on *Angry Penguins*. Ern Malley became renowned as the author of such portentously cryptic lines as

> In the twenty-fifth year of my age
> I find myself to be a dromedary . . . .

The story of the hoax was widely published, abroad as well as in Australia, but perhaps the most spectacular consequence of it was the prosecution, in Adelaide, of Harris, as co-editor of *Angry Penguins*, for having published indecent literature—the Ern Malley poems. He was fined five pounds.

Today Max Harris bears no scars of that experience and nothing about him shows that he was once hailed as a young genius. His frame is blocky and powerful, and he wears his dark curly hair cut short. His roundish olive-skinned face has a blunt nose, alert bright eyes, a good-humoured mouth. He is a prolific talker, although never an overbearing one. When he discusses himself, as he was at the Ern Malley period, it is with the kind of detached amusement that any tolerant man in the forties might feel for any brash, but reasonably talented, youth. He knew when he returned to Adelaide in 1946, after *Angry Penguins* ceased publication, that he had to forget his literary past and try to make other people forget it also. He must have been tempted at that time to try his luck in some other city than Adelaide; it is never easy for a wonder boy to go home, admitting it has all been a mistake. That he should have had the mettle to do so says something of value about Max Harris.

He was born in Adelaide in 1921, grew up in Mt Gambier, and at thirteen won a scholarship which gave him three years as a boarder at St Peter's College, Adelaide. There his embryo literary talents excited the interest of the English master, J. S. Padman, a poet of some note. 'I was always interested in writing,' Harris says, 'but my chief delight at St Peter's came from my success at Australian Rules football—I was the school's first rover—and my winning of the 440 yards championship.'

When he left school he worked for the Adelaide *News*, first as a copy-boy, then as a cadet reporter, but Adelaide's then Jury Professor of English Literature, Professor J. I. M. Stewart*—better known as Michael Innes, the writer of detective novels—decided his talents were being wasted. Stewart arranged for Harris to work in the university library, and this job, while not a sinecure, paid a regular salary and enabled him to study also. That period was an unprecedentedly exciting one in Adelaide's intellectual history, and Harris and his friends, as champions of new concepts of thought and self-expression, were uuder suspicion by orthodox student groups. One day some of them, including Harris, were seized by their opponents, frogmarched to the nearby Torrens River, and flung into the water, clothes and all. It was not, however, a total victory for the reactionaries. Harris still remembers with pleasure the sight of a group of his own friends hurtling toward his attackers, who were presently gasping and spluttering in the Torrens beside him.

The spread of World War II caused a truce to be called in the intellectual war of the University of Adelaide. Max Harris joined the army, but the War Organization of Industry Department claimed him as an economist after four months, and he spent the next few years helping to organize Australia's industrial war effort. Through it all he continued to write prolifically and take a vigorous hand in literary affairs generally. He was one of the young men who launched the quarterly *Angry Penguins* in Adelaide in 1942; the magazine took its name from a phrase in one of his poems, '. . . angry penguins of the night', and his personality was stamped all over it. When *Angry Penguins* moved to Melbourne in 1943, at the invitation of John Reed, later director of the Museum of Modern Art of Australia, Harris went with it. 'We published some drivel,' Harris says today, with disarming candour. 'Quite a lot was meaningless nonsense, but the magazine did attract people who could find no other outlets for their work, and it helped to produce a new Australian culture. Out of *Angry Penguins* emerged painters like Sidney Nolan and Arthur Boyd, and writers like Geoffrey Dutton and Peter Cowan. We published oversea writers, too, including Dylan Thomas, who was considered a posturing crackpot then.'

Max Harris regrets nothing about his *Angry Penguins* period. He says if he could turn back the clock he would change nothing; he would not undo even the Ern Malley hoax. He doubtless realizes that his experiences then went to the making of what he is now and what he will become, precisely as his boyhood in Mt Gambier did, and the football he played for St Peter's, and his work as a newspaper reporter. But when he landed back in Adelaide in 1946 he had little to show for all his exertions, except the wreckage of his literary

* For other references to Professor Stewart see the profile of Nancy Cato.

reputation. He knew he had to start all over again, and he threw himself into work. His bookselling business grew, but it was seven or eight years before he began to re-emerge as a writer. His first significant piece of writing, after the Ern Malley affair had become a memory, was a longish set of verses called *The Tantanoola Tiger*, a retelling of the old legend in sharp, salty, unromanticized terms. He has published other verses since then, and these have won him new respect from serious critics.

As a writer, his major concern for some time has been with a study he is making of the non-fictional literature of Australia. He intends to put this out as a two-volume work, examining in one volume the literary (not the historical) value of all non-fictional Australian writings, and publishing in a second volume a collection of such writings; to do this he has made a critical scrutiny of every Australian reminiscent document, except fiction, from the First Fleet's arrival until today. Of his findings Harris says: 'They may well determine such things, for example, as which of the Australian explorers had the most highly developed literary talent. The same applies to the squatters, settlers, and writers of reminiscences from the goldfields periods. It also seems possible that, as a by-product, we shall unearth a few classics which have been lying round awaiting recognition.' He is working alone on a separate book, which will be a study of the Australian character, 'beginning with the old bushwhackers and the goldfields men and working down to the larrikins of Bourke Street and Woolloomooloo, and including a challenge to Henry Lawson's theory of the origins of mateship'; and with Geoffrey Dutton on a book about class in Australia—the way, he says, that class patterns, or their absence, determined the kind of culture Australia built up in the nineteenth century, and affected the directions of twentieth century Australian literature and poetry, as well as national habits, customs, and traditions.

While admiring the scholarly purpose behind these works, some of Harris's friends regret that he appears to have turned away, if only for the time being perhaps, from the kind of writing which would give full play to his powers of imagination. He published a section of a novel, provisionally entitled *Biography of a No-Hoper*, in a 1960 anthology, *Southern Festival*, and its quality roused hopes that he was about to produce a novel of importance. Discussing the theme, Harris says: 'I was a kid in Mt Gambier in the economic depression of the 1930s, and this is a story of the unemployed largely in that area. A character who was a kind of king among them is the central figure. The novel is dry, unsentimental, and humorous. It's a gesture, among other things, against status-seeking and conformism.' Harris said late in 1960 that *Biography of a No-Hoper* was more than half-finished, but eighteen months later he reported it at a standstill, adding: 'Highly frustrating!'

Whatever Max Harris has done or failed to do since he crept back to Adelaide in 1946, he has clearly travelled a long way since he wrote *The Vegetative Eye*, and was all but smothered—as a literary man—in the vortex of the Ern Malley affair. Looking back, he believes he enjoyed nothing in his *Angry Penguins* period so much as two months he spent, in collaboration with a woman writer named Elizabeth Lambert, 'ghosting' a book of memoirs for the great Australian vaudeville comedian, Mo—the late Roy Rene. *Mo's Memoirs* should have been an Australian best-seller, but it was a flop. Max Harris believes he knows why. 'We handled Mo's story badly,' he admits. 'To us, he was a sociological phenomenon, and that was how we wrote his story. The Bourke Street boys didn't understand it, while the highbrows said, "What are you doing, putting out this book by a lowbrow comic!" The result was a failure at all points.'

Harris's association with Mo—another Adelaidean, incidentally, although for most of his life a national figure as a music-hall comedian—remains one of his cherished memories. A more law-abiding man than Mo never walked, but, paradoxically, the Australian underworld idolized him. Through Mo, Max Harris, then twenty-three, and still naïve under a varnish of sophistication, met some of Australia's most notorious gunmen. They accepted him, because he came vouched for by Mo, and he spent many hours, drinking and yarning with them. 'Those experiences convinced me of the simple-mindedness of underworld people,' Harris says. 'They all insisted on telling me their life stories, and left me satisfied that all they want is recognition and affection.' When Max Harris says this you suspect that, one day, he might take the material he stored away in his mind when he entered the underworld as Mo's guest, and turn it into a novel. You also feel that, if he does so, the novel will more closely resemble the kind of novel Damon Runyon would have written if Damon Runyon had been an Australian than it will resemble *The Vegetative Eye*. Stronger evidence that the youthful Max Harris is dead, buried and past all hope—or danger—of resurrection would be hard to find.

FICTION

The Vegetative Eye (Adelaide, Reed & Harris) 1943

VERSE

The Gift of Blood (Adelaide, Jindyworobak Club) 1940
Dramas from the Sky (Adelaide, Adelaide University Arts Association) 1942
The Coorong and Other Poems (Adelaide, Mary Martin Bookshop) 1955

Harris edited, and contributed an introductory essay to, *Ern Malley's Poems* (Melbourne, Lansdowne Press: 1961).

Geoffrey Dutton

"WHY NOT A BIOGRAPHY?"

AUSTRALIA has bred many poets and novelists, but for some reason few biographers worth mentioning. One of Australia's only substantial biographers, Geoffrey Dutton, might never have written a biography at all if the idea that he should do so had not been planted in his mind by an Irishman. In 1952 Dutton was in Adelaide, his home town, in the grip of more or less impenetrable despair about his literary future. To him, the outlook was uniformly dreary, although he had some years earlier published a novel and a book of verse, and was about to publish a travel book. For he had just spent a year or so working on a novel, which his London publishers had rejected. Weighed down by a sense of failure, Dutton talked to his friend, A. Norman Jeffares, then Jury Professor of English Language and Literature at the University of Adelaide.

'Why don't you,' asked Jeffares, an imaginative Irishman and himself an author, 'try something different? Why not a biography?'

'A biography of whom?' Dutton asked, not much impressed.

'Why not Light?' said Jeffares, naming the man who, as South Australia's first Surveyor-General, planned and laid out Adelaide.

Dutton went away and thought about Light, and the longer he thought the more interested he became. He did not know much about Light except superficial facts, but he kept remembering Light's self-portrait hanging in the National Art Gallery, Adelaide. This depicts a handsome man in the early thirties with intense eyes, strong curling dark hair, a sensitive yet commanding nose, and a resolute mouth. The picture had haunted Dutton for years; such a face, he felt, could have belonged only to an unusual man. He decided to follow Professor Jeffares's advice, and so *Founder of a City*, Dutton's biography of Colonel William Light, was conceived.

Founder of a City is among the ablest Australian biographies yet written, but Dutton, who is humble about his work, claims nothing for it, except that it is as accurate as devoted research could make it. 'Its success,' he says, 'is a symptom of the change which has come over Australia in the last few years. In 1945 it would have fallen flat, but there is real hunger among us now to know the kind of people we are, and books like the biography of Light help us to discover things about ourselves. When the war ended I had a mad urge to get to Europe and explore the sources of civilization, and I did spend some years overseas. But once started on Light I soon realized it was more interesting to explore our origins here than in Europe.'

Few people have more reason than Geoffrey Dutton to be interested in Australia's origins and development. His great-grandfather, an Englishman, in 1838 founded South Australia's first stud sheep station, Anlaby, ten miles from Kapunda, and Dutton was born there in 1922. He is a lean man (although his body has thickened somewhat in recent years), six feet three inches tall, and prematurely grey, who looks at the world with tolerantly quizzical eyes. He can laugh at himself, as well as at other people. He tells the story of a woman who went into an Adelaide bookshop to buy a copy of *Founder of a City*.

'You're lucky, madam,' the salesgirl said. 'We happen to have a copy signed by the author.'

'No, thank you,' the customer replied. 'I came in to buy a clean copy.'

He was educated at Geelong Grammar School, and had eighteen months studying Arts at the University of Adelaide before enlisting in the RAAF in 1941. Anchored in Australia as a flying instructor for most of the war, he managed to get into the fighting, flying artillery-spotting Austers at Bougainville, only at the end. He found little satisfaction in teaching other young men to fly while the war was on, but an experience he had while working as a flying instructor was a least the inspiration of one of the most memorable short stories written by an Australian in the last twenty years. This story, *The Wedge-Tailed Eagle*, describes how two bored air force instructors hunt an eagle in the air and kill it, then recoil from the deed in shame. The story has been republished many times, and appears in English, American and Soviet Russian anthologies, as well as Australian. '*The Wedge-Tailed Eagle* isn't a story, but a report,' Dutton says. 'The episode happened when I was flying Tiger Moths at Parkes, N.S.W.' To Dutton, the pursuit of the eagle was 'one of the idiotic things you do in wartime'. He brackets it with another incident in which he flew under a bridge over the South Esk River at Longford, Tasmania, where he was stationed for a while. 'I've always wanted to go back,' he says, 'and take a look at that bridge, to see how close I went to breaking my neck. To the wartime flying instructor, working with unskilful trainees, the temptation to test his own skill by diving under bridges or chasing eagles was nearly irresistible.'

Dutton was luckier than many young men were who had years of war service, because when peace came he knew what he wanted to do: he was determined to become a writer. He had already shown some talent; a volume of his poems, *Nightflight and Sunrise*, had appeared in 1944, and a few of his short stories had been published in literary magazines. Discharged from the RAAF, he returned to the University of Adelaide for a couple of terms; then in 1946, he and his wife Ninette, whom he had married late in the war, went to England. He took a B.A. degree at Oxford in 1949, moved into a cottage in the South of France and wrote hard. He turned out a number of poems and short stories, and wrote a novel, *The Mortal and the Marble*, which was published in 1950. He wrote another novel while he was in Europe, but his publishers did not like it; nor did he when the rapturous flush of literary creation passed.

And then he found himself hungering for Australia. There was one difficulty, though; both he and his wife detest sea travel, and they recoiled from the prospect of coming home by ship. They decided to make as much of the journey as possible by land, and set out from England in a car, along a route few Australians have followed, through Europe, Turkey, Syria, Iraq, Persia, Afghanistan, Pakistan, India and Ceylon. Dutton likes making such journeys, through out-of-the-way countries, by roads which are often little better than tracks; he has made several of them and hopes to make many more. They help to satisfy his appetite for action, for he is by no means merely the bookish and introspective academic his literary record might suggest. On the contrary he has a talent for practical, as well as aesthetic, things; for instance, he is a skilled automotive engineer and drives cars at high speed, yet without the slightest recklessness.

Back in Adelaide, after his car trip from England, he wrote the story of that journey, and it came out as a book eighteen months or so later as *A Long Way South*. It was at that time that he spent a year working on the novel which ended by pleasing neither his publishers nor himself. If he was ever tempted to forsake writing, it must have been then; and so Professor Jeffares's proposal that he should write a biography of Light was a kind of cross-roads on his literary journey.

Once started, he became absorbed, not only in Light's Australian period, from 1836 to 1839, but in everything which had helped to shape Light's character and actions from the day he was born in Penang, some fifty years before he came to Australia. Dutton travelled tens of thousands of miles, both inside and outside Australia, in search of material. In his own words, the hunt was 'a detective story . . . conducted with a very sparse set of clues'. The book was not completed for about seven years, but, while working on it, Dutton published two travel books, *Africa in Black and White* and *States of the Union*, and a book of verse *Antipodes in Shoes*.

His success as a biographer does not mean he has abandoned his interest in poetry and fiction. 'I still think,' he says, 'that poetry is the highest form of writing, with the novel close behind. I have for a long time been thinking over the novel I want to write—either one long volume or a trilogy, beginning in the Australia of the early 1940s and ending about now. I feel that period has been as significant as any in Australia's history. The composition and outlook of the nation have greatly changed in that time, and I want my novel to picture that change.'

He probably will not begin work on this big novel for some years. It is a work that will take time, and Dutton's time is heavily occupied at present. While meeting all the demands of his post as Senior Lecturer in English Literature at the University of Adelaide, he yet manages to put out a steady stream of art and book criticism for daily newspapers and periodical publications. He is a regular contributor of poetry to literary magazines, and a new book of verse by him, *Flowers & Fury*, was published late in 1962. Several other minor literary projects have all helped to keep him from the novel. In 1960 he accepted the general editorship of a series of booklets, *Australian Writers and Their Work*, published by Lansdowne Press, Melbourne; the series was launched in 1961 with a booklet by Dutton himself on Patrick White and one by me on Norman Lindsay. In 1961 Dutton published a booklet on Walt Whitman in a British series, *Writers and Critics*, critically examining the work of great modern literary figures; and in 1962 became Australian independent editor for Penguin Books—a spare-time post. A substantial literary undertaking also got in the way of his other ambitions. He found that he wished to write another biography, this time of Edward John Eyre, the explorer, whose life, like William Light's, was closely interlocked with South Australia's early days. Eyre's journey from Adelaide to Albany in 1840-41 is among the great feats of Australian exploration.

Professor Jeffares, who suggested the Light biography, is implicated in the Eyre biography also, but indirectly. Jeffares left Adelaide in 1956 to become Professor of English Literature at the University of Leeds, Yorkshire, and at his invitation, Dutton went to Leeds in 1960 to conduct a course in Australian Literature. One of the first people he met, after he and his wife and their infant son were settled, was a West Indian negro, who was working at the university as an anthropologist. Having discovered that Dutton was Australian, the West Indian asked, 'Why did you send us that scoundrel Eyre?'

'Eyre!' Dutton said. 'We had an Eyre in Australia, but he was no scoundrel.'

'Well,' the West Indian persisted, 'he put down the 1865 rebellion in Jamaica by the most savage measures.'

'There must be some mistake,' Dutton said. 'The Eyre I know of treated the Australian aborigines in the most humanitarian way. It couldn't be the same man!'

His curiosity was roused, however, and he looked into Eyre's record. To his astonishment, he discovered that his West Indian informant was right. As Governor-in-Chief of Jamaica, Eyre had quelled a native rising with appalling brutality; English public opinion was outraged and Eyre himself disappeared from public life. 'I still can't believe there wasn't some terrible mistake,' Dutton says. 'What apparently happened is so out of character with the Eyre Australia knew that I believe he must have been framed.' Dutton intends to discover the truth and, whatever it shows, print it in the biography he is working on. He knows moral courage is often required of the biographer writing of men who have lived in comparatively recent times. In writing *Founder of a City* he faced at least one challenge to his professional integrity. Light had a mistress, an English girl named Maria Gandy, who arrived in South Australia with him and lived with him until his death, then married Dr George Mayo, of Adelaide. Now Mayo is no less familiar a name than Dutton in South Australia; and Geoffrey Dutton was unsure when *Founder of a City* came out how members of the Mayo family would take the disclosure that Light's mistress was entangled in their family tree. Soon after the book was published George Mayo, Senior Lecturer in Genetics at the University of Adelaide, came to Dutton and congratulated him on the biography.

'I'm delighted,' Mayo said, 'to discover that my great-grandmother was such an interesting woman.'

Dutton hopes that whenever he publishes prickly biographical material the response of anyone it touches will be equally civilized and no less scholarly.

FICTION

The Mortal and the Marble (London, Chapman & Hall) 1950

VERSE

Nightflight and Sunrise (Melbourne, Reed & Harris) 1944
Antipodes in Shoes (Sydney, Edwards & Shaw) 1958
Flowers & Fury (Melbourne, Cheshire) 1962

GENERAL

A Long Way South (London, Chapman & Hall) 1953
Africa in Black and White (London, Chapman & Hall) 1956
States of the Union (London, Chapman & Hall) 1958
Founder of a City (Melbourne, Cheshire) 1960
Patrick White (Melbourne, Lansdowne Press) 1961
Walt Whitman (Edinburgh, Oliver & Boyd) 1961

Dutton is also the author of the introduction and commentaries in *Paintings of S. T. Gill* (Adelaide, Rigby) 1962.

G. M. Glaskin

A WORLD OF HIS OWN

WHETHER a stockbroker steps down or steps up when he becomes an author is a matter of opinion. Whatever one's view of the matter, Gerald Marcus Glaskin has made the step from stockbroking to authorship, for better or worse. Even though his books sell well, he is making less money than he made in his eight years as a stockbroker in Singapore, but he has no regrets. 'I was always fascinated by finance,' he says, 'and, never having had a penny of my own beforehand, I enjoyed handling big accounts as a stockbroker. But writing gives me deeper satisfaction.' Glaskin, who is candid about himself and his aspirations, admits he might some day go back to stockbroking, but this appears to be unlikely unless he writes himself out, as authors sometimes do. He is in a happier position, however, than most men are who adopt the fairly chancy career of authorship; if his books should ever cease to sell, he has all the experience required to earn a living in the tough and shifty financial world.

It is mildly puzzling that the name of this Western Australian should have been slow to register with his fellow-countrymen; none of his published novels has had in Australia anything like the popular success or critical notice it achieved in England. This must hurt him, although he denies any sense of hurt; for every prophet likes to be honoured in his own country, even if he rarely is. But Glaskin does not intend to change the style of novel he writes. 'The novels I have written,' he says, 'were written because I wanted to write them, not with an eye on their commercial success, although I'm pleased that some other people, as well as myself, seem to like them. I believe the success in London of my first novel, *A World of Our Own*, was due to its unconventionality. If I'd brought out a more orthodox kind of novel, it probably wouldn't have been noticed. I'm told I overwrite. Perhaps so, but I hope I always shall. As far as I can see, nearly every novelist whose work has lived has been accused of overwriting.'

The U.K. edition of *A World of Our Own*, which is set in Western Australia, and examines the efforts of a number of World War II servicemen to fit themselves into the post-war world, sold twelve thousand copies. Most of these were sold overseas, and British critics generally praised the novel more generously than Australian critics did; the English novelist, Sir Charles Snow, called it 'one of the most interesting manuscripts that has come into my hands for a long time. . . .' For reasons which nobody, including Glaskin, can explain, a Norwegian translation of *A World of Our Own* was even more successful; it became one of Norway's twelve most popular novels of 1957, selling fifteen thousand copies in a hard-cover edition and thirty thousand as a paperback.

Glaskin was born in 1923, and probably has his best work yet to do. He is tallish, with a regular profile, good teeth, and restless dark-brown eyes, and his stiff black hair is turning grey. His neck and face, and his hard-muscled slender body, are burned a deep shining brown, because Glaskin spends a lot of time out of doors, wherever he happens to be. In the middle of 1961 he went to Europe, and established himself in a studio-flat in Amsterdam. He did not know how long he would stay abroad; at least a year, but perhaps two, three or four years, or even more. He intended using Holland as a base from which to explore Europe, while keeping in close touch with his London publishers and agents. In a letter from Amsterdam he said: 'My routine here changes from day to day. There is so much to see and do, museums, art galleries, symphony concerts, opera, ballet, night-clubs, and the bars. On wet days I write.'

In Australia he lives—or at any rate lived before going overseas—in his own house, in the Perth suburb of Graylands, and nearly every afternoon he drove in his station waggon to Swanbourne beach, about two miles away, and walked on the sand, alone, for an hour or more, thinking out what he would write next day. 'At home, I work for about three hours every morning, and by noon I expect to have two thousand words written,' he said. 'After lunch, I always go down to the beach, unless I have something else I must do. The beach stretches for three miles, and it's an ideal place to think; there's no telephone to ring or people to get at me there. From the beach, I come home, edit whatever I wrote that morning, and send it off to be typed. At night, I sleep on what I've thought out while walking on the beach, and next morning it's bursting to get out and on to paper.' The method was obviously effective, so far as Glaskin was concerned; almost embarrassingly effective, because when I called on him at Graylands he had two novels and a book of short stories lined up with his London publisher, and was well advanced with the writing of a factual book about Australia's North. If he has an obvious fault as a writer it is that he is excessively prolific. On the whole, however, this is a fault most authors would envy him, and most publishers would put down to his credit, while his readers do not seem to penalize him for it by refusing to read his books. But it means his novels tend to accumulate, and often two or three years elapse between the time he finishes a book and its appearance in print.

The eldest of seven children, he was born in Perth. After a State school education, he had several youthful jobs before enlisting in the wartime Royal Australian Navy in 1941. He began to write professionally in 1943, while lying in Hollywood Military Hospital, Perth. He was recovering from injuries suffered in a wartime accident, which occurred when he was serving as a rating in the armed merchant cruiser *Kanimbla*. Coils of signal-halyard wire, under tension on winches, broke loose and wrapped like a boa constrictor round Glaskin's torso; they pinioned his arms and cut deep into his flesh, then snapped and freed him. Naval surgeons wished to amputate his right arm, but saved it in the end, and sent him to recover in Hollywood.

He could not use his arms, and the man in the next hospital bed, another war casualty, could not use his legs. They passed the time arguing about every subject under the sun, and reading anything that came their way. One day Glaskin grunted, 'I could do better than that myself,' after reading a magazine short story which seemed to him unusually piffling. 'All right,' said the man in the next bed. 'Why don't you?' Glaskin had played about with writing since he was nine, but did not know if he had any real talent. And there was one big difficulty in the way of his accepting the challenge: he could not use his hands to hold a pencil. That problem was solved easily enough, however; he dictated his story to the man in the next bed who wrote it down by hand. It was a naval story, entitled *Got Him!*, and though Glaskin does not consider it any masterpiece, it must have had some quality, because the Perth *Western Mail* published it. Since then Glaskin has never stopped writing for long. By the time he was discharged from Hollywood and invalided out of the Navy, he had written twelve short stories, dictating most of them to the man in the next bed, and sold them all.

Out of uniform, he took a job in Sydney with a soap manufacturing firm at the end of 1943; his work was to collate sales statistics and write radio advertising blurbs. Finding these tasks unexciting, he went down one day to the RAAF recruiting depot, thinking he might be able to talk his way past the medical examiners and enlist in a ground staff job; the doctors must have been drowsy, because they failed to notice his RAN scars, and passed him for aircrew. He trained in Canada as a navigator. All the time he was worried that his RAN past would catch up with him, but nothing happened until the day he graduated at Winnipeg. Then he was summoned to the presence of Air Vice-Marshal S. J. Goble, RAAF liaison officer in Canada. Goble handed Glaskin a sheaf of papers and asked, 'Any connection?' They were Glaskin's RAN discharge papers. Knowing he could not lie his way out of this one, he said, 'Yes, sir.' Goble looked severe, but his eyes twinkled. 'You've been a very very naughty boy,' he admonished. 'Don't do it again!' That was the only reproof Glaskin ever suffered for his irregular entry into the RAAF.

His war service ended tamely, however. The Axis was already crumbling when he graduated, and he finished the war, as a flying officer in a ferry crew operating inside Australia, far from any battle area. He remembers with no particular enthusiasm his early years back in civilian life. He had a year managing a Fremantle sports shop, then two years as sales statistician in Western Australia with the Ford Motor Company. About the end of 1948 another motor firm offered him a job in Singapore, and this he accepted. Not having to go to Singapore for six months, he felt this was his chance to do something he had wanted to do for a long time. His mind had been busy with a theme for a novel about young men like himself who had come home from the war and were trying to adjust themselves to the peacetime world; his problem had been to find time to write it. Resigning from Ford's, he took his RAAF deferred pay, and went to stay alone in his grandmother's cottage at Safety Bay, about forty miles from Perth. There, in about five months, he wrote his novel, four hundred thousand words long. The full story of this manuscript's adventures is too complex to be told here; it is enough that six years later, having been reduced to a hundred and sixty thousand words, it was published in London as *A World of Our Own*.

Glaskin had meanwhile settled into Singapore and grown to like the life. He had switched from motor merchandising to stockbroking after a year, and become a partner in his firm. He was busy with his daily work, and found little time for writing. Then, late in 1954, he fell ill with spinal meningitis and tropical infective hepatitis. He went home to Western Australia for treatment, and after a long struggle recovered his health—or most of it. And, as he had done in Hollywood Military Hospital more than ten years before, he used his idle hours of convalescence to work at writing, and produced his second novel, *A Minor Portrait*. It was less successful than *A World of Our Own*, but sold six thousand copies in hard covers, and seventy-five thousand later as a paperback. Glaskin still has some qualms about that paperback. 'The publishers,' he says, 'changed the title. They called it *The Mistress*, which seemed a little dubious to me. But the public evidently liked it.'

His doctors declared him fit in September, 1955, but they did not wish him to risk his health in Singapore. He had to find work, however, because he was nearly broke, and his father and mother were both ill; and all his efforts to find an acceptable job in Australia failed. He had another novel he wished to write at that time, and he applied for a Commonwealth Literary Fund grant, but, while he was still awaiting a decision, his money ran out, and, with his family needing help, he decided to defy his doctors and go back to Singapore. 'A week after I got to Singapore,' he says, 'the Commonwealth Literary Fund announced I'd been granted a thousand pounds to enable me to write my novel. It came too late, and I had to decline the offer. I'll never write that novel now; I've outgrown it.'

He wrote his third novel, *A Change of Mind*, in Singapore while working full-time at stockbroking; but when he started in 1957 on *A Lion in the Sun* (which he considers his first important novel) he realized he must choose between business and writing. 'I got ten thousand words done in seven months,' he says. 'At that rate it would have taken me about fourteen years or so to finish the novel, which is two hundred and fifty thousand words long.' So he sold his stockbroking partnership, and retired from the firm at the end of the year, buried himself on a friend's rubber estate in Johore, and finished *A Lion in the Sun* in a few months.

After returning to Western Australia late in 1958, he wrote two more novels, both of which were published overseas in 1961. One, set in Australia, is called *A Waltz Through the Hills*; the other, a story of Malaya, has the engaging title *The Beach of Passionate Love*—a literal translation of the name of a Malayan beach which Glaskin knows well. He also made a collection of what he considers to be his best short stories; these, all set in Australia, he put together under the title *A Small Selection*.

Late in 1960 he found himself committed to the writing of his first non-fiction book, *The Land That Sleeps*. This book about North Australia was commissioned by a New York publisher, who issued it in September, 1961. Glaskin did not expect its findings to strengthen his popularity with his fellow countrymen, and he said of *The Land That Sleeps* just after he finished it: 'This will be a controversial book. After spending two months travelling eleven thousand miles through the North, I concluded that something bigger must be done with the North than anything Australia could do with it. Many Australians won't like my solution, but I think it's a realistic solution, if one remembers that China's population will be a thousand million by 1965 and India's population heaven knows what.'

It would be idle to try here to give any up-to-the-minute picture of what Glaskin is currently doing as a writer or a man; most authors are reasonably predictable but he, a man of tremendous zest for work and life, is not. Only two things may be said about him with any kind of assurance. One is that he is a writer of both energy and talent. The other is that probably nobody—including, or even least of all, himself—could say at present precisely where he is going. He is, however, indubitably going there fast.

FICTION

A World of Our Own (London, James Barrie) 1955
A Minor Portrait (London, James Barrie) 1957
A Change of Mind (London, Barrie & Rockliff) 1959
A Lion in the Sun (London, Barrie & Rockliff) 1960
The Beach of Passionate Love (London, Barrie & Rockliff) 1961
A Waltz Through the Hills (London, Barrie & Rockliff) 1961
A Small Selection. Short stories (London, Barrie & Rockliff) 1962

GENERAL

The Land That Sleeps (New York, Doubleday) 1961

David Forrest

ELEVEN YEARS' HARD LABOUR

EVERY author knows the man or woman who corners him at a party and says, 'I think I'll write a book,' as if announcing a decision to mow the lawn. David Forrest has met many such enthusiasts since his first novel *The Last Blue Sea* won the Dame Mary Gilmore Award in 1958, and he says: 'The next time somebody tells me he's going to write a book, I'm going to take him upstairs and show him the stack of typewritten sheets which ended up, after long years, as *The Last Blue Sea*. If he still wants to write a book then, I might believe he means it.' Forrest does not know how many quarto sheets he filled with typing in his efforts to write *The Last Blue Sea*; probably about two thousand, which bear enough words, if printed, to make a novel as long as *Gone With the Wind*. They are awesome evidence of the labour a writer must do to produce a novel, unless he is lucky and takes every obstacle in his stride. The mere sight of them would dissuade most aspiring authors from pursuing literary fame. For David Forrest, that small mountain of paper represents eleven years' work—not eleven years' constant work, to be sure, but constant enough, possibly five thousand hours in all, which he spent trying to say the things that were in his mind.

In *The Last Blue Sea* he got something out of his system which had been there for a long while. He liked doing it in that way, for, at a time when some popular novelists are given to making pronouncements on every conceivable subject from decimal currency to the decay of manners, Forrest has a refreshingly clear conception of the writer's mission. 'I believe writers should say anything they have to say through their work,' he says. 'A man isn't necessarily qualified to step out into other fields and tell people what to do merely because he has written some books. In short, I believe a writer's first business is to write.'

Forrest's real name is David Denholm, and he is a descendant of pioneers, German on one side, Scottish on the other, who settled in Queensland in the 1870s. He is not sure why he decided to use a pen-name when he began publishing his writing. The most practical, if least convincing, explanation he can find is that people seem to have difficulty in spelling Denholm. He is six feet in his socks, but slender, and weighs only eleven stone. His brown hair is straight, and his pale-skinned face thin, with regular features. The brown eyes are lively behind his glasses, and the mouth suggests a wry sense of comedy. At the time of this writing, he lived with his mother in Brisbane, and worked in a Brisbane branch of the Commonwealth Bank. He has been a bank officer since 1949, when he transferred from the Queensland State public service. He likes his daily work, and even in private does not complain that the need to earn a weekly salary is a barrier between him and artistic fulfilment. 'I'd like to devote all my time to writing, of course,' he says, 'but it remains very much a nice idea. Anyway, if a writer draws his inspiration from real life, he must stay in real life. If I got a cactus-patch somewhere and sat down to write I'd soon lose contact with life. One sees this happen with some writers; they move into isolation or semi-isolation, and the stream of their work dries up.'

He was born at Maryborough, Queensland, in 1924, the eldest of three children. His father was a State school teacher, and David's childhood memories are, first, of the Gympie district, and, later, of the Burnett area, near Kingaroy. He was ten when his father died; his mother moved the family to Brisbane when he was fourteen, and there he finished his education at the Church of England Grammar School. He passed the Junior examination, but says he was lucky to do so. 'At that time,' he says drily, 'I used to tell myself my English marks were low because my ideas were different from those of my teachers. Now I'm inclined to think they were low because I didn't know as much as I thought I did.'

He had no ambition to write for publication then. English and English literature did not even interest him much as subjects, and he preferred geography and history. He joined the State public service in August, 1940, but his adult life really began in May, 1942, when he was called up for service in the wartime militia. In 1943 he went to New Guinea with a draft of a hundred and fifty infantrymen, some AIF, some militia, and some, like him, in the process of transferring from the militia to the AIF. He was nineteen. They travelled from the Australian mainland in a tank landing ship, and disembarked at Milne Bay, expecting to be sent on at once to an operational zone. Nobody seemed to want them, however, and only an imperturbable lieutenant on whom they were foisted appeared to care whether they stayed or went, ate or starved, lived or died. Even the lieutenant did not care much, and intimated that, on the whole, the less he saw of them, the pleasanter life would be. They wandered about for some days, fed enough food for their needs by the lieutenant, and wondering when someone in authority would presently take notice of them and tell them where to go. One day a RAAF administrative officer intercepted them.

'What's your unit?' he asked.

'Haven't got one,' they said.

'Don't be —— silly!' he replied, with acerbity. 'Who's your commanding officer?'

'Haven't got one,' they said.

This question-and-answer game went on until the RAAF officer, defeated, stalked away.

'He thought we were having him on,' says Forrest, 'though we weren't. We were stating the plain and simple facts. But he was fit to explode.'

They were sent forward at last, and arrived at Salamaua a week after the Salamaua campaign finished. Although Forrest did not take part in that fighting, he heard of it from other men, and the story captured his imagination. 'So, years afterwards,' he says, 'I dug into the Battle of Salamaua, and dug and dug and dug, and out came *The Last Blue Sea*—which isn't, as some people seem to think, about AIF and Chocos,* but about a generation of Australians who went to the wars.'

The hankering to write about the war, about the men he had served with in the islands, and specifically about the Salamaua operations first took hold of him in 1947, and when he sat down at his typewriter and went to work he did not guess he was starting something he would not finish for eleven years. 'I don't think I knew then what I wanted to write,' he says. 'I didn't even know where to begin. *The Last Blue Sea*, as published, was about the fifth novel I wrote against the Salamaua background, and each was a different novel, not just a rewritten version of the same events.' For one period of two years he did no work at all on the novel; feeling he was getting nowhere, he abandoned the idea, but then he dragged what he had written off the shelf and started again. It was, he says, one of those things that won't lie down.

Most critics were friendly to *The Last Blue Sea*, but the conclusions some of them reached about it puzzled Forrest. One described it as military history dressed up as fiction. Forrest says he adhered to the history of the Salamaua campaign in general terms, but that in detail his story is purely imaginative. 'I even,' he says, 'shifted topographical

* "Choco": An Australian slang term used in World War II as a derisive label for militiamen and military conscripts generally.

features, for motives of my own, and invented a few places which don't exist at all but were essential to the story. Some men who fought at Salamaua would be surprised if they read *The Last Blue Sea* and believed I intended it as history.'

In 1961, after a period of being 'in neutral', as he phrased it, Forrest finished a novel, *The Hollow Woodheap*. This novel takes its title from an incident in Henry Lawson's short story *The Drover's Wife*, in which the woman pulls one stick of wood from the heap and the whole heap collapses. Forrest says *The Hollow Woodheap*, which was published in 1962, is 'a mixture of things—the satirical, the sardonic, a couple of dobs of slapstick, some deadpan'. It has a Brisbane background. In his desk he also has a half-finished book of short stories, and this, he says, could remain half-finished for a long time yet; he has no intention of flogging himself into turning out a sequence of half-baked short stories merely to bring the collection up to publishable length. Forrest is also making a study of German closer settlement in south-east Queensland, which began just over a hundred years ago and ended two or three years before the outbreak of World War I. 'Some of my forebears were among the early settlers,' he says, 'and personal curiosity started me digging into it. I don't know what I'll ultimately do with the mass of notes I have accumulated. I might turn them into a history book, a novel, or a collection of short stories, or perhaps just hand them over to the Historical Society.'

Forrest's short stories, in particular, have been experimental, and for this reason, he says, 'a lot have fallen on their faces'. He has, however, about a dozen which satisfy him reasonably well. One of his most memorable short stories, *That Barambah Mob*, which first appeared in the literary quarterly, *Overland*, in 1959, is built around the feats of the aboriginal fast bowler, Eddie Gilbert, who played for Queensland's Sheffield Shield team in the 1930s, and once, at Brisbane, bowled Bradman for a duck. Gilbert was reared on a mission station at Barambah, near Cherbourg, Queensland, and played his early cricket with the local team at Barambah. *That Barambah Mob* purports to record a discussion in a pub between the author and a local farmer, Mr Stulpnagel, who batted against Gilbert in his Barambah days. It is rich in such deadpan passages as this:

> Mr. Stulpnagel rolled up his left sleeve above his biceps and we examined the corrugated and dotted scar imprinted there by the seam of a cricket ball.
>
> Mr Stulpnagel said, 'It wasn't Larwood done that.'
>
> He inclined his head and we studied the scar on the top of his head. The mark was old and brown and still recognisably a diamond in shape. Enclosed in the diamond, in reverse, were the words, '. . . nufactured in Austra . . .'

Mr Stulpnagel straightened up and said gloomily, 'Larwood never done that, neither.'

'Gilbert?' we whispered.

'Thirty years ago this summer,' said Mr Stulpnagel.

That Eddie Gilbert was a demon bowler is incontestable; the cricket record-books prove it. That there is a township called Barambah in Queensland is also incontestable; the gazetteers prove that. Whether there was a Mr Stulpnagel until *That Barambah Mob* was written is less certain, but there undoubtedly is a Mr Stulpnagel now, no less real in his own way than is the indubitably flesh-and-blood Eddie Gilbert. In short, David Forrest has a talent for creating fictional characters as believable as the man next door, but more entertaining. All that remains to be seen is what, in the end, he will do with it.

FICTION

The Last Blue Sea (Melbourne, Heinemann) 1958
The Hollow Woodheap (Brisbane, Jacaranda Press) 1962

Elizabeth Harrower

PEOPLE BEFORE PLACES

NEARLY every author tells how he began itching to write books soon after his infant fingers first clutched a pencil. Elizabeth Harrower is an exception. She did not know she wished to write a book at all until she started her first novel. She was twenty-five then, and on an extended visit to Scotland. One day, having never before written anything more substantial than a short story of fifteen hundred words, she started writing a novel set in Sydney. After getting the novel well under way, she put it aside, and did not think much more about it for a year or so. She was then living in London digs and awaiting the result of an entrance examination to London University, where she intended reading for a degree in Psychology, and, perhaps to ease the tension, she took up the draft of the novel she had begun in Scotland. 'By the time the examination results came through and I found I had passed,' she says, 'I had decided to go ahead with the novel and abandon my idea of qualifying as a psychologist.'

She hardly expected that first novel, *Down in the City*, to be published; when she wrote it she was, she says, chiefly teaching herself 'to put one word in front of another'. It appeared in 1957, however, and was reasonably well received. Her second novel, *The Long Prospect*, set in an Australian industrial city which she called Ballowra and admits is modelled on Newcastle, came out in 1958, and her third, *The Catherine Wheel*, in 1960. *The Catherine Wheel*, which is built around the infatuation of an Australian girl named Clemency James, living in London, with a vain and amoral young man of considerable charm, testified, among other things, to her ability to write convincingly about people in a non-Australian locale—something few Australian writers manage to do. Reviewing this novel in *Meanjin* (No. 4, 1961), H. P. Heseltine wrote: '. . . *The Catherine Wheel* offers its own version of the destructive power of love. It does not offer a pattern but a painfully special and unrepeatable instance. All the petty hates, the quarrels, the reconciliations are set down to create the image of an unendurable but unbreakable relation. What is perhaps most remarkable about Clemency's narrative is that, while it deals with emotion pitched to the point of hysteria, it never itself becomes hysterical. "I listened like a scientist, I listened like a lover," she once says; and in the justness of that claim resides the very considerable merit of this book. The appropriate comparison is surely with that other expatriate Australian novel of destructive Romantic love, *Maurice Guest*.'*

In Australia Elizabeth Harrower's novels have attracted some substantial notice in Sydney but, at the time of writing, astonishingly little in any other State. This is puzzling, because many Australian authors whose work is less arresting than hers are better known and better respected here. She came back to Australia in July, 1959, after eight years abroad, and took a job in the programme department of the Australian Broadcasting Commission in Sydney and worked hard for eleven months, saving up. Then she went to live in a pleasant small house at Neutral Bay, sharing with her second cousin, Margaret Dick, a large bed-sitting room and kitchenette, with the use of a bathroom. They contrived to live together in complete amity, and this is worth remarking, for Miss Dick is also a professional writer, and writers, being individualists, usually tend to clash if they are much together. These two are manifestly both tolerant people in their personal relationships. At Neutral Bay Miss Harrower worked at a table in the kitchenette, on a portable typewriter she paid twenty pounds for in London when she started writing, and Miss Dick at a table in the bed-sitting room. Since each observed nine-to-five working hours, six days a week, taking only Sundays off, they managed to avoid getting in each other's way. Both worked on novels about Sydney—Miss Harrower also wrote several short stories and a three-act play—and these novels should make an interesting comparison, because she had lived in Sydney from the time she was twelve until she was twenty-three, while Miss Dick, who is Scottish, had never seen Sydney until 1959.

Elizabeth Harrower, who was born in 1928, is a slim brunette, about five feet ten inches tall in medium heels. She has responsive hazel eyes under strong brows, a high-bridged nose, and a sensitive, though slightly ironic, mouth. She belongs to a still small, but growing, school of Australian novelists, who are more concerned with people than places, and with cities than the bush, and who take the Australian scene for granted, instead of describing it in conscientious, and often wearisome, detail. She says her knowledge of Australia is limited anyway; she knows something of Australian

* By Henry Handel Richardson (London, Heinemann) 1908.

cities, but little about the country, and nothing about the outback. One of her chief reasons for coming home was to refresh her local knowledge; after eight years in London, she felt she was losing touch with the way Australians think, talk and live.

For her first few months back in Sydney she lived with her mother in a house overlooking Balmoral Beach. The house had every device for making life comfortable, and, from its front windows, she looked out on a superb panorama of harbour, heads and ocean. Any writer, she says, would have been able to work there if physical comfort and beautiful surroundings were the secret of writing well, but she found herself able to write nothing at all. 'I've concluded I can't write in comfort,' she says. 'I was comfortable for the first twenty-three years of my life, and also extremely restless all the time, and now I associate comfort with restlessness. From the time I was on my own in London, I was never restless, though rarely comfortable, and I found no difficulty at all in working.'

She was born in Newcastle, and her first twelve years were spent there, but she looks back without enthusiasm on Newcastle, and especially on Mayfield, the suburb she lived in. Sydney was different. She lived at Manly, with her mother and stepfather, and Sydney enchanted her. When, in Scotland and London, she wrote *Down in the City* she poured into it all her enthusiasm and affection for Sydney and, in doing so, believed she had worked Sydney out of her system. After being back in Sydney for two years or so she realized she was wrong about this, and admitted that her liking for the city and its people was deeper, and probably more enduring, than she had dreamed.

She had most of her schooling in Sydney, then worked as a clerk in a city office, but she was unsatisfied with herself and with life. She knew she wanted to do something, but did not know what, except that somehow 'people were mixed up in it'. From the time she could think for herself people always interested her more than anything else, not merely for their superficial actions, but also for their motives, their secret impulses, the working of their minds. She was always watching people, trying to discover what went on behind their masks. To her, they were an absorbing study.

Seeking light on human behaviour, she read every textbook she could find on human psychology. Then, as an extension of her practical investigation of the subject, she consulted two Sydney psychologists, not together, but separately, because she wished, in truly scientific spirit, to check their findings one against the other. Both psychologists were middle-aged men, each with an array of letters after his name, and she wanted their guidance in discovering what she should do with her own life. But also—and this she did not tell the psychologists—she wanted to find out what psychologists were like. So, although they did not know it, while they were analysing her she was no less cold-bloodedly analysing them. Both reported that she was of bright intelligence and could 'do anything', but they did not help her to decide on a career for herself. Though she retained her respect for psychology, she now has reservations about some of its practitioners.

Perhaps she should have known, without prompting, where her talent lay. From the time she was twelve she kept an enormous diary, spending many hours every week writing down in exercise books the details of her experiences, thoughts, fears, hopes. She did not imagine, however, that anything she might write could possibly interest anyone but herself, and much less that it might be worth printing, so she drifted along, observing people, wondering about them, wondering about herself. Then, in 1951, she went abroad. 'Having been born in Australia,' she says, 'was one of the best things that ever happened to me. But leaving Australia was one of the next best.'

She does not pretend life was easy in London. In a material sense, it was far harder than her life had been in Australia, but it taught her many things, including self-discipline. She learned, for instance, how to live 'on very little a week'. She lived in digs or, when she had more money, in flats in different quarters of London—Lancaster Gate, Sloane Gardens, Chelsea, Wandsworth Common—and took in typing to help pay expenses, while working thirty or more hours a week at her novels. By denying herself many luxuries—and, she says, some necessities—she travelled fairly extensively in Europe several times. It all helped her to see people and life with clearer eyes.

She has always used the same method in writing a novel, drafting it straight on to the typewriter, then rewriting it four or five times. She cuts without mercy anything which seems to have been written for effect, instead of to further the narrative. 'Deletions,' she says, 'are always an improvement. I sometimes think if everything were deleted one might have the perfect novel.' She likes writing novels, but is interested in other literary forms also. She might well in the end make her deepest mark as a short story writer or a playwright, but at present the novel is her chief concern.

Where she will ultimately make a permanent home—that is, if she makes a permanent home anywhere—is uncertain. Much as she likes Sydney, she finds life there too pleasant, and fears she would become a 'mental beachcomber' if she were to settle in that environment. 'I have a lot to learn,' she says, 'and I find one doesn't learn much in pleasant circumstances and surroundings. I don't know why learning always has to be done the hard way, but it does.' Her personal interests are wide. She likes the theatre, ballet and opera. She also likes reading, and Stendhal, Tolstoy, Mauriac, Colette, Saul Bellow, Truman Capote, Elizabeth Bowen, and the South African Nadine Gordimer are among her favourite novelists.

She writes in what she calls 'a ruthless way', pursuing the truth of her characters, and she says not everyone likes what she writes. It disturbs many people, she finds, to have the truth presented to them in cold print; they seem to prefer the philosophy expressed in the satirical song, 'I Want to Hear of Beautiful Things'. Elizabeth Harrower has nothing against beautiful things but she doesn't aim to spend her life writing of beautiful things alone. To do so, she feels, would be dishonest, unintelligent, and—for her—boring.

FICTION

Down in the City (London, Cassell) 1957
The Long Prospect (London, Cassell) 1958
The Catherine Wheel (London, Cassell) 1960

Randolph Stow

YOUNG MAN IN NO HURRY

RANDOLPH STOW's walk is the thing that practically everyone who knows him mentions when describing him. His friends and acquaintances sometimes differ about other of Stow's physical characteristics, but they all give the same picture of his walk. He covers the ground with long-legged strides, head down, shoulders hunched, his eyes fixed in front of him—'as if,' says one of his friends, 'his mind had just sidled around the corner on a journey of its own.' Perhaps the key to Stow lies in those words. His novels—*A Haunted Land*, *The Bystander*, and *To the Islands*—and his poems could have come only from the kind of mind which often goes sidling off 'on a journey of its own'. Stow's personality cannot of course be captured in a few revealing words, for he is at least as complex as any character in his own novels, and more complex than most of them. One of his friends puts the matter in rough-and-ready terms when he says, 'Mick Stow'—this is the name which Stow himself favours and the one by which all his familiars know him—'has two selves. You might begin to know something about him if you could discover where Mick Stow ends and Randolph Stow begins.'

Either as a man or a writer, Stow cannot be ticketed, in accordance with some approved and easily recognizable formula. This makes him a little disconcerting to those people who like their writers to fit neatly into established pigeonholes. Some daring—or, more likely, brash—critics have attempted now and then to pin one or another of the conventional labels on him, but any literary label looks wrong on Stow, even though, like every writer, he has been influenced by the work of other writers. He acknowledges a debt, for instance, to Elizabethan and Jacobean dramatists, and to a few modern poets, including Eliot, Pound, Rimbaud, St John Perse, Garcia Lorca, Whitman, and (as a poet) D. H. Lawrence, while Judith Wright, he says, 'has had a profound effect on my way of looking at the Australian landscape'. Novelists influenced him hardly at all until in his mid-twenties he came to Conrad and Patrick White. He says,

'I admire White enormously, and his influence is very likely to appear in work I may publish later.' This does not mean Stow will ever be a mere echo of Patrick White. He will never be a mere echo of any other writer. The thing that stamps all his published work is not its similarity to anything anyone else has written, but its immense and imaginative originality. What his ultimate achievement will be is only to be guessed, but it will be something of himself, not something borrowed or adapted. It is not surprising at all events that some of his admirers consider him to be, in the words of one of them, 'touched with the blighted hand of genius'.

Stow, fine-boned and delicately cast, is five feet eight inches tall, but his slender build makes him appear taller. (He weighs only nine stone, and this led a drunk in a country pub a few years ago to offer him a job as a jockey.) His naturally brown curly hair is prematurely grey, and his skin fair. He has a fairly full mouth, and exceptionally bright blue eyes which are often fixed in a somewhat puzzled expression. His eyebrows are incongruously heavy—one of his friends calls them 'stage Irishman brows'—and he tends to twist them when concentrating on a conversation. In a group he is apt to listen rather than talk, confining himself to an occasional comment, but with two or three friends he talks well. He has a good sense of humour, and his remarks, although never the weighty pronouncements of the intellectual, are often penetrating. Like many shy people, he is a man of strong convictions. He does not obtrude these, but if necessary he will resolutely defend them. His politics, like most other things about him, cannot be readily labelled; when pressed to declare himself politically he once said, 'I'm a human being.' Music—especially classical music and folk songs—is among his major interests, and he has a fair collection of recordings. At some of his parties, if drunk enough, he extemporizes on the piano, often quite brilliantly; he cannot read music, but has a true ear and plays with feeling. He sometimes sings also in a voice which some people find agreeable, even though it is hoarse and not particularly melodious.

What Stow thinks of himself and his abilities is less easy to discover than what other people think of them. (To a direct question, 'Which of your books most satisfies you?' he replied, with obvious sincerity, 'I couldn't say. I don't like any of them much.') He is almost pathologically humble. Although his three novels and his verse had been highly praised by responsible critics, he decided in 1959 to abandon writing, and went to New Guinea, 'meaning to settle down,' he says, 'to a non-literary career'; at that time he was twenty-three. In New Guinea his work, as an assistant to the Government Anthropologist, was mainly linguistic, and this interested him, because he has a gift for languages; he majored in French, which he reads fluently, at the University of Western Australia, and is hardly less fluent in Spanish. His health was poor in New Guinea, however, and he resigned his post after eleven months, and came back to the Australian mainland. He went to England in 1960, and stayed for nine months, living in Suffolk. He did no writing in England, but while there agreed with his London publishers to make a new collection of his poems. The appearance of this volume, *Outrider*, with illustrations by Sidney Nolan, was delayed for several reasons, but it ultimately came out late in 1962. Stow came home in 1961 to live in Western Australia, and went back to the University of Western Australia to do post-graduate work in English. Early in 1962 he returned to England as assistant lecturer in English at the University of Leeds.

While back in Perth, he shared a flat in the suburb of Nedlands with a former college friend, Mike Thornett. He enjoys city life well enough, but says, 'I've always vacillated between town and country, never quite a countryman but a constant weekender and vacationer. I'm still in much the same position, though I now know bigger towns and wilder bush.' If forced to make a definitive choice he would probably choose the bush. This is suggested by a passage in an article he published in the Western Australian literary magazine *Westerly* (No. 2, 1961). 'In the cities,' he wrote, 'personality is fenced in by the personalities of others. But alone in the bush . . . a phrase like "liberation of the spirit" may begin to sound meaningful.'

He was born at Geraldton, Western Australia, in 1935, the son of a country lawyer; the only other child was a girl, two years younger than Stow. His forebears on both sides were early Australian settlers; his father's people helped to establish Adelaide and his mother's were pastoral pioneers of the Geraldton district. He was educated at State schools in Geraldton, then went as a boarder to Guildford Grammar School, near Perth, and there he discovered Christopher Fry's plays. The major literary influences in his life until then had been the romantic poets and the Scottish balladists. Fry was something new, and Stow, inspired to emulation, wrote, in his own words, 'a string of bad plays in bad verse'. He took two of these plays to the Western Australian author and literary critic, John K. Ewers, who was impressed with their facility and soundness of construction, but in handing them back said, 'But, Micky, why don't you write on Australian themes, on something you know?'

Stow says that any writing he did until he was about eighteen was not an expression of himself, but an imitation of the styles and thoughts of those writers whose work he admired. Then he went to the

University of Western Australia (where he started out to study Law but switched to Arts), and soon afterwards he discovered his own creative faculty. 'I became a writer,' he says, 'for two reasons. One was that in National Service I first collided with the facts of life in the atomic age. The other was the death of a friend. He was not a particularly close friend, but we were at school and college and Law School together, and to me his death, coming at that time of my life, was a pretty world-shaking experience. I felt it was terribly necessary for me to do something creative and do it quickly. I expressed this at the time in a poem called *Madame Yuan Ying Disoriented*, and that was really my first poem—the first, that is, that wasn't simply a literary exercise. Later in the same year I began *A Haunted Land*.'

A year earlier he had worked on what he calls 'a Goonish sort of novel', *The Pink Elephant*, but did not finish it. It was, he says, important only to the extent that it showed him that writing novels was 'not impossibly difficult'. An interesting aspect of *The Pink Elephant*, even though that novel came to nothing in a public sense, is that unlike Stow's published novels it was humorous in treatment and theme. One of his friends says: 'His favourite radio show is the Goon Show, and as a script-writer for that kind of show he would be incomparable. I'd never read anything so funny as a sketch he wrote about English and Australian intellectuals being interviewed on the BBC and the ABC respectively. He was surprised and pleased when I laughed like a madman. He said he couldn't judge it himself. This gives a clue to his basic uncertainty about himself and his work, and also to his personal humility.'

Stow had to look outside Australia for his first substantial encouragement as a writer. In the middle of 1954, when he was eighteen, he found he had enough poems to make a book, and someone suggested he should try them on the Commonwealth Literary Fund. He did so, and got back 'a rather bored letter indicating that someone had read the first half-dozen poems and didn't like them'. Irritated, he sent the poems to London, and there they impressed Macdonalds, who eventually published them as *Act One*. When he finished *A Haunted Land* he sent it to Macdonalds who published it; they published his two later novels also. This anecdote explains why Stow has been known to remark with mild irony, 'I feel warmly friendly to the Commonwealth Literary Fund.'

He says he is equally interested in poetry and prose; to him, they seem to be 'quite different ways of speaking—not just the obviously different ways of managing language and cadence, but more that a poem is about the writer himself, while a novel is about other people'. Feeling this way, he sometimes doubts the value of publishing his verse at all. He reworks his poems a good deal, but his novels are planned so minutely beforehand that he hardly ever makes structural changes, only improvements in the style. He is not interested in writing short stories, because the short story is 'on too small a scale, and the characters are gone before one has a chance to know them'; nor in plays, because the stage is 'constricting', and 'there are too many other people interfering with the author's vision'.

When Stow writes a novel he likes to have a few months absolutely free; he wrote his first two novels, *A Haunted Land* and *The Bystander*, in university vacations. On novels he works only at night, between ten o'clock and four in the morning; he seems more comfortable when most other people are sleeping, whether he is putting down words on paper or mentally communing with his own gods. In writing a novel he works to a strict plan, which he has gradually built up beforehand, over a period of at least a year. He sometimes uses graphs to map character development, and a sort of stage lighting plan in which the central theme is the stage with the various incidents of the plot arranged around it like spotlights. '(I think, but I'm not sure,' he says, 'that I stole this idea from Henry James.')

Readers of Stow's novels know he is more interested in extraordinary than ordinary human beings—the 'monster', Tommy Cross, in *A Haunted Land* (the only character in that novel that was not fictitious, Stow says) is a good example. But he does not agree with one critic who claims he has chosen abnormal psychology as his field. Stow says that no doubt some of his characters are abnormal, but he considers 'genius without a province', a phrase he used in *A Haunted Land*, to be a more sympathetic description. He also disagrees with those critics, beginning with Elizabeth Bowen, who discovered in his work the influence of Emily Brontë. He believes his novels and Emily Brontë's have one quality in common, however: that their picture of their characters is perhaps (in Charlotte Brontë's words) 'too exclusively confined to those tragic and terrible traits of which, in listening to the secret annals of every rude vicinage, the memory is sometimes compelled to receive the impress'.

If Stow were a less complicated man his future would be fairly simple to forecast. Such a man, with his talent and achievement as a background, would almost inevitably settle down to a successful novelist's career. But Stow's future is unpredictable, if only because he is temperamentally incapable of ever becoming one of those well-ordered, and professionally admirable, writers who sit down at their desks at a set hour every day and, having written a set number of words, rise at a set time and go out to play a round of golf. Perhaps

Stow would never wish to be such a writer; at any rate he never will be. When he and I were discussing this profile toward the end of 1961 he remarked that he had done no writing, except for a handful of poems, for three and a half years. He had then been maturing in his mind for five years a novel about a fictional town called Tourmaline, 'constructed out of bits and pieces of decayed gold-mining townships in the Murchison country, east of my home town', but he was in no haste whatever to get it written.

'I don't think,' he says, 'that, once I begin to write a novel I have much difficulty in framing individual thoughts, but my experience of that novel, when completed, is miserably less than my mental experience of it before writing. This is also true of a completed poem. I don't know what my "ultimate aim" as a writer is—just, I suppose, with a bit of luck to produce something as grand and perfect and beautiful as the conception usually is before I set pen to paper.'

When he does that—and his admirers believe he will do it—the literature of his own country and of his own time will be enriched.

FICTION

(Published by Macdonald, London)

A Haunted Land 1956
The Bystander 1957
To the Islands 1958

VERSE

Act One 1957
Outrider 1962

ACKNOWLEDGMENTS

I wish to thank Mr Oswald Syme, chairman of directors of David Syme and Company Ltd, proprietor of *The Age*, and the board of directors, for their generous agreement to let me adapt for this book thirty-eight profiles, from the original series, 'Australian Writers in Profile'. Without the facilities given me by *The Age* to visit other States and interview writers, I could not have undertaken the work of gathering the material for profiles.

Photographs in this book are, with a few exceptions, those which were used to illustrate *The Age* series; prints of these were supplied by the company, which also owns the copyright of nearly half these photographs. The authorship of other photographs is acknowledged as follows: Paul Brickhill (Wynyard de Luxe, Sydney); Nancy Cato (Jack Cato, F.R.P.S., Melbourne); Henrietta Drake-Brockman (Hollywood, Perth); Mary Durack (John Dent, Nedlands, W.A.); Geoffrey Dutton (Colin Ballantyne, Adelaide); John K. Ewers (Frank Evans, Perth); David Forrest (Edmond Bourke, Brisbane); G. M. Glaskin (George Britnell, Perth); Max Harris (Colin Ballantyne, Adelaide); Elizabeth Harrower (Jill Crossley, Sydney); Ion L. Idriess (Jenkins, Horsham); Gavin Long (Australian News and Information Bureau); Leonard Mann (Dickinson-Monteath, Melbourne); Alan Marshall (Adrian Boddington, Melbourne); Mary Mitchell (Athol Shmith, Melbourne); John Morrison (Brendon Studios, Mount Waverley); Walter Murdoch (West Australian Newspapers, Perth); D'Arcy Niland and Ruth Park (Kara Feldman, Montgomery Dunn Studios, Sydney); John O'Grady (John Hearder, Sydney); Katharine Susannah Prichard (West Australian Newspapers, Perth); Olaf Ruhen (Peter Godwin, Sydney); Colin Simpson (Max Dupain and Kerry Dundas, Sydney); Randolph Stow (Mark Gerson, London); Morris West (Pamela Chandler, London); Patrick White (Boris Cook, Sydney).

The bibliographies are drawn from a number of sources. In compiling them I made frequent use of Green's *A History of Australian Literature* (Sydney, Angus & Robertson, 1961) and the revised and extended edition of Miller's *Australian Literature* (Sydney, Angus & Robertson, 1956). Many of the authors took considerable trouble to assemble and confirm bibliographical facts about themselves, and the help Mr Bert Iliffe, of Angus and Robertson, gave me in compiling two of the longer bibliographies, those of Ion L. Idriess and Walter Murdoch, and in tracking down elusive details for a number of others, was invaluable. My aim has been to make each bibliography a complete record of books published by each author up to October, 1962, when *Forty-Two Faces* was listed for publication. A number of publishers have helped me to do this, and I wish to thank them.

J.H.